The Kiss

Angels, Liars, and Thieves
Boston 1946-2000

Book Two: 1983 to 1988

Memoir by David Scondras
Second edition, January, 2018

Dedicated to my mentors and friends Mel and Joyce King

Introduction to Book Two

When I was a hippie, I never voted and I thought government was an enemy. Then I got elected.

I discovered love; I discovered power; and the city discovered that gays wanted a lot more than just gay rights.

Like most people, we cared about having a job; raising kids; getting into good schools; finding housing; getting medical care; and putting an end to homelessness.

I took them all on. This book tells that story.

Table of Contents

Chapters 118 through 131 appear in Book Three.

Chapters 132 through 142 appear in Book Four.

55 / The Kiss

Boston gained its first openly-gay city councilor in 1983 with David Scondras' dramatic November win. Television prominently covered the victory kiss David got from his lover Bob.

BAY WINDOWS • Jan. 5-18, 1984 19

During the election of 1983, our goal was to get our city back. It was fair for our opponents to say, "Get their city back from whom?"

The answer to that question depends on who you are. Most progressives in 1983 subscribed to an answer best summarized in the book, 'Who Rules Boston?' Its author, Peter Dreier, claimed Boston was run by a wealthy group called "the Vault." (Dreier became a Boston mayoral appointee in 1984).

For gay people, we wanted our city back from those who taught hatred of others based on sexual behavior, who supported discrimination against gays, who painted gay men as child molesters. Those in power in Boston in 1983 were either wealthy, or homophobic, or both.

For me, my particular target was to get our city back from Mark Roosevelt, my opponent in the district City Council race. Mark Roosevelt was the child of generations of famous, legitimate leaders, related to Teddy Roosevelt, FDR, and Eleanor Roosevelt. Mark characterized the election as a difference between styles: he would persuade, while I tended toward confrontation. He would be able to bring people around to liberal ways of thinking; I would alienate.

He was ultimately correct in that I was a two-humped camel and he was a one-hump camel. What I mean is that some people like myself create strong friends and strong enemies, virtually no one is lukewarm. A two humped camel. He fostered a general positive feeling, not too deep, and a mild negative one, not too deep. The one-humped camel dominates most legislative bodies in the world.

The good gays, the 'well-to-do' queers who tended toward assimilationism, supported 'legitimacy' that would lead to acceptance by those who ran the place, as opposed to being self-accepting and demanding others become tolerant. For this reason, they lined up behind Roosevelt, in spite of my being openly gay, or rather, because I was openly gay. They might well have supported a well-dressed, well-connected closet case over Mark, but in the absence of one of them running, Mark was a good fit.

Our campaigns for District 8 City Council, plus the mayoral race, got to be the only game in town. Radio talk shows, television, street corner hawkers, lit drops, house parties, rallies, visibilities (when many campaign workers for a candidate stood with signs outside subway stations and other places where people passed) all made sure that no one could miss the fact there was a big election going on.

Part of the scale of the election was due to the fact that Kevin White, the Mayor of Boston, had decided to step down after 16 years and, for the first time, the city had districts. This meant that for the first time in a generation, whatever happened, change was in the air and people responded. Part of it was, no doubt, because the culture wars of the 60's had finally reached the voting booth.

My campaign was actually the campaign of the people who put it together. I personified the result of a team effort, and I got used to the idea that it wasn't about me, really. It was about us.

We worked hard toward November 15th, Election Day. Robert took it upon himself to organize two visibilities. The first was two weeks before the election, getting at least two sign-holders at every intersection in Back Bay. The second was to put a person holding a sign every 30 feet all the way from the Arlington Street entrance of the Boston Public Garden to the Park Street T stop, across the entirety of the Boston Common, where foot traffic was very heavy.

Election Day

We grew optimistic toward Election Day. We could feel the energy, the momentum. On Saturday, November 5th, the *Boston Globe* endorsed me. Mark got a bit demoralized as Election Day approached.

The November 23rd issue of the *TAB* said Mark felt that he had done all he could. I disagree. The day before the election, the schedule for Mark included "a few phone calls and teaching a class at Mission High School: 'I didn't do anything the day before the preliminary, either,' Roosevelt said. 'I stayed home and I was so nervous that I read three novels.' " That does not mean Mark's campaign was inactive. Just before the election Mark's campaign sent a mailgram to all the registered voters, signed by the chairmen of all three of the ward's political committees, endorsing Roosevelt. The mailgrams cost some $6,000 in postage.

But we began to make national waves. A November 8th *New York Times* article included a picture of me; headlined, "Increasing Political Influence of Homosexual Citizens is Sensed Across U.S." Across the U.S., gay people were starting to organize and vote. In other words, on some level, come out and fight for themselves. The article spoke of Boston:

I know that a reader must wonder why so much fuss was being made about my being gay. To remember what it was like then, look at an official city survey of over 1,340 gay men and women which was reported out that November, and painted a picture of a kind of society that has since undergone change:

- 53% of the people surveyed expressed having had been the victims of overt acts of discrimination.

- 24% had been physically attacked in the city of Boston due to their sexual orientation.

- 75% had been subjected to verbal abuse.

- 28% said they would be fired if their co-workers learned of their orientation.

My number of events immediately preceding Election Day itself was amazing, in comparison to Mark's nervous at-home reading. For months now Gary had been driving me around the district to events in what we called 'Mobile One,' an ancient, falling-apart Volvo that I learned to love. On Election Day, among many other things, we went to the Mel King rally joining some 50,000 people who came to show support for Mel at Grove Hall. Mayor Harold Washington, the first black mayor of Chicago, who campaigned for Mel, joined us.

Back at campaign central in the West Fenway, my home base, people were phone-calling voters who had said they would support me. We got school buses with loudspeakers to bring people to the polls.

We had an endless recording of Frank Curley saying, in his inimitable Irish accent, "This is Francis Curley. My father, James Michael Curley, was the Mayor of the Poor. I pray you go out today and vote for David Scondras for City Council." Mark Roosevelt hated the tape. He asked Gary to pull it. Gary told him 'What, you could make a tape of your dad, Kermit Roosevelt, telling everyone that when he was CIA Director he personally engineered the toppling of the elected government of Iran and installed the Shah.'

In Ward 5, John DeVillars, who worked for the state at the time, challenged voters at the poll, to make it impossible for everyone to vote. This was the part of my district where the largest single bloc of my votes came from. We had to rush lawyers over to straighten out the mess. I guess if you can't win the race, you try to break the other guy's leg.

My Mom had spent a lot of time on Mission Hill so we put her at the polls in Mission Park where she talked to every person asking them to vote for 'her son.' She was elderly; so were they. Mom had called every Greek-surnamed person in the district over 65 years old and spoke with them in Greek to vote for me. My aunts came to the polling places to hold signs and give out literature.

Robert and I had rented a car for the day so he could help deliver lunches and snacks to poll workers and giving rides to the polls to people who hadn't voted yet according to our "ID and pull" operation. Finally, the polls started to close but at least 150 of our voters hadn't voted yet in the Fenway. There were long lines and it was a freezing-cold day. We desperately tried to convince poll workers to stay open longer and the people in line not to leave.

But finally the day was over our people started to converge on the campaign headquarters. Early results came in from ones Back Bay and Beacon Hill, as those well-to-do precincts usually produced tallies sooner after closing than the grittier Fenway, Mission Hill or Allston precincts. It seemed pretty clear then that Mark had won the race. Based on those early precincts, his base, he was over a thousand votes ahead and the Fenway, my base, historically had very low voter turnout. With ever growing pessimism, we started totaling the precincts.

But while some campaign workers were adjusting to the idea of losing, French Hill, my numbers guy, answered the phone with "City Councilor David Scondras' Office." He had just tallied the numbers and realized something no one else did at that moment: He knew we had won. He had the spreadsheet, the computer program, and astonishingly, the Fenway not only landslided for me, it also cast as many votes as the more heavy-voting parts of the district. I had trounced Roosevelt in the Fenway 2,637 to 1,111, winning 70% of the vote. It meant I had won by 103 votes out of 14,311 cast. Seven-tenths of one percent of the vote. I had lost Mark's half of the district by 1,334 votes but won the Fenway by 1,526 votes and when the dust settled I had won the election.

Mark Roosevelt appeared at 10:30 pm to congratulate me. The room had a bit of booing which I immediately shushed. He got up to the mike and congratulated us on our victory, promised to work with us in the future and was extraordinary in his genuine and statesmanlike remarks. He would eventually be the Democratic nominee for Governor of Massachusetts and a good one. We shook hands, which made it onto the *Boston Ledger's* front page.

Robert rushed back to the office from his assigned Mission Hill polling place, and by then, the campaign staff, volunteers, supporters, neighborhoods, and press people started to congregate taking pictures, rolling film, turning the victory into a media event. The storefront was packed, almost impossible to move about. I kept waiting for Robert to return, when Jack Hall decided we had to give the victory speech now, before the press headed out to other venues. So I began, very elated but sad that I couldn't share this moment with Robert. We had worked so long and so hard and given up so much of our time together to secure this victory. I was in the middle of my acceptance speech when Robert returned. When he walked in, the crowd – everyone was quite fond of him – started cheering and clapping! Almost all the cameras turned toward the door to see what the commotion was.

I was accustomed to him always being in the back or near the wall or with a small group of friends and I could see him looking for a spot in the back to stand, but the crowd parted to form a path up to the hastily made platform I was standing on. He reluctantly came up and when he stepped up onto the platform gave me a most innocent kiss on the cheek.

Kissed me on the cheek. That's the picture on the cover of this book. It made the front page of the *Boston Herald*, and was shown on most local TV. Our friend Rosaria Salerno said she saw us kiss on television in Chicago.

I wasn't even in office yet and that "peck on the cheek" became the first "issue." Channel 7 got complaints it was sensationalizing the news so they ran it again to show that they had not. A week later we held an event at Avalon, the large gay/straight venue. At the press conference, we waited for everyone to focus on us. Then we kissed again, only this time on the mouth, turned to the cameras and said, "Get used to it."

A year later walking up Boylston Street one evening by cafés where diners sat watching the night come on, we followed a group of young gay guys who were chanting "We're Here; We're Queer; We're Fabulous; Get Used To It." I heard "our phrase," and turned to Robert and said, "I think we helped start Queer Nation." They became a radical gay group that pushed for coming out and being yourself. I got uncomfortable with what I had possibly had a hand in starting.

The November 26th edition of *Gay Community News* had me and Robert holding our hands in the air like prize fighters who had just won in the final round, which was taken at The 1270, the gay bar where I first came out for real, and the place that made it possible for me to survive being gay in a straight world. When Robert and I walked into the bar, we knew that we had won. The place erupted.

I got the mike and said "the City of Boston now has its first openly gay city councilor!" The crowd applauded and cheered. "What's truly important to me is to thank the coalition that made this possible," I said. According to Larry Goldsmith in *Gay Community News,* I said it was the combined efforts of tenants, women, blacks, Hispanics, and members of the gay community who stuck together with me and pulled this thing off.

"What about straight white males?" yelled a supporter.

"Oh, listen, there were a lot of straight white males that helped us all the way through," Scondras acknowledged. "Have I left out anybody?"

Mel King lost but won more white votes than any other black mayor in America. His 'rainbow coalition' was the future for our country. Robert Jordan wrote the *Boston Globe* lead story for Wednesday, November 16th, 1983:

When Melvin H. King stepped to the podium at 11 p.m. the
cheering crowd of more than 3,000 supporters at the Sheraton
Boston Hotel treated him like a winner. When the cheering died
down, he said: "You all obviously haven't seen the results."

"Tonight the city of Boston has taken a giant step forward.
Because of all of you, Boston will be great again. I have lost the
Mayor's race, but I have been privileged to represent the
Rainbow Coalition." a reference to the collection of blacks,
whites, Hispanics, homosexuals and women from who he drew
his support. He got 66,992 votes. "You have given me the
privilege to be able to guide us through what the historians will
recognize as the turning point in the social cultural and political
history of Boston."

Ray Flynn was quoted as saying "We have proven that the hopes that unite us are stronger than the fears that separate us". In the November 28th *Newsweek* article that covered the election, it mentioned that Mel symbolically pinned a Rainbow Coalition button on Flynn's lapel that election night. The voter turnout for Boston topped 66%, the highest in its history.

From "A Kiss is Just a Kiss," *Boston Globe*, January 21st:

Had the kiss been bestowed in the dining room of the Somerset
Club on Beacon Hill of the ballroom of the Ritz-Carlton in the

*Back Bay, it doubtless would have led to some unpleasantness.
Some old codger might have thrown a punch in defense of
Edwardian manhood and an otherwise flawless dowager or two
might have uttered an unaccustomed oath.*

*But the big smooch David Scondras gave Robert Krebs Tuesday
night was delivered on a platform at Metro, the flash and dazzle
disco in the Fenway. Many of the guests, who paid $3 for the
inaugural party and fundraiser, had been doing a fair degree of
untraditional affectioneering on the dance floor of Metro and
were hardly in a position to take umbrage. In fact, the kiss was
applauded, even by those few among the estimated 1,300
guests who did not already know that Robert Krebs and David
Scondras live together.*

*Scondras represents the city's silk stocking district, and also the
frontier neighborhoods of the Fenway, Mission Hill. Scondras
observed that his district was a silk stocking with a hole in it.
Increasingly gay, black and Hispanic, Boston's WASP image, and
WASP power is molting. Repeating a theme he struck several
times during his formal remarks to his guests early in the
evening he said, "We've made a start. The city will not tolerate
bigotry."*

*If that's where all this kissing leading to, then who's to
complain?*

One of the letters I got concerning the kiss came from a gay
group. Throughout the struggle for freedom, the gay community, like all
other oppressed minorities, struggled constantly with the danger of
coming out which all groups essentially do when they fight for freedom,
making them a target for hate. It is in this context that the content of this
assimilationist letter needs to be understood.

January 28, 1984

Dear Mr. Scondras,

*We, the South Shore Gay and Lesbian Alliance, think the
behavior at your victory celebration could have been done in
better taste.*

The 'flaunting' referred to was Robert, kissing me on my cheek for winning the election. Kitty Dukakis did the same thing to Mike Dukakis, under roughly the same circumstances, during roughly the same time. I was not actually aware that this was sexual or flaunty.

56 / The Decade of Enlightenment 1984-1994

A friend of mine who writes intense poetry knows of the effort I am making to share myself in my writing. The seers think of this as creating a legacy. I think of it more as creating a story sung around a fire as I heard the story of my family's village sung by my grandfather's brother. It lasts longer than legacies, better informs, is entertaining and can sometimes change the world.

Nick said I could pick a poem to share with you at the beginning of this part of my trip. I chose this one, with an echo of both Robert Frost, the dark poet, and the exhortations of Pericles — 'we do not imitate others for we are to set an example for the future.'

A Walking In The Woods

By Nick Hattam

I have the greatest want inside of me
And that is to grow arms like centipedes' legs,
Hundreds of them and with half-moon claws for nails
And I want to dig those claws into the middle of your skull,
All of them,
And peel you open.

As you force molt, I will see your insides,
Finally.
And then I will whisper my thoughts into you,
Sew you up again with my tongue,
And sooth your scar with my night-terrors.
And when you open your eyes again,
You will see things the way I do.

You will see how green the grass is when it gets hit by a
Downward facing sun, how it might burn by that orange
eye's stare.
You will see the tiny garden spider hanging from a branch,
No bigger than a grain of dust with eight legs,
And you will smile as it twists in the wind with an aphid
in its jaws.

It's blunt but honest. Nick is young and perceptive. He is a new model of the old ones who have always changed the world from Thermopylae to the boats that circumnavigated the globe, from the exhortations of Alexander to end strife between religions and sects to the election of Corazon Aquino.

We all were blunt and honest in 1983, the gang that took over Boston, the product of the 60's, the effort of the poets to run the real world. Some of it worked.

I began writing this section on June 25, 2009, the day Michael Jackson died. He was 50 years old. Amidst the circus of speculation, the voice of a reporter who knew him well said:

> *He was coming out of a long and troubled retirement following*
> *acquittal on the 2005 child molestation charges...this is the*
> *person I saw transform within an hour from confident public*
> *person to frightened manchild curled up on the couch in a fetal*
> *position and unable to face the world.*
> — *Geraldo Rivera*

I cried. For myself. We torture each other with our public paranoiac rages about sex — in this case with children — that have led to the latest national witch hunt against the hundreds of varieties of 'sex offenders' we have invented. It makes no difference that Jackson was acquitted of child molestation charges because the media paints pictures which resonate with cultural obsessions and cause such extraordinary damage that judges and juries are actually side shows, as public hangings and social ostracism have long ago, perhaps always, replaced any rational effort to mediate disputes or analyze behaviors.

Michael Jackson died from stress which is the price paid by people who do not fit into culturally prescribed roles or hold the culturally predetermined beliefs about good and evil, neither of which is a particularly good tool toward understanding life. We all need love. The trouble is, if you try to get it from society instead of a few close friends, the world will kill you for your deviances of which we all have plenty.

This all begins with an atavistic world view that designates behavior and people as good or evil, which they rarely are. The lion is not evil when it eats you, it is hungry and you are available.

Sex is not dangerous, evil, sinful, sick or unnatural. It is simply a part of nature. Not long ago there was a movement in Boston to have animals wear clothes to preserve modesty and a condemnation of public copulation of dogs.

There are so many myths.

Looking at just one of them, no one has ever proven that sex play among children has ever caused any actual harm to anyone. It is a cultural precept that goes unchallenged because to challenge it is to be categorized as a demon. And yet no less a giant than Sigmund Freud made psychology's most controversial observation, clear to any nanny in history, that children have a sex life. I know because I was once a child and so were my friends and trust me, we all had sex lives.

I remember my Uncle Andy having to stop my mother from freaking out when she discovered I masturbated. He explained to her that he had too when he was a kid, and that everybody does. My mother had threatened to "cut it off" at one point.

Miscegenation was once a crime punishable by lynching. Adultery is illegal notwithstanding its omnipresent reality. There are many, many examples of things past and present that are illegal or culturally unacceptable which attempt to dictate to nature what nature has dictated shall happen in this world of ours.

None of this is to say that people cannot or should not decide to live life in ways that make them feel good, safe, happy. But to impose these arbitrary and completely hypothetical cultural norms which violate what nature dictates this species will and must do, leads to an underground in which they are constantly violated, a lack of self esteem stemming from engaging in their violation, and becoming a target of hate when society suspects you of violating their latest sacred nonsense. This runs the gamut from the false modesty of wearing a veil in Islamic cultures, where the veil once was a step toward women's liberation, to creating sex offender registries and jail sentences for children who play sexually with people of any age, which they have done for as long as there has been puberty and bodies.

Legal and cultural norms are not based upon reason and data but rather on mythology, history and custom. These are three systems that have always failed to protect any of us from anything and have always led to injustice, suffering and death. Throw the virgin down the stairs of the tall pyramid and the gods will bless you with a good crop. This led to dead kids, grieving parents, an exploitative class of clergy, and no help for the farms. It is not all that different now.

I do not say these things to shock or upset, but rather to say that we fish must eventually discover water. We are the last to see what we are really doing to each other when the veil of normalcy cloaks it. When we feel really good about some idea we have with no foundation in experiences, data, study and reason we should chuck it into the wastebasket.

Few people more than a gay closeted man understands how the endless repetition of a self-congratulatory lie can kill, the worthlessness of trying to build a person or a society on things that are fake. And much of what has been built is fake. To stop repeated historical mistakes we have to begin by admitting that they exist, which for the most part has really not happened yet.

I talk about sex for the same reason a black activist might talk about color — until we get can get over it, I have to talk about it. But knowing that one part of a culture is fundamentally broken gives you eyes to see the other broken parts, and I became an activist on a host of issues addressing many institutions, laws, and practices that belong in the grave.

So when Michael Jackson died today, I was feeling pretty down about the number of people who I have known over the years who have suffered so much because of such ignorance and arrogance among the purveyors of fake wisdom which include virtually everyone in a position of power within our culture.

I remember that I was determined to change all this when I went to City Hall. I was a radical of reason, a soldier in the army of the Enlightenment, arrogant as shit. I would eventually see the new left as filled with the same old tired fundamentalist attitudes toward the newest 'politically correct' point of view as the Supreme Ruler shows toward those who, God forbid, want some freedom in Iran. But when I first came to City Hall, I was a true believer.

I was idealistic, and in my 38-year-old youth had a pretty big picture of what I could accomplish.

57 /   Inauguration

"You campaign in poetry. You govern in prose."
— Mario Cuomo

"Our theory of government will be trickle up, not trickle down."
— Ray Flynn

On January 2nd, 1984, we were all sworn in. Change had begun.

Ray Flynn, the son of a longshoreman and a former cleaning woman, was inaugurated as Boston's 46th Mayor. Anyone in Boston who could walk in and out of the City Hall and see the Mayor without an appointment would testify that an upheaval had happened. Ray promised to help the poor. He offered Mel King a position as deputy mayor which Mel declined. He echoed the theme I had grown to hear from Boston's Democratic politicians when he said the test of greatness is the protection we afford the weak. He had an inaugural ball, of course, but seven thousand people came and it was free. There was no dress code. The *New York Times* compared his inauguration with that of President Andrew Jackson in 1829, when Western frontiersmen and Eastern factory workers trooped through the White House.

In the afternoon, his first act was to sign an executive order to assure equal rights and equal pay for women in Boston.

Day One at Boston City Hall

I walked as a City Councilor into the huge concrete building that looked like an upside down grey ziggurat, which we call 'City Hall' in Boston, and tried to figure out how to get to my office. It was on the fifth floor, which I assumed would be above the 4th floor, silly, me. There is no fourth floor on that side of the building.

The city had built new offices for the new councilors (the total had changed from 9 to 13) out of what was once the art gallery on the 5th floor. I knew it well.

The building vaguely scared me. it felt like it might fall on my head.

The redone gallery had four council offices all of which looked pretty much the same. Concrete bunkers with high ceilings, perhaps 14 feet tall, walls of concrete with the ghosts of the wooden forms still embedded in them, fluorescent lights high above that made everything seem cold, and gigantic wooden doors that announced a room of importance. Inside the door, there was an ante-chamber housing the support staff – usually of 2 or at the most 3 – and after that, another door to the inner room where the councilors desk sat. But instead of 2 or 3, we had 13 staff, some paid for by stretching the councilor staff allowance, some paid out of my pocket, some from campaign funds, some as local universities' interns, and some were volunteers giving their time.

From hollow core doors and modular cubical panels, Robert designed work stations for 10 people in the large room usually reserved for the councilor. We had the reception desks in the reception area in the outer office and I was able to put a little desk for me behind the entrance door. Most people entering would walk right past me into the main office.

Robert installed 8'-high Homasote panels on the concrete walls so volunteers could paint them – the color elected was a warm pink – and thus humanize the space. I was very excited about helping, but Robert forbade it. He had already experienced several painting disasters at our house related to my skills including one involving cat-paw-shaped paint-steps on the carpet from where our cat Nixon inadvertently stepped in the paint tray and then ran to hide when we heard him coming.

Still, I objected. I was the master and I would paint! And I promptly ran the roller off the Homasote onto the concrete. I was immediately reassigned to vacuuming but during that job accidentally knocked a can of paint off a chair onto the brass radiator grill which was impossible to clean up and I was promptly banished, putting an end to my painting career.

My mother was there talking endlessly until the big shot radio personality Howie Carr walked into the office, meeting my mother and making snide remarks about having a child molester in office. My mother did not lambaste him as he used the language of the cowardly innuendos that characterized the right wing signals to haters that flew under the radar of less sex-obsessed folk.

"How does it feel to have your son in office," he said, implying, "How did it feel to have a deviant in office?" But that was not how he put it. It was how he meant it.

The first few weeks of building a team at City Hall were filled with work that reminded me more of moving day at college than a 'transition to power.' We tried to get permission to build a loft the big room, but there just wasn't room for the staircase and besides it would go beyond the ability of the building department to look the other way... too far out. So we suffered with cramped quarters housing at all times over 10 people in rooms designed for 4 at most.

Eventually, over the years, posters, letters, pictures, and awards would decorate the walls of the otherwise cold surfaces. I figured the City Hall architecture, called "brutalist," was an effort to intimidate people. It was big, solid, hard, cold and confusing. The red brick desert you had to walk across to get to it was cold and windswept much of the year, and there was nothing that made you feel welcome, not even a chair in the lobby.

But we were to change all that.

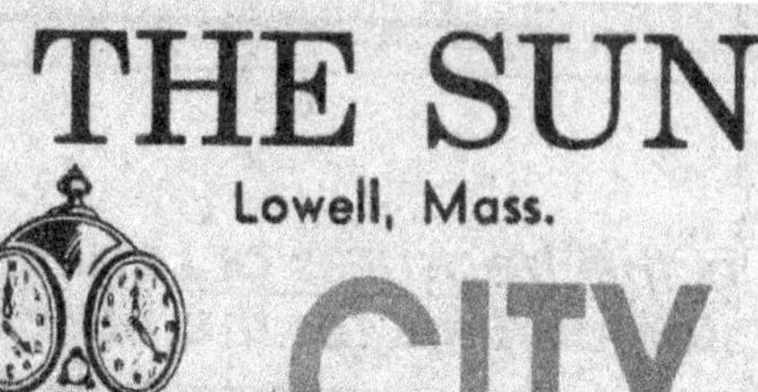

THE SUN

Lowell, Mass.

CITY

Wednesday, November 16, 1983   17

Lowell native edges opponent in Boston City Council race

LOWELL — Lowell native David Scondras headed toward victory today as one of Boston's nine new district city councilors.

Scondras, 37, a gay rights and housing activist, was locked in a tight race last night for the District 8 council seat.

But he emerged today with a slim lead over Mark Roosevelt, 27, a lawyer who served on former President Jimmy Carter's domestic policy staff.

The district includes the neighborhoods of Beacon Hill, Back Bay, the Fenway and Mission Hill.

"I'm very happy," Dorothy Scondras, his mother, said this morning. "We worked very hard."

Scondras said her son received campaign help and funds from several Lowell residents.

He had a fund-raiser at the Olympia restaurant that netted him between $3,000 and $4,000, she said.

Scondras is best known for founding in 1975 the Symphony Tenants Organization, a group recognized nationally whose arson investigations led to 31 arson convictions.

He also helped draft an anti-

David Scondras

arson law that was signed by Gov. Michael S. Dukakis during his first term.

Scondras graduated from Lowell High School in 1963 as the class valedictorian. He attended Harvard University on a scholarship and later won a fellowship at Northeastern University.

Scondras now teaches mathematics at Northeastern.

Councilor Scondras

One thing I could not get used to was the name. They changed my first name from David, to Councilor. I heard it every minute for ten years. It was a matter of respecting the office I suppose, but it made the role more relevant than the person, and I had to remind myself that I was David not 'the Councilor.'

In the ten years I was in office we handled over 9,000 individual crises, passed 70 percent of all the legislation, set in motion all the major public initiatives which today are still the cutting edge of public discourse from the green revolution and electric cars to sex law changes to reconciliation with Communist regimes to the end of apartheid, to novel uses of eminent domain, changes in the school system, an end to the sick 'vice squad' of the police department, the first successful balancing of our budgets, protecting people from evictions and building new affordable housing and on and on.

We also established urban foreign policy, and we passed the first gay rights laws in our history.

58 /   The Vision: Homonia

In January 1984, we created the *District Eight News*, which we circulated every month for ten years in the District I represented. I focused on a theme of unity, a majority of minorities, a plan on how to get power that by its nature would share power with those who needed it. For example, in a piece about the New Year I wrote:

> *We are a people whose time has come. Our community has within it members who are Black, Hispanic, disabled, members from every religious persuasion. This kind of coalition is what the larger society needs in order to overcome bigotry, so we shall become a model for others.*
>
> *Because we understand what it is to be left out, and because we understand that to be poor is to be left out, a central theme throughout our politics will be support for every measure, which will reduce poverty.*
>
> *We have spent a lot of time looking for a home, and much of it in places and with people who dislike us. We made some mistakes, but we have grown from them and it is very clear that our only real home is each other.*

In the meantime, the city council divided along lines familiar to most Americans. Jimmy Kelly, who opposed racial integration, gay power and liberals in general, by January 18th, had picked a Presidential candidate: Ronald Reagan. In contrast, I picked Jesse Jackson.

On January 9th, Mayor Ray Flynn signed an executive order at the general meeting of the Alliance, prohibiting discrimination on the basis of sexual preference in public employment and city services. I was there. The applause was loud and sincere. The executive order was a first step from a boy from Southie, the most conservative section of Boston, and that gave a signal that a gay rights bill was a real possibility. The state had failed to pass one for 15 years.

In the meantime I put together task forces to work on gay and lesbian rights, financing of AIDS resources, the development of alternatives to nursing homes, and many other issues, especially housing.

Flynn Signs Executive Order

By Larry Goldsmith

BOSTON — Mayor Ray Flynn attended the general meeting of the Boston Lesbian and Gay Political Alliance on January 9 to sign the second Executive Order of his administration, a policy prohibiting discrimination on the basis of sexual preference in public employment and city services.

"Signing this order is certainly not going to resolve all the problems that people in the city of Boston face with regard to human rights," Flynn said, "but it's going to set a tone...that this is a city that respects the rights, that respects the dignity of each and every citizen."

Flynn signed his first executive order on inauguration day, shortly after his swearing-in ceremony. That order prohibited discrimination on the basis of sex.

The new executive order replaces a June 1982 order by former Mayor Kevin White. Flynn's order is identical to White's, except that it omits a section outlining the duties of the Mayor's Liaison to the Lesbian and Gay Community. A committee in the Flynn transition organization is now writing a new job description and searching for a replacement for White's liaison, Brian McNaught, who is scheduled to leave at the end of January.

Flynn left the meeting after signing the order, and the Alliance proceeded to enact changes in its by-laws and elect new officers. Eric Rofes, who ran unopposed, was elected to a second term as chairperson. Mission Hill resident Connie Apple was elected over Dorchester resident Will Hutchinson as Vice Chairperson. Denise Fetonte of Brighton will be Alliance Secretary and Back Bay resident Bill Freeman will serve as Treasurer.

Six people were elected to two-year terms on the steering committee: Richard Burns, South End; Joyce Crowder, Dorchester; Ellen Simons, West Roxbury; Kevin McFadden, Dorchester; Krista Jackson, Allston; and Will Hutchinson, Dorchester. As chairperson, Rofes has the authority to appoint four more steering committee members.

David Scondras applauds Mayor Ray Flynn's executive order.

As we became visible as gay people, we also became targets. In New York City, the Rabbinical Alliance of America, Citizens Against Sacrilege in the Media, Catholic war veterans, and others filed suit to stop the June 27th 1983 Gay Pride March down 5th Avenue. District Court Judge Robert Ward dismissed the case pointing to the First Amendment.

Self-hate and its repercussions continued, the dilemma of the closet continued, suicides among young gays continued to a greater extent than in any other group of people, and hate crimes against gays and lesbians continued to lead the pack of hate-based violence so that the FBI was eventually was pushed to keep track of such incidents.

Across the country, gay groups tended to pick a path of making ties with the existing power structure rather than making new demands upon it. I saw the possibility of organizing a 'majority of minorities.' I often said, 'You don't have to like the people you're working with when you rob the bank, just agree on your share of the take.'

The revolution had begun. The enemy was not what most people thought, not bigots and bankers, bullies and boors. It was assimilationism, the desire of those left out to be allowed into the club, even if "the club" was the KKK.

59 /   Day to Day

Where would we sit? The council chamber had nine big desks in a squarish horseshoe arrangement and councilors were seated alphabetically given the rules of the council.

Dapper O'Neil, his nostrils flaring, could see it coming. The twelve others elected to represent the city were, besides me, alphabetically:

- Bruce Bolling, handsome black, articulate, talkative, energetic;

- James Byrne, the quiet, smart and conservative one;

- Maura Hennigan, whose father had been a judge and who almost killed all of us for holding a council meeting on her wedding day;

- Christopher Iannella, who was constantly in search of being elected council president, the elder of the group;

- James Kelly, a recovering alcoholic once in jail for illegal possession of a firearm who led the forces in Southie against busing and liberals and who fancied himself a working class hero;

- Michael McCormack, who had slowly moved from a public housing kid to becoming a member of the landed liberal gentry;

- Brian McLaughlin, sweet, closeted, quiet, thoughtful Irish guy who lived with his mom and dad;

- Tom Menino, who was once State Senator Joe Timilty's driver, and later became Mayor, and who was always the last to decide how to vote, maybe for good reasons;

- Albert "Dapper" O'Neil, blustery, red nosed charmer with a low voice, big bark, small bite and who hated gays;

- Joe Tierney, the President of the moment with his sharp sense of humor reminiscent of characters in Oscar Wilde's plays;

- Robert Travaglini, handsome, young, a believer in God and the Church but also a practical ward boss with a gift for cutting deals;

- and Charles Yancey, a black man with a penchant for smiles, numbers and careful thought.

Oh-oh. With me, that made it B B H I K M M M O S T T Y which obviously meant I would be sitting next to Dapper O'Neil.

Dapper worked himself into a fluster. He left me a huge lollipop in my desk, He made a habit of smooching his lips at me and asking if I wanted a kiss. He complained. Tierney mediated the dispute, and by chance the chairs were arranged so that a large square concrete column blocked our desks from contiguity. This did not stop Dapper from making it clear he did not want to be sitting next to the homosexual.

Tierney called me to the presidential suite. "Don't get mad about it, you two need each other. Every time he opens his mouth about you, you both get votes." It turned out Tierney was right.

The Dapper/Scondras feud started on day one and lasted more or less continually for ten years, driving me nearly crazy but providing great copy for the local press.

The Team

Being a district councilor, given the new districts, meant being the person anyone with any problem in the district called for help. During the first two days I dealt with complaints about ten people who were evicted from public housing, a trash collector who punched someone, two homeless people on Mission Hill looking for help, some arson fires and a noise problem. We dealt with them easily. The hardest problem we faced was that there was no heat in the office, but the mayor gave me his old space heater, so we dealt with that issue as well.

During my ten years on the council, my office dealt with over 9,000 individual problems one at a time, and usually solved them. They were all recorded in detail on forms we put together enabling us to create bar diagrams of types of problems which we published each month in the newsletter we sent to all our neighborhood groups, leaders and friends. They served a management function: when the graphs showed a statistically significant increase in a type of problem we changed from handling each problem one at a time to using our powers to identify the underlying causes of the change in the expected numbers and framed city policy or changes in the budget or in department's work priorities to reduce that bar back to a normal level.

Rosemary and Robert early on had developed a constituency service form that had codes for every type of problem, and we noticed with smug satisfaction that over time everyone stole our forms, changing only the name of the office owning the form. We know that they were plagiarized because they copied our codes without knowing what they meant (they were routing numbers for our staff).

We wrote and passed, according to the *Boston Globe*, over half of all city legislation passed during the decade we were in office. We wrote and got state laws enacted, impacted national issues, affected decisions of foreign leaders and affected the gay rights movement nationally.

Roughly speaking the office was divided between constituency services that handled problems and complaints and public policy issues involving shaping, influencing and implementing how government worked.

Constituent services gave us a window into what was and what was not working and informed our public policy debates. The staff (including Robert, who would come in from his office if he wasn't too busy) met every week as a group, all of the people who worked for our office, usually on Friday to review what had happened during the week, and what direction the group wanted the office to move.

None of this could have happened except for the core of people who worked with me. In particular, Jackson Hall, Robert Krebs, Rosemary Whiting, Gary Dotterman, Jack Mills, Elizabeth Conner, Shelagh Flynn and Chris Norris spent many years on the team. Each of these amazing people has their own history which they brought with them to the office and to the efforts we made as a team to make a difference for people.

I remember Attorney General Frank Bellotti once saying at a fundraiser at the Harvard Club in Back Bay that my becoming a city official only meant I got a chance to rock more and bigger boats. I could do this because I had more and better boat rockers.

A picture of my staff taken at our house during one of the years on the Council. Jack Mills, Steve Talan, Robert Krebs, myself, David Steinberg, Greg Foley, unknown, below Priscilla Gray, below her Lisa Wilcox Shelagh Geoghegan, Rosemary Whiting, Jarrett Barrios, Kim Donahue, Chris Norris, unknown. There were many others like Gary Dotterman and Jack Hall but this is the only picture of much of the crew I could find.

The first six people in my office during the initial years were:

- Rosemary Whiting — a get it done no nonsense fixer
- Christopher Norris — a lawyer's lawyer, smart, workaholic, focused
- Gary Dotterman — sees the forest, resident Commie, well connected
- Jackson Hall — make it happen, quarterback, team leader
- Jack Mills — brilliant, intense, focused
- Robert Krebs — partner, friend, lover, architect, politically pragmatic

The people who spent years of their lives on our team are why we could do what we did, why we even cared to do what we did. So the next few sections of the book outline in some detail some of the members of the core team, how they came to be with us and where they came from.

Rosemary Whiting, Constituent Services

Rosemary hired and fired, took care of thousands of complaints, and never once complained. The 52nd item on the work experience section of Rosemary Whiting's resume reads:

> *1986-1993 Boston City Council — Organized constituent services for City councilor Scondras who is openly gay and rather progressive. The office trained interns (usually students from B.A. to Ph.D.) to perform ombudsman and research services. We deal with about 800 cases a year. I supervised both paid and unpaid staff.*

I met her while running for office in 1983, door-knocking on Beacon Hill. She struck me as a member of the Boston Blue Bloods, not particularly prone to parley with a plebe, because her accent was suspiciously English. Turned out the worry was a waste of time. Rosemary was blunt, practical, and the antithesis of impressed with station or any other kind of decorative foliage designed to identify class standing.

One day, Robert asked me if I would be interested in Rosemary handling constituent services for our office. I told him we were broke. Didn't matter, Rosemary was not. She wanted to work on a regular basis. So I decided to meet her and decide together how to work together. Constituent services were driving everyone nuts.

Rosemary cut to the chase. "I am willing to work on certain conditions," she said. "First, I get to do all the hiring and firing. Second, I get to manage the staff and I am the boss. If we can agree on these things, I will work for you for as long as you need me".

Yikes. And I thought I was the boss but hell. Delegate power and you get results.

In practice, she always asked me (or shall we say, suggested to me) what she felt might be that was appropriate to each case, and she became the most effective person in Boston in handling issues as complex as finding a person who could translate Nepalese to deal with a person's problem, to getting housing for the homeless.

She sometimes said "Sorry, we can't use you" to a volunteer because the college they went to was not up to her standards. She sometimes decided that a person was just not up to the work and dismissed them. She made it clear from her advertising in college papers to her personal appeals for help that working for us required a person to have a good resume and a great deal of intelligence that was documented. She felt that since we were working for 'the people' that they deserved the best and that if you wanted the best to work for people even for free, you had to have high standards.

I was shocked. But she was right. We had more applications for volunteering than anyone had ever had in City Hall. We turned away perhaps a thousand people over a ten-year period.

Gary Dotterman, the Communist

Gary drove me everywhere, kept my daily schedules, interfaced between me and many people who wanted to talk to me, set up meetings, gave advice, listened to me kvetch and made lots of phone calls. Gary gave me a context for everything I did and encouraged me when I was down. The fat man had guts; eventually white hair, a loud voice and a twinkling eye. He played Santa Claus every year in Tulsa, where he was born. And he played the role of jovial demon that could grind down an enemy into his grave and grind salt into the dirt to keep him down. He is a great man.

He became important to me during the elections of 1981 and 1983 and for the next fifteen years of my life. He is still an important part of my life and was with me doing politics every day for the ten years I was on the Boston City Council.

Gary was not just a schedule keeper, driver, advisor, and someone who made me laugh. He also gave me a foundation of political wisdom and experience. He joined us after a long life of politics, before he even met me, writing articles supporting my election in the gay "Guide" long before knowing who I was. Best to leave Gary speak for his self (from tape recorded interviews):

I was born in Tulsa, Oklahoma, the oil capital of the world. Tulsa is a city with no respect for the past, and lots of respect for money. If you want something new, just tear down the old and build new. When I grew up 1,600 families made over $1 million a year. And 16,000 families didn't have indoor plumbing.

You knew the class you were in, from the neighborhood you were born into. If you were on the east side you were middle class, and if you were south of downtown, you were rich. If you were too far out, you were a dirt farmer. If you were North of Archer you were black, and if you were west of Main, you were white trash. I was west of Main Street.

My parents believed that the road out of poverty was through education. They put me into Holy Family grade school and junior high, and then Bishop Kelly High School. I spent one year at the Horace Mann public school where I skated the whole year. It was my only 'A' year.

When I was 12, I became involved in politics. I passed literature out for a fellow running for District Attorney, J. Howard Edmonson. It was something to do to kill time. They gave us free cokes. And also, I felt important because I was with adults.

When I was 14, I met a man by the name of Charlie Pope, who was a Tulsa attorney, who liked me and understood that I had learned the mechanics of electoral politics. Charlie decided to run for city council in Tulsa. He paid me to spend two weeks to do campaign stuff: lit drops, posters, but not in normal neighborhoods, but the black community, and I was asked to live with Ed Goodwin's family. Ed was the son of big Jim Goodwin, the owner of the Oklahoma Eagle, *the oldest black paper in the state.*

Ed and I distributed literature for two weeks and I lived at their house. That was the best education for a poor white boy that I had ever had. Suddenly I was the only white person in an all-black community. He put me there because he had no one else to send there.

The black vote was big. I figured I had a background that would resonate in the white community (I was white trash), but to get black support you needed to be there for a long time. The only black issue really on the burner at the time was the civil rights issue. Being who I am, I couldn't be passive. I also involved myself with labor issues to get the white working class vote.

By the time I reached the 1960 presidential campaign, I was well known in the communities making up the basic Roosevelt coalition. I was in the Democratic Party because my parents were. In Oklahoma, if you're rich, you're Republican; if you're poor; you're a Democrat.

I always had gay feelings, but I was so repressed, I couldn't even express them. I had the feeling I was gay but there was no way to act on it because I also wanted to be governor of Oklahoma.

I served in the Navy, and upon returning, I became known as an antiwar speaker around Tulsa and a Democratic activist. I worked on a lot of political stuff in Oklahoma. I was the head of the draft Kennedy committee for Oklahoma in 1968. The committee was organized in 1967 to push the Senator into running.

I worked on the Kennedy campaign from Indianapolis to California as an advance man. On Election Day in California, Bobby Kennedy came down to the ballroom about 12:30. The emotions were euphoric. It was big win. A decisive win. He makes a little speech and thanks people... onto Chicago. I was onstage right holding people off the stage. He was in the center stage. I was just about to leave... as Bobby was shaking hands in the kitchen, I heard this pop pop pop pop and suddenly I looked and the guy on the right of me had been shot in the head (the treasurer of the UAW) and to my left a guy was shot in the leg and he was screaming, and so I grabbed the guy shot in the leg, because he was about to fall down, he put his arm around my shoulder and I took him out of the hallway. I put him in a cab and told the driver to take him to the closest hospital. He was an ABC radio reporter. As I was walking back in, the police were taking Sirhan Sirhan into custody. I felt terribly angry. My first words were that I hoped they burned this city down.

I ran for state rep in 1968 after coming back from the Kennedy assassination. I ran and lost. So I moved to DC. I was asked to go to New York by a group called Jews for Urban Justice. I was in New York for about two years. I came to Boston to run a senatorial bid for a guy named George Samaria. George didn't care if I was gay or straight. He failed to make the ballot. I met Barney Frank who was working for Mayor Kevin White at the time, and Barney was campaigning for Samaria at the state convention. I opened a couple of gay bars in Boston, and stayed.

When Barney Frank decided to run for Congress, I ran for special election for state rep to replace Barney. I eventually dropped out of the race.

I decided to make a job for myself, so I met with a couple of guys running a magazine and we put together a magazine called a Gay Guide to New England. This publication made money from the day we hit the press. From 1981-1983 I supported myself on this magazine.

In 1981 there was this crazy guy running for city council named Scondras. I put in an ad but never met the guy. David got elected. Then I campaigned for Mondale and when I got back I was looking for a job. Scondras gave me a job.

Robert Krebs

Next on the list of core staff at the office was Robert Krebs. Robert was my partner and was my other half, including within the context of my political life, but he also had his architectural career and his own tumultuous life. During the year we campaigned for City Hall, Robert rehabbed our four-apartment home in the Fenway, and during part of the year his downtown office had a huge fire, which interrupted his work. I interviewed Robert so that he can have his own voice in this autobiography undiluted by the vagaries of my memory:

D = David
R = Robert

D: We should start at the beginning — where were you born?

R: In Newton, Iowa. It's about 30 miles east of Des Moines, past home of Maytag Washers and Dryers.

D: Is it fair to say you're an Iowa fellow then?

R: Well, it is fair to say I was born in Iowa.

D: Ok, how long did you stay there?

R: Well, mom and dad got divorced when I was four and then we spent summers in California after that; then mom remarried and I started the 6th grade in North Dakota.

D: Why did you go to North Dakota after Iowa?

R: Because mom got married there, because that's where mom's husband lived.

D: How did the divorce affect you?

R: When you are 4 years old your life is just your life; I think kids just take for granted what's happening to them. I think in retrospect it was at a time when very few people were getting divorced. In fact, nobody in my class for years was divorced so that made me, I suppose, a bit of an anomaly and always feel like I would stick out. But the worst trauma I remember is they would ask for your address and then I would never know what to put; I just didn't fit into the paperwork that they always wanted you to fill out, because it said put your mother and father's name and just, you didn't fit in the form.

D: Did you like North Dakota? Going there?

R: Mmmmm, no, I was not happy.

D: Why?

R: Because I had four amazing grandparents and two amazing great grandparents and aunts and cousins and...

D: In Iowa?

R: So, I did not want to go.

D: But you spent a lot of your life in North Dakota?

R: Yeah, and every summer in California, and every minute I could in Iowa; I spent sometimes a few weeks in the summer there and sometimes the holidays in Iowa.

D: Talk to me about your upbringing. Were you a religious person?

R: Not too much. In Iowa we were members of the Methodist church and we went, and I did Bible study and catechism and stuff; when we went to North Dakota, Ted was a member of the Evangelical United Brethren which I think was some tangential branch of the United Methodist Church.

D: Were you always an architect?

R: My grandparents built a new house when I was about five or six and from then day on I pretty much wanted to be an architect. When I was a kid I would build suspension bridges on the couch from one arm to the other see if I could do it without having any supports in it down onto the cushions.

D: Did it work?

R: Yeah! I got pretty creative: I used dominoes or Lincoln Logs; I found out that if used rubber bands, I could keep the dominoes in compression and then I could use them. But most of my architectural energy went into my train set. It had very few box cars and mostly it was an excuse to build the town around it. So then I would spend weekends building models to scale for the town of the railroad.

D: When did you find out you were gay? Did that happen once or was it in a slow cluster?

R: No, no, no; I sort of always knew I was gay from day one; I don't think that was ever a surprise. I think the question is when do you come to the realization that that is different? It had to be around the time when I was four because it was around the time that my mom and dad got divorced. We had a babysitter named Shelby and she would take us over to her mother's house and her brother would come out to eat breakfast in his pajama bottoms and I remember very clearly just wanting him to hold me. I mean, I don't think at that age it is necessarily sexual but it was definitely an affectional preference and I very much wanted him, you know, to be friends with him.

D: What happened with you and your religious stuff, the minister? At some point you had a girlfriend and...

R: That was after college, yeah.

D: What happened before college?

R: Well, I'd say by the time I was 15 or 16 I had a born-again experience.

D: What does that mean?

R: Well, there was a revival going on in at the Methodist Church, in North Dakota. I went forward…

D: Which means what?

R: That is when you go up to the altar, you accept Jesus as your personal savior…

D: So you went through that?

R: Yes, I did, and I got pretty adamant. I became a deacon at some point. I took that quite seriously.

D: In those days, did you have any issues around your sexuality? Did you tell anyone?

R: No, totally not, but I certainly knew I was attracted to guys. I was on the basketball team, and I was the student manager for the football team, so I knew that I was attracted to guys. I just didn't think I put it in the context of guys being attracted to women. I don't think I knew enough at that time to know about it. I mean maybe at that time it just seemed like a curiosity – I was just curious about guys. I also know that some of my friends had been kind of curious and had fooled around a little bit.

D: With each other?

R: With each other, and I didn't really see it as out of the ordinary, but the older you get, the more you engage with the social norms, and you realize that something is not right.

D: Ok, so talk to me about college. Where did you go to college?

R: North Dakota State University at Fargo. North Dakota State University of Agriculture and Technical Science – that is its formal name.

D: So when did you first have a girlfriend?

R: In graduate school; I mean after college, between then and graduate school.

D: Tell me about that?

R: Well, I worked really hard in college. I had done a lot of stuff – I was in a lot of activities. I think looking back on it, it was mostly sublimation – like I just had a lot of sexual energy to sublimate into something. By the end of school, I was exhausted and I was also incredibly discouraged because I had been praying day in and day out – 20 or 30 times a day at least – for God to make me straight and it wasn't happening. I was getting more and more attracted to guys and maybe the yearning was more and more intense. I was very discouraged because I just didn't think that God was helping me.

D: God wasn't making a good effort?

R: Well, He just wasn't answering my prayers in a way that I could understand. So I got accepted to graduate school, but I had no money left – so I decided to take a year off which drove my dad just totally crazy. I just felt like I needed a year off but that was a very bad year. I got quite lonely. I was living in a three-bedroom house just by myself.

D: Where?

R: In Roseville, which is a suburb of Sacramento. Dad had just got divorced, so the house was empty.

D: What about God's effort?

R: I was going to the Methodist church and finally I decided – I don't know, it was maybe desperate measures – I decided maybe the Methodist church was the problem. The church I was going to was very unfriendly – no one talked to me during the service; no one had ever said hi to me or said "I see you here periodically" so I switched to another church that I saw an ad for, called the Mission Valley Church which I think turned out to be the Assembly of God. I got to be happy there – I met people and we started hanging around we had a really intensive kind of young adults program. I immensely liked all the people there so that was really great.

D: What about your attraction to guys?

R: Near that Thanksgiving, my dad had his car in the shop and came up to get a ride from this medical building I was working on to the dealer where his car was at. When he got in the car I had been talking to the paver and he said, "That paver is hitting on you." I hadn't noticed that in the slightest but it was a first time that there was a connection between the fact that I was attracted to guys and that guys might be attracted to other guys, me in particular. Before then I don't think I had a realization that anyone else on the planet might be attracted to other guys.

D: So did you follow through?

R: At some Christmas party that I think the developer put on – although I don't quite remember where I was at – someone hit on me and I recognized that they were hitting on me and that really panicked me because suddenly all the stuff that had been fantasy became real. Suddenly it was a possibility and that was in stark contrast to my beliefs and what I kind of wanted for my life. And so as soon as I could, I made an appointment with the pastor at my church. On New Year's Eve, right before the church party, I went and talked with him. I said, "You know, look, I think I am gay, and, uh, you know, it is really making me crazy, and I don't know what to do. I have been praying for 7 or 8 years."

D: And the pastor said…?

R: He said that of course I wasn't gay; that I probably had a lack of experience; that what I needed to do was meet a woman and get more dating experience; and when that happened I would switch back from those feelings. So he actually introduced me that night to this girl who was in my youth group – kind of formally introduced me and kind of orchestrated our ever-increasing dating schedule or whatever you want to call it. He was the one who kind of put that together and said, "Okay, so tonight you are gonna call her and ask her out on a date," and blah blah blah. On Wednesday night, while she was at choir practice, I would come and get counseling and he would coach me on what to do the next day, or that night after church or whatever, so he pretty much orchestrated that, and then we talked about getting married.

D: Did he tell you what to do sexually with her?

R: Well, we were Christians so there wasn't really like a big choice about that – although he did say things like, on the way back from the ice cream store, "Put your hand around her shoulder, fondle her breast" – well "fondle" is maybe a bit of an over exaggeration – but to caress her breasts and stuff like that, but vaguely. We were Christians so it wasn't really like there was going to be any real intercourse, or anything.

D: So he is setting you up with a girl just to give you some encouragement…

R: Right, which again was horrible because she was being basically a guinea pig in a situation that had pretty huge consequences, but I was so desperate that I would have done anything the pastor said. You know, at that time I just so anxious to get to stop having these feelings, that I would have done anything he said.

D: Because you thought they were not Christian, is that the problem?

R: Yes, because I knew they were not Christian. I am sure that Carol had fallen in love with me at that time, but about that time this guy Erik started coming to church and all of a sudden, we spent a lot of time together because he didn't have a lot of time so Carol encouraged me to…

D: Help him out, basically?

R: Yeah, to give him rides and things like that. After a very short period of time, I suddenly realized that what Carol had been feeling for me, I was now feeling for him, and it was the first time that I made the connection about why loving someone was really amazing. And then I felt even worse because I realized that that was what she clearly was feeling for me.

D: Ok…

R: I don't know how this really worked, but I think what happened is, I don't think I told the pastor – that was just beyond the pale – so I think what happened is this: We had a retreat in Yosemite and we had all gone down there to some church camp and on the way home I stayed with Carol's roommate's fiancé at his house because it was another hour on to North Sacramento and my house. I think the pastor found out about it and must have thought that there was something prurient and gay. I never talked to him about it, but very shortly after, the pastor said "I found you a certified counselor." He said that that guy was going to help me out, and – I'm not kidding – I think after 2 or 3 sessions he said, "You know, you might just be gay; you may have to just deal with that fact. You can pick a lot of choices: you might want to be celibate; you might have to be in a committed relationship. There are choices but you may have to come to grips with the fact you're gay."

D: A church counselor said that?

R: You know, I've learned since then that the Lutheran church is incredibly – not maybe all of the congregations – but the theology behind the church is incredibly progressive in this area. It's not a surprise that it took a Lutheran minister to say, "You know, we are living in the 20th century, and, you know, these are the ways you might have to deal with this." Because my cousin's Lutheran and he showed me a document that the church had written: they had reanalyzed the bible – they had tried really hard to get a good teaching around sex and love and relationships and things like that. They had come up with this doctrine that was incredibly progressive.

D: *Did you ever tell Carol?*

R: *Well, yeah, but not right away. I mean, it took a little while to get my head around, you know, that I might have to deal with this. I mean my* modus operandi *that whole time had been that God would make me straight and that that would be the end of it. So I think that that was the first time I had to face the idea that I might just be gay and have to deal with it and come up with a strategy for my life.*

D: *So that church counselor...*

R: *He also said something else that stuck with me which was that God had created me in his image and that if that were true, then I had to have respect for myself and that other Christians would have to respect for me as well. Because if we were created in God's image, then that meant that whatever I was struggling with, was also something that God knew about intimately. That was the first time, I think, anyone in my life had explained the connection about caring for yourself in a way that would play out in your life. Do you know what I mean, that those are connected: that if you have a good self esteem that if you feel that you are a good person – that could be theologically based. And that was a huge step.*

D: *And Carol?*

R: *I eventually told Carol; we might have agreed that I was gonna finish a year of graduate school; she would have her nursing degree and she would have her license by then – that we would get married that summer. She would move out here for the last year and a half of my graduate school and then we would go back to Sacramento – that was the plan. Somewhere I had found the wherewithal to say that I was gay and that I didn't think that getting married was a good idea. And unfortunately for her, I don't think she even really quite knew what I was talking about and she felt it was something that she did, she actually said "What did I do?" I had a lot of effort to convince her that that was really nothing to do with her.*

D: *How did she handle it afterwards?*

R: *I heard later that she went back and had trashed me. It sounded like [the Pastor] set her up with someone who had started coming to the church that was kind of a gold digger. She had already – once I said I didn't think we should get married – she'd already bought a house on her own and I'm sure that it was a really hard really hard transition for her especially without knowing what the reason might be.*

D: Sounds really sad.

R: Oh, I think it was, and I was really sad because I had been incredibly lonely and I felt – especially at the beginning – I confused the companionship with her, because I liked her – I mean it wasn't like I didn't like her – I really liked her a lot – but I think I confused that companionship and being less alone with love.

D: So now you are at Harvard; you are upset; Carol is gone; you must have been upset at the time. How did you end up meeting me?

R: At the end of my first year I, um, again – in an incredibly courageous move given my personality at the time – came out to the guy across the hall to me from me.

D: Kevin Cathcart?

R: Kevin Cathcart.

D: Now in New York City? Running GLAAD I think?

R: Running GLAAD. But anyway, I came out to him and he said, "Here's the name of some bars," and I said to him "Hey, I'm still coming from this Fundamentalist experience; I don't think I can do that." Then he says, "Well, the Old West Church has a gay and lesbian coffee hour afterwards; maybe you should go there; you really need to meet people." During midterms, he must have spent, I don't know, hours and hours with me after I came out. It was like just this phenomenal question. We actually went to see this movie called "Word is Out."

D: Yeah, I know the movie...

R: ...and it was amazingly poignant because it was exactly the most perfect thing to do as I was coming out and I got to hear all these other stories and hear these lives and relate to all these people. It sort of made that connection for me, and so a couple weeks later I went to the Old West Church for the first time and that is where I met you, that first night that I went.

Others

There are many, many other people who worked with us, many volunteers, people with special projects, work-study students, people who worked on re-election campaigns or specific public policy issues, and without them a great deal of what was accomplished could not have happened. The people whose backgrounds I have given you stayed with me for many, many years and they were the scaffolding within the office which supported the efforts of everyone else.

It would not have been possible to do what we did without people like Helen Cox, the town crier of the Fenway, and Matt Thall, the voice of reason at our Community Development Corporation, who could imitate Julia Child so well he did a skit playing her at a fundraiser in the Fenway. It would not have been possible without a host of other people – I don't want you to get the idea, a variation on the American 'superman' view of how things happen that a few people in our city council office were responsible for everything that we came up with.

We often were the people, who were given credit, and often were the people who gave words to explain feelings and interviews to spread news, but we were not the only people involved in making things happen by a long shot. We were often the witness to the event, the minister who comments upon work requiring far greater powers than ours. Many, many people are responsible for what we accomplished.

I talk about this because there are several theories about how the world works that have done us great disservices — one of them is that the world is made better (or worse) by supermen and super demons. This world view is reinforced by religious traditions and is connected to the notion that if you succeed it is because of your efforts, that if you fail it is because you have flaws, and that becoming a cheerleader for a superhero can substitute for doing something toward a cause we say we believe in. People are thus divided into winners whom we applaud and whose heads swell, or losers who feel terrible about themselves because they are clearly deficient in character, people whom we shun.

It is another of many myths, which keep the hierarchy of power stable, and you in your place.

We began our decade with a simple idea: that if you don't support people's right to be really different from you, and then you will eventually lose your freedom to be who you are too. That only a majority of minorities is a safe power block, that every other kind of organized group demonizes someone who eventually undermines the stability of the organized group. That no matter how 'sensible' it seems, the idea that you're putting down anyone who is different from you is dangerous to your freedom.

Robert, at a Gay Pride parade in Providence, was confronted by a group of people who were teachers in a parochial school. They commented to him that the nearly naked men on a float were disgusting, and were ruining it for everyone else. Robert said that his grandfather thought Catholics were disgusting. And that if the churchgoers did not understand why it was important to support the men kissing on the float, they should understand that if left to people like Robert's grandfather, the day would come when they would stop Catholics from doing their thing, and on and on until we would all learn again what the word "fascist" really means. To his amazement, they said they had never thought of it from that perspective and finally understood why prejudice is such a slippery slope.

61 /   The Trenches

City Hall was an endless series of hallways filled with people who had all sorts of issues, some easy to deal with, some difficult, all important to those affected, and for the most part no one else. The hardest part of being in office, of managing, was to simultaneously set an agenda which laid out goals toward which we worked every day in one way or another while having enough legislation or other vehicles on hold waiting for the right time, the right circumstances that would make them viable, while simultaneously handling issues brought to our attention by people who supported us — a liquor license here, a parking ticket there, institutional expansion, rent control, being evicted, a homeless veteran, lights that burnt out on public ways, rats and thieves — and we developed systems to handle them all.

Meanwhile my personal life became increasingly public.

February 2, 1984 Bay Windows *Valentine's Day article*

There was a huge article in the Valentine's Issue of *Bay Windows* about Robert and me. It was the first of hundreds of articles that built me up, trashed me, tweaked Bob or extolled him for dealing with my shortcomings. There was an avalanche of media that ensued in the wake of our becoming a gay elected couple.

In the same November election, two cities, Santa Cruz, California and Key West, Florida elected openly gay mayors. John Laird, the new Mayor of Santa Cruz would become our friend. Richard A. Heyman was elected Mayor of Key West and said that support from the black community was critical to his success. Eventually Steven Shulte and I would form the Gay Officials Conference — Steve was a gay city councilor from West Hollywood which seemed to me to be a gay city. Of the over 500,000 elected officials in the U.S.A. it would seem perhaps 5 were openly gay prior to my election. If we assume some correlation between percentage of gay people and percentage of gay representatives, we should have had 5,000 openly gay elected officials if gays are even one percent of the population — a very conservative figure. Ten times that given the usual guess of 'one in ten.'

I mention this because what caught me and perhaps many others by surprise is that becoming the first openly gay elected official North of Key West and East of the Mississippi made me known via the gayvine, the intricate web of local newspapers and person to person conversations, to many, many thousands of people and places across the nation. I became a loud voice for the most despised of a nation sexually schizoid, and soon I would be asked to speak in many cities across the country and around the world.

So it was natural to see columns and interviews on television and in newspapers about our personal life.

In an article called "An Intricate Web of Love, Accommodation and Support" *Bay Windows* shared my life with Robert with everyone else in the local gay community. It was a puff piece, but fun to read. Some of it was revealing. It begins:

> *David Scondras leaves his socks over the entire floor. His lover
> said so.*
>
> *"I didn't allow myself to depend on anyone," Scondras said, "not
> financially or emotionally. I felt that I had to be totally
> independent. Many of my past relationships were short. They*

were all very important to me but that kind of unreliability keeps you on guard." Before meeting Krebs, Scondras had assumed he would be alone for the rest of his life. "I wasn't upset about it. I just accepted it as a fact."

Kissing Scondras on the head, Krebs concluded, "I made my decision. I wanted David to fulfill my fantasy. I had a lot of expectations. I made a choice. I could either accept David as he is and work on us, or I could move out and get a clean apartment"

That was what I told the paper, but the truth was that I could have had long relationships before. I was just too conflicted about being gay. I mean, I had gone to a mental hospital and asked them to cure me of being gay while I was at Harvard! I had spent years of my life trying to exorcize what I had been taught was a sin or sickness. To this day I am left with the damage done to people who are taught they are sick or evil for being what nature made them.

Gay people were still mostly closeted (as they still are today), still made fun of, still beaten up, still harassed by cops, still arrested for sex. They are to this day the most common targets for hate crimes according to the FBI hate crimes statistics. It is intriguing that our 'sex offender' lists are disproportionately people of color or people who are engaging in sex that is socially not acceptable by born-again prudes. For example, a blowjob with your heterosexual wife is just as illegal as one in the woods with a same-sex partner, but the former is ignored and the latter is the subject of police sweeps befitting the search for a serial killer.

The culture had begun to change but a lot of the world continued on like nothing had happened.

Meanwhile I got used to dealing with a seemingly endless set of demands on my time. Tuesday, March 6th, 1984, was a typical day:

- *8 a.m. meeting with Jim Shannon at Club Café (U.S. Representative Shannon would become Massachusetts Attorney General for a term)*

- *9 a.m. meeting with Vince Perrelli (still working at the Fenway Health Center as one of its doctors)*

- *10 a.m. Public Safety Committee Meeting on taxi killings and guns*

- *12:30 lunch with Jack Mills re: Arson Hearing*

- *1:30 meeting with American Legion and Triangle Association at the Legion post re: residential parking*

- *2:00 p.m. Meeting with Representative Tom Valleley about New England Life (I was opposed to their construction project without some benefits to the city)*

- *3:30 meeting with former city councilor Larry DiCara*

- *5:30 Michael McCormack fundraiser at Anthony's Pier 4*

- *6:00 p.m. Ruggles St. Baptist Church*

- *7:00 p.m. District A Police meeting with Beacon Hill businesses*

- *8:00 p.m. Barney Frank and friend, dinner*

…and on and on day after day after day. A 13-hour day; 18-hour days became typical during the ten years I spent as a City Councilor.

In this chaos keeping our team focused on a set of goals and moving toward them was extremely difficult; the political wind kept blowing and we had to tack, take bearings all the time, decide which way to move, when to move, what to move, who to move.

We got into the habit of meeting every Friday, all of us arranged around the big tables in the Piemonte room. We would each review what we had accomplished during the week, what we felt we had to do to make progress on our tasks, what unforeseen crises had occurred, and any movement on our major goals, advice on political decisions, etc. Robert tried to attend because he said it made planning our personal lives easier, coordinating our schedules more efficient and keeping informed on my efforts less time consuming.

These meetings made it possible to bring order to what otherwise could easily have devolved into a reactionary, directionless mess — a common ailment in elected offices.

62 /   Car Alarms

It was really late in the evening around November of 1981. The damn car alarm just would not stop. It went on and on competing with the sound of torrential rain. I lay in bed trying to figure out how to block out the noise, but it cut right through the pillows. Robert was up, having been very ill. I was very worried about how this would affect him so after about an hour of ceaseless, high-pitched noise, I got up and dressed and went out, ignoring the pouring rain.

It turned out that a group of neighbors had formed on the street, all looking at the car, not knowing exactly what to do. I notice that they were carrying a hammer and a crow bar. We had already called the police who said they could do nothing — no one could touch it. They clearly felt that "property" was more important than our sleep.

We began to feel like warriors of the dark. It was a very small car, a Le Car by Renault, so several of them tore open a part of the cloth sun roof in hopes of pulling the hood latch open. When that failed, two of them pried open the hood but pulling the wires off of the battery did nothing. Then I remembered the police said the only way a car would be removed was if it were blocking a fire lane.

So, they started bouncing the little car, up and down, moving it inch by inch until the front blocked Edgerly Road enough that cars, and more to the point, a fire truck, could not get by. The Fire Department was called, and within a few minutes came and just took the car away. We all speculated that the car had been parked there by rich Symphony-goers, who didn't worry that they had parked illegally in a resident space or about getting a ticket since Traffic and Parking never seemed to ticket or tow in our neighborhood on a concert night. But we were sure they would remain clueless as to why the car was damaged in such a curious way.

We got to sleep, finally. All committed to silence about the mystery of what happened. You notice I know no names. Who knows how long memories last and I want to make sure no one gets in trouble.

It made me realize how much noise was the enemy of peace in the city. Keeping the noise down was a huge part of making a city livable but it was not well appreciated in government. The memory of this event led to one of the first things I did as a lawmaker on the City Council.

Back to 1984. Gary's horn tooted outside my apartment, too early as usual. I struggled bleary-eyed to get into that stupid suit that my staff had me wear every day. I still have that green suit after 25 years. Guess it was well made. I remember getting it at a store near Newbury Street, I forget the name, one of three suits that would be the mainstay of the uniforms I had to wear but never liked.

Anyway, Gary and Mobile One, our ancient Volvo sedan, were waiting. We rushed through the streets. Gary would tell me the news of the day and what I needed to do. As usual I griped about everything, and in particular about car alarms that never, ever stopped.

We got into the City Hall garage where we had a coveted parking place, where, over and over the building staff complained that our car was giving the seat of government a bad name because it was such a piece of junk. Gary eventually caved in and bought a brand new Ford Escort that came to be known as Mobile Two.

Chris said, "Hi," from the computer he lived behind, Jack Hall had some project he wanted me to look at, Gary got me my schedule as I hid behind the cardboard wall we erected behind the entrance door where no one would imagine the Councilor would be located. Our work-study students were working, getting direction from Chris and Jack, I think.

But I hadn't forgotten that car alarm from 1981. So when I got elected, one of the first things I did was write a law to stop it. My law to stop this noise from happening again would precipitate a fight with Council President Joe Tierney. It would be my first fight with Joe, although to this day I can't figure out why Joe cared about protecting car alarms. Anyway I wrote a law, which nobody but a city lawyer could figure out, which was meant to stop the damn car alarm noise in Boston. It was "An Amendment to CBC Ord. 14 Chapter 11, Sec. 354" and read, in part:

> *Whereas in the City of Boston there are both automobile alarms which terminate automatically within two of three minutes and those which do not; and*

*Whereas the Boston Police Department does not have the
authority to terminate the nuisance created by such alarms
which do not automatically terminate after a reasonable
amount of time, by towing or disabling; and*

*Whereas numbers of complaints concerning this problem have
come to the attention of the Council, therefore be it ordained by
the City Council as follows...*

The rest basically said that you couldn't have a car alarm unless it shuts off automatically within five minutes or you get fined.

March 7th, 1984 I got the council to vote on the law, and got another law sent to the state house to get the police the power to disable the noisemaker or tow the car. Both laws passed.

I felt good. The era of car alarms that went on for hours would soon be over, not so much because the police would intervene, but rather because insurance companies would not want to have cars run up bills for repairs when they had their endless alarms 'disabled' and would require self-terminating alarms to minimize insurance costs. I figured that over time, the endless alarms would end.

Tierney didn't like the law, but voted for it anyway. I think he objected to government interfering with private property, even private property that made very public noise. Anyway, I loved it. I finally got back at that car alarm.

I thought about it for awhile and decided that in the end, the whole issue of noise in a city was one of the biggest ones for people, because it was the single most common problem with the quality of life when people lived in highly concentrated areas. Although it seemed like a small thing, it astonished me how many people loved this law, and it made me quite popular. Of course it was useful that the vast majority of people who voted for me did not own cars.

This would be the first of 107 new laws I would write, 310 orders and 319 resolutions, more than all the other councilors combined and more than any person had written in the history of the City of Boston.

63 /   The Gay Rights Bill

In 1973, State Representative Barney Frank introduced the Massachusetts Gay Rights law. But in 1984, there was still no gay rights law in Massachusetts. Wisconsin actually became the first state to enact a gay rights law, and even today in the 21st century the majority of states do not have one.

Massachusetts would have to wait until November 16th of 1989, to watch then Governor Michael Dukakis sign the Massachusetts bill into law soon after it had finally passed the Massachusetts House and Senate.

Mark Roosevelt (my opponent in chapter 45 in book I) introduced the bill as a State Representative from Beacon Hill that awesome year that it passed. Mark Roosevelt lost the city council race to me, but the gay community gained a fighter in Mark on the state level not long after.

Prior to the 1989 state law, I knew that everyone expected me to get Boston to pass a city gay rights law, a Human Rights law, and it was the first big piece of legislation I undertook in 1984.

Sorry, I am falling into the idea that big men strut across the stage and change the world singlehandedly. It would be more accurate regarding the gay rights bill to say that the many gay people who had struggled to get me elected had set a gay rights bill as one part of my agenda. In fact at one point there were 47 people who were working on drafting the bill — and that was just writing it.

There was a legitimate concern that if I could not get this bill through the conservative City Council of Boston, it might damage the efforts to get the state law passed. So I went to Mayor Ray Flynn to discuss the bill with him. He looked up at me and said, "What's a transvestite?" There was a reason he wanted to know.

I had been at a union celebration for the new mayor. I was trying to butch it up, to fit in and I wanted to show Flynn what a great a guy I was. Then in walked a drag queen with a low voice named Sylvia Sidney. All 6'7" of her decked out as Cleopatra. She walked over to me and said, "David, darling, I insist you to introduce me to the Mayah."

Sylvia Sidney, whom I introduced to "the Mayah," Mayor Ray Flynn

So I introduced a transvestite to the Mayor. Surprisingly, Ray Flynn was amazingly cordial and talkative. He offered her a new costume and suggested an appropriate job at City Hall. He introduced her to other people around him and his sweetness got me confused.

During my meeting with the Mayor, I came to grips with something that had not occurred to me. I wasn't powerful because Ray Flynn liked me. I was powerful because a drag queen named Sylvia Sidney (who wouldn't give Ray the time of day) had worked extremely hard on my election, had raised money for me, got me a union endorsement, and had talked me up to anyone who would listen. It was my connection to this drag queen that was what made me powerful, not being another sycophant hopping for favors from a mayor. Because Ray Flynn couldn't get her on his side on his own — for that he needed me.

I began to see that what I had been hiding from for all my life was what gave me strength, what made me special, what made it possible for me to connect with thousands of institutions each of which had quiet gay people embedded in them. It was what helped my connection with communities of color in which circulated my gay black friends, what helped me raise money, make phone calls, talk to power.

I felt ashamed then, that I had been so ashamed for so long, and I knew that the thing that made me unique meant that I could get the law passed because there were a lot of gays in Boston, and they had money, and votes, and Ray knew perfectly well that in a voting booth you didn't have to come out of the closet to do yourself a favor, that the gay community would support the people who supported the gay community.

Sylvia, in asking me to introduce her to Ray Flynn, taught me a lot about loyalty, power, love and quid pro quo. It was this love that brought me to City Hall. And she made me remember not to assume anything about anyone. Besides being a fabulous comedienne, she was the long-time shop steward of a very important local labor union-Local 26!

> *"I'm not considered a drag queen, per se, trying to impersonate another woman. You've never seen a woman that looked like me! I look more like a hardcore madam, sort of a Mae West caricature. When I hit the stage, I'm coarse, loud and vulgar."*
> *— Sylvia Sidney*

If support from those who were just like me were not the basis of my campaign, Boston would not have had an openly bearded, Greek gay Commie on the Boston City Council elected from a district predominantly by people of Irish descent, Beacon Hill white liberals, union members, gays and people of color.

Ray told me he would sign the bill if I could get it past the 13-member council.

64 /   Getting It Past the Council

The old Boston City Council was a bit like the court jester except that a court jester was supposed to tell the king the truth albeit in humorous metaphor. The Council had no truth to tell and its humor seemed to be of a slapstick variety.

The new 'district' council actually had brains and depth but certainly not much common ground. And because most of its members had never been elected to anything nor even had any training, we pretty much invented our own set of interactions.

I'll never forget the day we got sued because we were not supposed to be hanging out with each other unless there was an "open door," the ability of anyone who wanted to listen in to our conversations. This was even true of council committees, so when two of us took an airplane flight together and if we were the majority of a smaller committee, we were violating the "open meeting" law. We figured out more ways to get around that piece of nonsense, from musical chairs meetings, to sequential meetings, to phone conferencing to plain out-and-out to hell with it.

There are folks called lawyers who are taught that truth, justice, fairness and goodness proceed from rules, regulations, and an adherence to form. This is an error. Good things proceed from good people no matter how horrible the rules, and good rules will never save you from the twisted machinations of the greedy or the prudish.

The older, pervious members of the Council did not disappear. Councilor Freddy Langone came to my office and spoke with me about the budget, giving me loud, clear advice although I did not really understand what he was saying at the time.

Shortly after the new council was seated, Freddy invited everybody to a dinner, which he put together. Everyone showed up, including Mayor Flynn. Dapper was in great form, joking about each of the new councilors. Freddy looked around and said that there were too many of us without spouses. He looked around the room and pointed us out. There was Brian McLaughlin (who for good reasons I suspected was gay), Maura Hennigan (daughter of a state senator), myself, Bob Travaglini, and me, who all were, according to Freddy, unattached. He said looking at Maura "look at the beautiful woman, you should have someone! We have to find people for Brian and David..." I said that perhaps it would not be necessary for me. The councilors chuckled. Dapper himself was unmarried although he had a 'girlfriend' that no one seemed to have ever met.

To understand how important the gay rights bill was, it is important to understand that in 1984, the world was different than it is now. It was far worse for gays.

The world of heterosexuality had dozens of venues for people to get together, from parking areas where people watched the 'submarine races' at night by rivers, to dates at local places, to dances, to the Senior Proms, to television shows that gave endless lessons on dating and love, to homes where parents expected and fundamentally supported their children's right to heterosexual love even if they were skittish about it.

Nothing though for those of us who were gay. At home we were silent. On the street we were invisible.

For example, one of my classmates at Lowell High School told me, "Don't do it. Be careful. If you get caught your life will be ruined." I had fallen for the head of our track team, a blond boy named David, so deeply that I spent time in the yard next to his house painting pictures hoping to see him. I had joined the track team mainly to watch him run. Years later I went back to Lowell hoping to meet him. I stood in the same empty lot for a while, where I had painted my pictures. No one would tell me what happened to him. He was dead. I know that he must have committed suicide as I had tried to do, and as 1/3 or so of gay teenagers try to do. To this day I wonder what my life would have been like if the world had been kind and I had been able to ask that boy out for a date.

In the absence of any other outlet, gays would check each other out in bathrooms, and have sex there. You couldn't do it at home, in parks, or on the beach. Straight people did it everywhere but everyone pretended not to notice. So gay people tried to cruise, have sex, and connect socially wherever it could be sneaked. A life of hiding, looking over your shoulder constantly. A life full of fear.

Police would raid bathrooms and arrest guys for having sex or luring gays into having sex with them and then after the sex was finished, arresting them. What sickies — you can be sure that having sex was not just 'part of the job' for these pathetic people. Gays' biggest problems came from closeted gays who were twisted by their need to punish themselves for who they were. This included the famous queer cross-dressing FBI director J. Edgar Hoover.

The woods, where straight people kissed and made love, were also raided constantly by the police who targeted gay people, chasing them away or sometimes beating them up or arresting them.

Some numbers might help paint the picture. As recently as 1995 the Fenway Community Health Center compiled anti-gay incidents. In 1995, 2,212 anti-gay incidents were documented in which over 2,900 gay people were attacked. The National Coalition of Anti-Violence Programs' eleven tracking programs compiled these incidences. These programs did not keep track of all incidences because reporting them is voluntary on a local level. The vast majority of acts of violence against gays were never reported for several reasons, including legitimate fear of the police.

In Massachusetts there were 173 incidents. Overall, 34% of the incidents resulted in serious injury and 4% in death. Nationally, 382 incidents reported in the few states that kept track of acts of violence against gays, involved weapons of one kind or another used against gays.

Some examples which paint the picture of a homophobic society, which commits acts of violence against gays, a society in which as recently as the year 2000 has more acts of violence against gays than against any other minority group:

- *Washington D.C.:* as bystanders watched, an ambulance crew rushed to save Tyrone Hunter (a cross dresser), injured in a car crash, until one paramedic cut open hunter's trousers and learned the victim had a penis. The rescue workers stopped treatment, backed off and started ridiculing Hunter to colleagues. Hunter died later that day in a hospital.

- *Jackson Heights, Queens, NY:* On June 18, a 24-year-old gay man who was distributing condoms and HIV related information to street workers at 1 a.m. was assaulted with a knife by a 17 year old resident. The victim sustained a severe cut to his elbow. The perpetrator repeatedly referred to the victim as 'faggot'.

- *New York NY:* On November 24, a lesbian couple was severely assaulted on the dance floor of a lesbian nightclub by a heterosexual couple. The assault occurred after the lesbians refused the sexual advances of the straight male. The man struck the lesbian repeated to the face causing fractures to her facial bones and severing an artery. He then dragged both lesbians by the hair across the dance floor.

- *Jamaica Plain, MA:* A lesbian couple was repeatedly harassed and neighborhood adolescents vandalized their home. Anti-gay signs were placed on their porch and their car was repeatedly vandalized by anti lesbian/gay graffiti and stickers with slurs such as 'gay bitch'. The tires of their car were slashed. The women chose to move, having little faith that the environment would improve.

The reports go on and on detailing rape, murder, theft, harassment, act after act in city after city in state after state.

I remember how dangerous it was, just being what I was. I was once in a subway, and watched a guy across the chasm of the train bed because he was beautiful. He disappeared. Later he appeared coming down the stairs, walked by me and kneed me in the groin. I bent over in pain and shame and half ran, half crouched away. The fact he would go so far out of his way to hurt me was not lost on me.

We had gaydar and played poker with everyone in our environment. To make a mistake invited violence. Gaydar was our ability to distinguish quickly whether someone was gay or straight. This was a survival mechanism. If we could not quickly and accurately distinguish between the two so that the poker face could be invoked, we stood a real risk of being beaten up.

In all these years, after all these reports, there is still no end to the punishments meted out to queers for being what nature dictates that they must be.

I was beaten up by a cop on a police car next to the Fenway park area, where I cruised, one of the few places I could do that. After all, if you cruised in most places you would be attacked.

If the hormonal surge caught you and you used a bathroom to play with a guy, you stood a real risk that you would be humiliated at best, arrested and beaten at worst, and have your name displayed in local papers.

Society had no space or place for gays, and yet demanded the right to punish them for being what they are wherever they could. It would be like stopping a person from ever eating at a restaurant or dining room table, then beating them up for sneaking scraps in an alley.

Today on the Internet, that place of meetings that is more anonymous, police lure men and beat them up, as do occasional homophobes. When I am in a chat room on occasion there are crazy Christians who try to 'save us' from talking to each other and arranging rendezvous.

When I was young the TV series "I Led Three Lives" was a favorite of mine because I was a kind of spy, at least understanding the constant fear of exposure which is what it was like being gay.

Our newspaper, the *Gay Community News* and its sister *Fag Rag* had an office which was burnt to the ground. I remember going over the ashes hoping to help figure out what happened.

I tell you these things to help explain that putting on public view a 'gay rights bill' was not just another bill, it was a moment for an entire community to say "we are here and we have the right to be here." Or, as I said at my real debut in John and Peter Lyons huge disco club Avalon to reporters and friends, with Robert by my side: "We're here, we're queer, get used to it."

It was a time for a fight for freedom, for a push for privacy and respect. I remember the poem that motivated me.

Let America be America Again

Originally published by Langston Hughes in *Esquire* and in the International Worker Order pamphlet *A New Song* (1938)

*Let America be America again. Let it be the dream it used to be.
Let it be the pioneer on the plain Seeking a home where he
himself is free.*

(America never was America to me.)

*Let America be the dream the dreamers dreamed — Let it be
that great strong land of love Where never kings connive nor
tyrants scheme That any man be crushed by one above.*

(It never was America to me.)

*O, let my land be a land where Liberty Is crowned with no false
patriotic wreath, But opportunity is real, and life is free, Equality
is in the air we breathe.*

*(There's never been equality for me, nor freedom in this
"homeland of the free.")*

*Say, who are you that mumbles in the dark? And who are you
that draws your veil across the stars?*

*I am the poor white, fooled and pushed apart, I am the Negro
bearing slavery's scars. I am the red man driven from the land, I
am the immigrant clutching the hope I seek — And finding only
the same old stupid plan Of dog eat dog, of mighty crush the
weak.*

*I am the young man, full of strength and hope, Tangled in that
ancient endless chain Of profit, power, gain, of grab the land! Of
grab the gold! Of grab the ways of satisfying need! Of work the
men! Of take the pay! Of owning everything for one's own
greed!*

*I am the farmer, bondsman to the soil. I am the worker sold to
the machine. I am the Negro, servant to you all. I am the people,
humble, hungry, mean — Hungry yet today despite the dream.*

Beaten yet today — O, Pioneers! I am the man who never got ahead, The poorest worker bartered through the years.

Yet I'm the one who dreamt our basic dream In the Old World while still a serf of kings, Who dreamt a dream so strong, so brave, so true, That even yet its mighty daring sings In every brick and stone, in every furrow turned That's made America the land it has become. O, I'm the man who sailed those early seas In search of what I meant to be my home — For I'm the one who left dark Ireland's shore, And Poland's plain, and England's grassy lea, And torn from Black Africa's strand I came To build a "homeland of the free."

The free?

Who said the free? Not me? Surely not me? The millions on relief today? The millions shot down when we strike? The millions who have nothing for our pay? For all the dreams we've dreamed And all the songs we've sung And all the hopes we've held And all the flags we've hung, The millions who have nothing for our pay — Except the dream that's almost dead today.

O, let America be America again — The land that never has been yet — And yet must be — the land where every man is free. The land that's mine — the poor man's, Indian's, Negro's, ME — Who made America, Whose sweat and blood, whose faith and pain, Whose hand at the foundry, whose plow in the rain, Must bring back our mighty dream again.

Sure, call me any ugly name you choose — The steel of freedom does not stain. From those who live like leeches on the people's lives, We must take back our land again, America!

O, yes, I say it plain, America never was America to me, And yet I swear this oath — America will be!

Out of the rack and ruin of our gangster death, The rape and rot of graft, and stealth, and lies, We, the people, must redeem The land, the mines, the plants, the rivers. The mountains and the endless plain — All, all the stretch of these great green states — And make America again!

Langston Hughes 1938

America was never America to me either. I understood this. I lived in two worlds, the world I wanted and the world that existed and they were not the same. I did not long to belong, I longed to be left alone, free to be who I was and the law I was writing was my own blow for freedom's sake. Even Hughes had to hide —

In the 1989 film, "Looking for Langston," by British filmmaker Isaac Julien, Hughes is reclaimed as a black gay icon from where there is a consistent attempt to ignore or at least downplay his homosexuality because he is such a towering figure in African American literature; his icon status among the African American community is contingent on his heterosexuality.

It was always a mystery to the pundits why I got so many black votes in Boston. It was because my black friends, many, many of whom were gay, had networks within the community of color. It was a side effect of being a white gay man who not only organized but also socialized with black gay men.

This poem said with more eloquence than I can muster how I felt, what I wanted, what I tried to do in spite of the pain I felt constantly, the fear, the anxiety, the self doubt and the desire to run away, to hide.

Anyway, the City Council was a collection of people who were not about to pass a gay rights law without a lot of pressure, and we decided to provide that pressure. Faneuil Hall was the location of the rally the Alliance put together in support of the gay rights bill I was proposing to the council. Hundreds of gays and their friends showed up.

San Francisco Chronicle

Gay America Enters the Political Mainstream

By Randy Shilts
Chronicle Correspondent

Bunceton, Missouri

Mayor Gene Ulrich nervously eyed poll officials as they tallied hand-marked ballots in Bunceton's one-room City Hall, deep in the part of Missouri known as "Little Dixie."

A near-unanimous vote came from both the south side of Main Street, where descendants of the area's freed slaves live along dirt roads, and north of Main Street, where the city's predominant Southern Baptists live behind white picket fences.

The vote count showed Ulrich's mandate for a third term was complete — an 88-to-6 victory.

Gene Ulrich's re-election in this two-gas station, one-grocery town of 419 said nearly as much about the nation's changing politics as the outcome of many of this year's presidential primaries.

Bunceton's popular mayor, as it happens, is unabashedly gay and lives quite openly with his lover of 11 years in their small home on Olive Street. Their relationship is accepted so matter-of-factly here that the two were given a married couple's discount when they joined the Chamber of Commerce.

In 1984, gay America is moving into the political mainstream nationwide.

Although San Francisco's gay rights movement has captured most of the limelight in recent years, a visible movement has emerged in every region of the United States. Gays are enjoying political advances and a degree of social acceptance that could not have been imagined a decade ago — although they still face some of the sternest challenges to confront their movement's brief, 15-year history.

"If you said a generation ago that there weren't a few hundred or a few thousand homosexuals, but millions, and that they would be standing up one day and saying they were gay, people would have been wide-eyed. People just would not have believed it could happen," said Mervyn Field, author of the California Poll.

"It is a phenomenal change in a brief period of time."

The movement of gays into the nation's political mainstream is demonstrated on many fronts:

■ All three major Democratic presidential candidates have endorsed gay concerns.

■ After years of ignoring all homosexual issues, the U.S. Supreme Court is expected to rule soon on the constitutionality of statutes against gay sexual activity.

■ Although no acknowledged homosexual was serv-ing in any public office 10 years ago, openly gay people now serve in Congress, the Minnesota Legislature, the boards of supervisors of San Francisco and Dane County, Wis., the city councils of Boston and Minneapolis, and as mayors of Key West, Fla., and the California communities of Santa Cruz and Laguna Beach.

■ Gay voters are now an established element in the liberal political coalitions that have elected the mayors of Philadelphia, Houston, Seattle, Birmingham, Washington, Denver, Atlanta, New Orleans, Chicago, Los Angeles, Minneapolis, Miami and Charlotte, N.C.

"It's amazing when I think back and realize that I never heard the word gay or homosexual even spoken aloud until I was well into my 20s," marvels Bunceton's Mayor Ulrich, 39.

"Gay politics is almost the least of the change — the whole way America views gay people has changed 180 degrees in just a handful of years."

Presidential Politics

The most visible symbol of gays' melding into America's mainstream has come in this year's presidential campaign. Each of the major Democratic candidates has aggressively sought gay votes as well as campaign contributions from the growing coffers of gay political action committees. Gay rights has been integrated into the platform of key elements of the traditional Democratic coalition, such as the AFL-CIO, which voted to endorse gay rights legislation last year, and the Congressional Black Caucus, most of whose members are co-sponsoring gay rights legislation.

Like former presidential candidates Alan Cranston, Ernest Hollings and Edward Kennedy, Senator Gary Hart recently became a co-sponsor of a bill to amend the 1964 Civil Rights Act to include gays. Walter Mondale and Jesse Jackson have also announced their support for federal gay rights legislation and campaigned among gays across the country.

The presidential candidates still approach the gay issue cautiously, if not uncomfortably. Both Jackson, who has referred to the gay rights issue as "that sex thing," and Mondale have showed some reticence in directly addressing gay concerns even while courting homosexual voters.

"This is still a very controversial issue and politicians can still get in trouble either way, by supporting gay rights or opposing it," said Minnesota state Senator Allan Spear, who has been re-elected three times since disclosing his homosexuality 10 years ago.

"As it's worked out, however, you can get in more trouble by coming out against it than for it, as John Glenn found out," a reference to the way the Ohio senator's effort to use opposition to gay rights to attack the "special-interest" candidacy of Mondale backfired.

Gay leaders now are split almost equally between Mondale, who has added gays to his traditional Democratic labor-ethnic coalition, and Hart, who appeals to

Gay City Councilor David Scondras of Boston believes 'passing laws doesn't change attitudes'

By Steve Ringman

See Page 27, Col. 1

Other politics did not stop just because we were engaged in the gay rights fight. Some examples:

Anti-gay actions were often clothed as public policy. For example on May 9th there is an article in which I am defending my refusal to allow the Parks Department to tear down the reeds (phragmites) in the Fens which protect the privacy of gays using the Fens for cruising and sex mostly after midnight for the past 100 years. They said the reeds were an invasive species. I said 'In other words you want to tear out a plant that needs no fertilizer or gardeners, and replace them with wussy plants that costs us money and the time of our limited parks staff. They have been there for a century and because they need very wet ground they stop at the waterfront areas, they don't bother you and they are beautiful. You want to tear them down because you are once again attacking a place gay people can come together."

I protected the reeds and their benefactors for ten years, stopping the police from harassing gays every night, getting rid of gay bashers etc. Even the state Supreme Judicial Court weighed in, ruling that what people do sexually in a park having made every effort to conceal themselves without trying to impose it on anyone is a matter of privacy. Later this would become the basis of ending the terrorizing of men in rest areas, at least for a while.

Mayor Flynn chose Ann Maguire to be the city's gay liaison, which did not sit well with people who were pro-choice. She had supported Ray Flynn in his election bid and Robert said that she knew with unerring instinct who would get power and make sure she was there. She came to my office and told me not to object to her appointment. Despite the fact that she had supported everyone else but me in the city council race, I had no intention of objecting to her appointment. She had a strong personality and could do a lot of good for a lot of people and I felt that Flynn needed a woman who could bring her weight to bear on the concerns being raised by the gay community. It made sense for her to have the job. Yet she assumed that I would be opposed to it.

I had come to believe that there are no friends or enemies in politics, just common interests.

In spite of my 'progressive' credentials, I also fought for building a substantial office tower that would bring jobs and taxes into the city on Small Park where once a parking garage existed built by Carolyn Park's dad. He had built the old garage to help out a previous recession by investing in the downtown. Carolyn owned Town Taxi, the largest cab fleet in Boston, and she lived alone with her South American lover in a beautiful house in the suburbs. She was an amazing liberated woman. Robert and I spent some time at her house, swimming in her pool and getting to know her and her lover. The liberals wanted just a big park with no tower. We proposed burying the ramp and putting the park on top of it; it still exists today. I said, "I thought I was coming here to shake things from the left, but I didn't know how bad things are. I feel as if I'm a capitalist asking for reform in a feudal barony."

In the meantime, the fight for the gay rights bill continued unabated. By July 1984 so many gay people had reached a point of taking action to free themselves and over 100,000 lesbians and gay men marched through the city's streets to demand equal rights. The Democrats at their national convention in San Francisco passed a strong gay rights plank in their party's platform.

A gay discrimination suit against Disneyland was filed, other cities passed gay rights ordinances, executive orders banning antigay discrimination were filed, more money was raised for gay causes than ever before.

It was also the beginning of the great sadness: the killer disease AIDS had killed 3,000 Americans by then, controversies erupted over closing gay bathhouses, and the use of soon to be available AIDS tests (some wanted forced testing in the USA).

By June 16th besides all the groups, maneuvers, lawyers and lobbying, 17,000 people came our and marched in Boston's 1984 Gay Pride Parade. Harry Hay came from Los Angeles for the occasion. He gave the keynote speech. Harry was once in the Communist party and quit in order to "protect the reputation" of the party during the McCarthy Era by protecting it from being labeled queer. He started a group called the Mattachine Society, which had a newsletter "One," which was traced by the FBI, which visited people who were recipients of the newsletter. It took a U.S. Supreme Court case to get One allowed to be mailed freely in the USA. In the early days of the movement, two organizations, the Mattachine Society and the Daughters of Bilitis, fought for ending harassment and hoping that someday gayness could be cured. Hay said that we were more than what we did in bed, that our ability to see society from a different point of view had contributed mightily to society's well being. Precisely because we were different and could therefore see what the others could not see.

I followed Hay with a few words about the Human Rights Ordinance that was pending in the city council saying "I expect it to be passed because this human rights ordinance is the most American bill in the history of this city."

We distributed post cards to write letters of support to city councilors. The Boston City Council received more letters on my bill than any bill in its history.

Apuzzo Stumps for Local Bill

400 Rally For Boston Rights Ordinance

Virginia Apuzzo addresses Boston gay/lesbian rights rally at Faneuil Hall.

By Larry Goldsmith

BOSTON — A crowd of 400 people gathered in Faneuil Hall on June 7 for a "Community Action Evening" sponsored by the Boston Lesbian and Gay Political Alliance to demonstrate support for the proposed Boston Human Rights Ordinance.

Alliance Chairperson Eric Rofes, in his initial remarks to the crowd, addressed himself to the context of the ordinance.

"It is our awareness at the Boston Lesbian and Gay Political Alliance that the ordinance is not an answer in and of itself to homophobia," Rofes said. The elimination of homophobia, racism and sexism, he said, "also involves public education of politicians, public health officials, our neighbors and others in the Boston area."

Rofes outlined a three-point strategy for educating politicians. First, he said, politicians must be convinced that lesbians and gay men exist. Then, they must be convinced that discrimination exists, and finally, they must be convinced that "discrimination is morally wrong."

"This education requires us to be upfront about who we are and not be different from who we are," Rofes declared. "It means being upfront with our neighbors, it means keeping the sex in homosexuality, and it means coalition-building with other minority groups."

District 8 City Councillor David Scondras, the sponsor of the ordinance, emphasized that the legislation was designed to benefit everyone in the city. "This bill is as much for Catholics and the Irish as it is for anybody else," he said.

Addressing himself to a concern that the goal of lesbian and gay rights might be diluted in a broadly-worded "human rights ordinance," Scondras stressed his view that the ordinance should be all-inclusive.

"We made it broad because we have members [of the lesbian and gay community] who are black, and to not be concerned with racism is to not be concerned with ourselves," he said. "We are everywhere, we belong to every group and our freedom must belong to every group."

Scondras aimed a portion of his remarks specifically at District 2 City Councillor Jim Kelly. "I want to call upon my colleague Jim Kelly and ask him to take this opportunity to heart," Scondras said. "This is an opportunity for the councillor from South Boston to show the city and planet that he can overcome the bigotry that is the cause of the most human suffering on the planet."

Kelly, whose district comprises both conservative South Boston and the substantially gay, racially-mixed South End, has spoken out in previous years against non-discrimination legislation, saying it offered no protection to whites who were discriminated against by blacks, and that "landlords [would] have serious problems if they deny an apartment to homosexuals." He has not publicly stated his position on Scondras' current proposal.

"People can change," Scondras hinted, "and when they change we will forgive them."

To emphasize the problem of homophobic discrimination and violence in the city, a panel of eight people representing a cross-section of Boston neighborhoods spoke from personal experience about the forms of harassment they encountered as lesbians and gay men.

The bill I introduced created a Human Rights Commission and prohibited discrimination in public and private employment, housing, credit and services on the basis of race, color, sex, age, religious creed, disability, national origin, ancestry, sexual orientation, marital status, parental status, ex-offender status, prior psychiatric treatment, military status or source of income. It prohibited "practices and policies which by their nature are sexually or racially harassing." At a press conference at which I introduced the bill were many people. Councilor Bruce Bolling called the law "historic" and "universal in scope." I said, "The only difference between American society and any other is that important thing called freedom. The thing that is important to remember about freedom is that you are always free to do as the majority says. The freedom to be different is the crucial point about this society."

I managed to get the council to vote 11 to 1 for the bill, an astonishing accomplishment given the lobbying against the bill by the Catholic Church and the underlying homophobia that characterized much of the city. As each councilor voted, the audience held its breath. When the vote was finally over, 11 to 1, they broke into cheers and hand waving, crying and smiles.

195 years after the bill of rights, Boston had added "gays too."

When the bill finally passed, Dapper grabbed a copy of it and slammed it against a stone pillar in the council chamber, yelling, "Welcome to Cuba!" revealing not only his bigotry but his deep understanding of the sociology of Cuba.

I remember how I felt. There was noise everywhere but I couldn't hear it. I was stunned. I had spent so much of my life not being myself that I could not quite grasp what had just happened. I was exhausted. I had spoken for hours, on my feet, running back and forth, getting agreements to change this or that, making sure the maneuvers to kill it would fail. And yet, it was somehow over. I felt oddly as if the passage of the bill had been anticlimactic. The grueling days, the thousands of letters directed at my colleagues, the endless meetings and arguments were at an end.

I smiled. I think my eyes watered. I know they did.

The bill was a landmark, yet on some level it was a reiteration of the promise of America to be fair, fair and equal treatment under law was something that had yet to happen.

But I wondered if I would ever give myself the freedom to be me. The love and respect I had never really taken inside.

The fight with Dapper continued unabated for many years. O'Neil commented about me on radio and television, conducting tirades against me. City Hall insiders said that it was the most vicious and longest ever running personal controversy ever to take place within council chambers. O'Neil called me 'disgusting, a nuisance, ridiculous, and homophobic.' When I was asked to comment, I said there is no disagreement between Dapper and me because "you have to have two sides to have an argument and Dapper is capable of having both sides himself."

Robert and I got a card from Don Babets, one of my campaign workers who spent a lot of time encouraging me to run and be strong.

Inside he wrote:

"Free at last, free at last; thank God Almighty we're free at last" Thank you, David! Love, Don Babets.

Dapper eventually died in December of 2007. I was told by the media that Dapper said he, of all the councilors he had known, had the most respect for me, because I was honest and always kept my word. I do not know why he said this but suspect his sexuality was far more complex than Boston was led to believe.

65 /   The Beginning of the Fight for Gay Marriage

"I was against gay marriage until I realized I didn't have to get one."
– James Carville

3,742 letters were sent to Boston City Councilors from the people who voted for them, pushing them to pass the Human Rights Bill — what we ended up calling the bill that established non-discrimination for all of the folks who are treated with disrespect by society including gay people. In most instances, councilors got more letters from voters than their margin of victory. The anti-discrimination bill was politically dangerous to tamper with. Yet it turned out I actually caused the biggest threat to the bill by an act, which in retrospect reveals how naïve I was.

In Boston at the time, people who got health insurance had their spouses covered. So I sent a private letter in a sealed envelope to the city Corporation Counsel, Joe Mulligan, asking him if, given our non-discrimination policy in Boston, Robert Krebs – who is my legal companion (we co-owned our house, shared our finances, have made out our wills to each other, live together) – can be given coverage as he is "my immediate family and my spouse." I was asking for his opinion.

The insurance division, Blue Cross Blue Shield, sent me a note saying, "Blue Cross Blue Shield rules stipulate that employees must be married to be eligible for family coverage." Of course, at that time, Robert and I could not be married under Massachusetts law.

The issue should have ended there, but the letter was leaked to the press and all hell broke loose.

I was caught by surprise. My ingenuousness was real — I did not expect private communications would get leaked and I certainly did not understand why I would greeted one morning by three TV stations camped out at City Hall. The reporters seemed surprised. "Did you really ask for coverage?" they asked. At a quick office strategy meeting, we decided it was better to take up the cause than suggest it was exploratory

Things have changed enough that it is hard to remember what the world was like in 1984. People like me — everyone who was unmarried or childless — were being forced to subsidize health insurance for our colleagues' spouses and children. Yet when we asked for equal treatment for our unmarried families, you would think the world was endangered, that the pillars of society would collapse.

The *Boston Globe* had the headline "Councilor Scondras seeks benefits from city for 'domestic partner.' " In the article I am quoted saying: "A married couple can have medical benefits extended to them minutes after they are married. I want my domestic partner to receive the same coverage. What's fair is fair."

The *Herald* on September 13th had a huge headline: *"GAY COUNCILOR ASKS 'SPOUSE' INSURANCE."* The article begins "Boston City Councilor David Scondras has jolted City Hall by asking that his gay lover be covered in his city health insurance policy."

The press and politicians speculated that I was trying to set up a "test case" as if my question was some kind of malevolent raid on the justice system. A lawyer from the city's Corporation Counsel's office said: "We're reviewing this very carefully because he may be trying to establish a test case."

Nobody seemed to think that I was simply asking if Robert could get health insurance so we wouldn't have to buy two separate health policies, or for that matter that I was simply asking for what every other family got — a family plan.

Dapper, my City Council colleague, wrote me a note saying "You have really embarrassed this City Council with your ridiculous request. All I can say is that you have one hell of a nerve to even suggest insurance coverage for your lover or spouse as you call him. You make me sick."

Joe Tierney said: "He's rubbing our noses in it," and "It's one thing to accept and tolerate certain lifestyles. It's another to ask us to support it with taxpayers' dollars."

I said that I agreed with the councilor. By his own logic, *none of us without wives and kids should have to support his lifestyle by subsidizing his wife and kids with our taxes.* Tierney proposed amending the human rights law to stop unmarried couples from receiving family plan medical insurance coverage. I made sure it went nowhere by getting the matter referred to a committee for hearings that would never actually happen.

To Tierney, the issue was not health insurance, but the redefinition of the human family, which I had not immediately realized was what I was up to, but in fact I did define "family" differently from Joe Tierney. A family to me is people who love each other, support each other, and act as an economic unit — in other words, act as a family. Joe said, "It is important to the survival of the family and the human race" that we leave things as they are. He clearly felt that *our* families were not real or important to the survival of the human race.

The Hotel Workers Union got involved on my side of the issue, and the news spread across the country. Mayor Flynn spoke to me in his office. He asked me to please retract my request, feeling that it was precipitating a storm which might negatively impact the progress represented by the gay rights bill that he had signed and might jeopardize the action on the state level needed to empower the Human Rights Commission I had created to enforce the new law. I felt boxed in — I did not want to reduce the support from Ray Flynn that I might need for more items on the agenda for the coming years.

By September 29th I tried to stop the tsunami by withdrawing my request, but it was too late. I had somehow hit some cultural nerve that I was unaware was so raw.

Change is like peeling an onion, each time you think you have arrived, there is another layer beneath. I had reached another layer with my question about health insurance. Kissing Robert in public was one layer tampered with. And asking for equal treatment was another layer of the onion of discrimination: upsetting the 'natural order' in which gay people were supposed to subsidize others without becoming uppity. Gay people paid more taxes and used fewer public resources than heterosexuals. We paid for schools for straight people's kids, medical services for wives and pregnancies, and the most expensive of all medical costs — having a baby. We paid more in income taxes having no spousal deductions, but we were not supposed to get what we needed for our families.

I was getting angry about it. And, the "traditional" concept of "family" was about something that did not and does not actually exist in America. In 1984, 70% of Americans were not in straight, formal marriages.

I spoke at the University of Pennsylvania in Philadelphia. I told the audience that gay people who had been brutalized by police had told me their stories during my first year in office, and my political peers had come to understand how pervasive hate was in America. But I had hoped that the power of a coalition of minorities would be the wind that blew hate away. I had written the gay rights law to include everyone, including people who had been in jail, because I wanted to move toward a society in which we all valued each others differences. Perhaps my upbringing in my church mattered here. I'm not sure.

At that talk in Philadelphia I found words to explain how I thought we needed to move. I said: "41 of the 47 groups that testified in favor of the Human Rights Bill were not gay or lesbian. The new law gives us a tool to use. It gives people protection to come out."

I still believed that Harvey Milk's push for everyone to come out was the answer to gay oppression, and for that matter every form of oppression.

In talking about the request for Robert to get health insurance I said, "I made the mistake of assuming I was normal for thirty minutes," during which I wrote the infamous letter.

In Philadelphia I talked with gay leaders, saying that trying to get politicians to like us would never work, that we would not get our freedom as a favor from those in power — that creating a fuss against the norms suffocating us was the road to freedom. "Don't get angry at boat rockers," I said, "They are our best friends. You don't get respect for anything except power. A coalition of those who historically desired access to power and respect — women, blacks, Hispanics, the disabled, former offenders — could together create a majority of minorities."

This is the only way I felt we could get all the groups out of the tunnel of despair, by uniting together. I didn't feel the groups had to like each other. "We can build coalitions with other hated groups who do not like us. We have a common goal and need only respect each other, not like each other." I felt and told the group: "All the hated groups share a whole history of experience in what it is like to be left out, to feel hostility directed toward you because you're different."

At my speech in Philadelphia I said that we have a hard time coming together because "we are good at acting straight. We are the best frauds on earth. Now this is not necessarily a bad thing. It is a defense." But it keeps us from coming out, a step toward coming together. "We seek approval constantly, from Mom, from Dad, from police, from politicians, an endless search for approval. We have to instead give it to ourselves. We continue to internalize perceptions of ourselves as no good. We cannot afford to do that. We need to feel good about ourselves. We can transform society out of that strength."

I said that as a result of this seeking approval we end up hurting each other. "We put down our brothers and sisters. We cut each other up. This is okay, roses must have thorns. But we must learn not to stab each other with them."

I explained that in my campaign these cleavages occurred, because gays were actually afraid of having an openly gay candidate: "They thought I was running for Queen and would outshine them or deprive them of their roles as gatekeepers to power, or end up putting too much light on things when what they wanted was the protection of invisibility, of darkness, to continue." I tried to convince them that I would end up opening more doors for them than secrecy and gatekeeping could.

"The age of bigotry is eclipsing and the age of coalition-building is beginning."

For years people felt I had made a mistake in asking for health insurance for Robert. While in reality it was motivated by my naïveté, it led us to gay marriage. In large part because of the national upheavals around this issue, by 2009 health benefits for domestic partners had become a pretty common part of health insurance policies.

66 /   Urban Foreign Policy

O accursed hunger of gold, to what dost though not compel human hearts!
— Virgil

I did not think having a foreign policy was the turf of heads of states, but rather cities or groups of people, and history bore me out. I thought Boston should have a foreign policy.

It is known by relatively few that in the United States, during the end of the 20th century, modern cities also had foreign policy initiatives and even a national magazine on urban foreign policy. I knew this because I have copies of the magazine and read it regularly.

Boston had such policies — especially Boston with its mixture of immigrants with international roots and politics as its biggest sport. Every city in the country which had immigrants who still cared about the places they came from, had a foreign policy. Miami certainly has a foreign policy toward Cuba and the Boston area has had many initiatives from dealing with the IRA during the war in Northern Ireland to helping the citizens of Armenia during the aftermath of the earthquake in Yerevan.

But perhaps the most well known foreign policy initiatives in Boston stemmed from the growing concern about apartheid in South Africa. In 1984, Councilor Charles Yancey (a black man who represented the majority-black Roxbury and Mattapan sections of Boston) put forth a bill that would boycott businesses doing business with South Africa. That was a response to a request from members of the African National Congress (ANC), that was struggling mightily to put an end to the economic, political and social segregation of South Africa by race.

On July 11th, 1984, the Boston City Council voted 10 to 3 to ban any city investments or depositing money in any banks doing business directly or indirectly with the Republic of South Africa or Namibia. This was Charles's bill, and the Commonwealth of Massachusetts followed suit with the same boycott of South Africa.

But the ANC needed us all to do more to put an end to apartheid. I was asked by the local emissary of the ANC to participate in a personal way, by blocking the sale of the Krugerrand, a South African coin that brought in cash to South Africa. That coin was sold in Boston by a company called Deak-Perera.

So I went with Mel King to the Deak-Perera office. Their lobby was, perhaps for security reasons, configured like the smallest banking floor in history. It had several windows with security glass and a couch. It felt crowded with just the two of us there. Mel and I approached the manager and asked that we meet with the company's president and that, until the meeting, the store stop selling the gold coins.

The manager, Christopher D'Elia, called Boston Police, but it took several hours before they would come. Seems I waited a lot for the police.

When the police finally arrived to the Deak-Perera office and told us to leave, we refused. We were handcuffed and put into a police wagon, and driven across the city to a police station. The ride was bumpy, the wagon careening from side to side. I held onto Mel, who was a huge African-American, for support, but I couldn't see him, it was so pitch black in the wagon. I said, "You can't tell who is black in the dark." Mel chuckled and said, holding me up in a kind of embrace, "And you couldn't tell who was gay if you could see."

We brought to fourteen the number of people arrested in Boston during the campaign of civil disobedience protesting business and government relations with the South African government.

I was finger-printed and my picture taken at the police station, and there were TV cameras and reporters after the arrest asking us to explain what was going on. We became part of a movement, which would eventually put an end to apartheid, but at that moment I wondered how much damage I had caused my political career.

It really didn't matter because I had always been a criminal, and this was just another example of it.

I said, "the sale of the Krugerrand is... the equivalent of selling gold swastikas." Our trial was set for December 21st.

Scondras Arrested In South Africa Protest

By Larry Goldsmith

BOSTON — Police arrested former state representative and mayoral candidate Mel King and District 8 city councillor David Scondras on December 10 during a demonstration at Deak-Perera, Inc., a downtown firm that sells South African Krugerrand coins.

King and Scondras entered the firm's Franklin Street office and presented the manager, Christopher D'Elia, with a letter requesting a meeting with the company's president. According to Scondras, they also asked the company to stop selling the gold coins, which help finance the South African government and its racist apartheid policies, until the meeting could be scheduled.

D'Elia called Boston Police, who arrived and arrested the two men. They were taken by police wagon to the District A police station, where they were booked, photographed and fingerprinted, and then to the Boston Municipal Court, where they were arraigned on trespassing charges and released on personal recognizance, pending a scheduled December 21 trial.

"Apartheid is morally repugnant to me and I think to all of us," Scondras told *GCN*. "The sale of the Krugerrand is emotionally and in point of fact the equivalent of selling gold -swastikas. It is supportive of the most outrageous kind of ideology on the part of the South African government and it is financially supportive of South Africa's oppression of Black people."

"I think it's important for the gay and lesbian community to be supportive of the concerns of all people who are oppressed including the Black and Latino communities," added Scondras, the city's only openly gay elected official, saying such support was necessary for "the continued development of a coalition with our own community and also because we have Black members of our own community and [need to] support them in all aspects of their oppression."

The two arrests brought to 14 the number of people arrested in Boston in the current nationwide campaign of legal demonstrations and civil disobedience expressing opposition both to apartheid and American business and governmental relations to the South African government.

Mel King (l) and David Scondras following their arrests at a Boston South Africa demonstration.

Then the trial was postponed. And then the Suffolk County District Attorney chickened out. I was pissed off. The Commonwealth of Massachusetts would not prosecute us!

We were prepared to turn the trial into a trial of apartheid, claiming that our actions were driven by necessity, the 'necessity defense' which was a common law defense which was rarely invoked. We had lined up expert witnesses to show that the actions were necessary including Navi Pillay, a South African lawyer of Indian descent, Nelson Tambini, a black South African labor leader, and Randall Robinson, director of Trans

Africa, a black organization trying to free the blacks in South Africa from their oppression. And we got Harry Belafonte, the great African American singer, to agree to speak on our behalf.

Harry Belafonte, Mel King and myself
(Photo Ellen Shub)

The Boston case was to be the first trial involving any of the 1,800 people arrested in 11 cities since the original demonstration at the South African embassy in Washington D.C. on November 21st. We wanted a trial because it would raise the issue to a higher level of awareness; keep the pressure up to put an end to apartheid.

I continued the work I was doing, realizing that the justice system itself was ultimately political and layered with concerns that were far more complex than adjudication of laws.

We would continue to work toward an end to apartheid in South Africa, and some amazing things would result. For me personally it would lead to my meeting that other felon, Nelson Mandela, at Logan Airport one day far into the future at the invitation of the ANC.

67 /   I Make Friends with Daniel Ortega

Dapper accused my office of using too many city resources. I was actually quite proud of that. David Passafaro, the Boston City Council's staff director, had tallied the offices' work levels. I came in first. On Dec. 12th, 1984, Passafaro released his analysis showing that my office averaged 28 calls per hour, 7 people who walked in for help per hour, 52 pieces of mail in per day and 53 pieces of mail out per day. During 1984 we tabulated 990 cases of people needing help, each kept in a separate file, each of which was serious enough to require us to take an action.

During that same year, we undertook a somewhat larger fight, involving Ollie North, the Contras, President Ronald Reagan, the junta of Reconstruction which pretty much led the political party popularly called the "Sandinistas" that at the time ran Nicaragua.

I didn't know where Nicaragua was. I did, however, know that Reagan was determined to overthrow its government, wherever it was. And interestingly enough, most Americans, who probably also had no idea where Nicaragua was, did not like Reagan's ideas. And I knew that I was pretty good at getting press coverage whether I wanted it or not.

On February 28th, 1985 the *Globe* published a poll of 1,506 people showing that Americans opposed by 4-1 Reagan's efforts to overthrow the "leftist" government of Nicaragua, using the U.S.-backed rebels called "the Contras." Reagan's efforts was opposed virtually everywhere across America, even by Republicans who opposed it by 60% to 26%!

On October 10th, 1984 I got a letter from the Lawyer's Committee on Central America, which began:

*We invite you to participate in a delegation which will be
visiting Nicaragua between October 30th and November 7th to
monitor the national elections scheduled to be held in that
country on November 4th. A major rationale for U.S. support of
forces seeking to overthrow the government of Nicaragua has
been Nicaragua's alleged failure to move toward democracy.
The scheduled vote itself has been dismissed in advance by the*

*Reagan Administration as a "sham." It is important that
representatives from this country judge for themselves at first
hand and report what they saw and learned.*

Wow. This sounded pretty interesting.

At the time, U.S. Rep. Chet Atkins was the Chairman of the Massachusetts Democratic State Committee. I went before their "Committee of Inquiry on Central America" and told them of my invitation to serve as an observer. I got a letter from the state committee that said:

*We are pleased to designate you as the official representative of
the Democratic State Committee for observation of the elections
in Nicaragua in November 4th. We are very excited that you will
go to Nicaragua to observe these important elections as our
representative.*

Bingo. I had a rationale!

Nicaragua was under an embargo that Reagan imposed on this poverty-stricken country. It was under daily attack including bomb-dropping war planes, paid for by Ollie North's diversion of funds to the Contras [a scandal which became known as "Iran-Contra"].

I was getting more and more involved in understanding the country itself, its pain, and I found myself more and more concerned about a world in which people demonized and destroyed each other rather than supported each other, even in their differences. Dapper O'Neil sent me off at the last council meeting before I had to leave with a statement: "I'm not an overly religious man, but I will say a personal prayer for the councilor to have a safe trip to Nicaragua," he said, tongue in cheek. He was quoted by Norma Nathan in the *Boston Herald*, saying "I'd like to see him detained by the Sandinistas or the Nicaragua (sic) government or anyone else, because to me he's nothing but a nuisance. Isn't it wonderful we have a city councilor to solve the whole problem!"

Our delegation to Nicaragua included: Fred Snyder, Assistant Dean for International Legal Studies at Harvard Law School; Manuel Rodriguez, professor of law at Northeastern University; Carol Doherty, past president of the Massachusetts Teachers Association; David Halperin, a physician; Margaret Leahy, professor of political science at Northeastern; Ralph Fine, a Boston attorney; and several others. We would travel across the country in groups, study the society, and meet with leaders.

<hr>

In Managua, we met with Miguel D'Escoto, an official of the Sandinista government, and I taped recorded all of my conversations with everyone I spoke with.

"Reagan says there are no blue birds," [short hand for a type of U.S. jet], said D'Escoto, who smiled after the building we were in shook as if we were in the middle of an earthquake, from those U.S. jets. It happened again and again. I taped the sounds of the planes buzzing the capital city of Managua, one of the many actions Reagan took to terrorize and demoralize the population of Nicaragua. In fact, Reagan lied about the planes. Butterflies did not shake buildings.

We had to be suddenly moved several times from where we were staying because the fighting was too close and the Sandinistas did not want anything to happen to us. I remember our guards coming into our room one morning and very politely asking us to please hurry. As we drove off, we heard the sounds of explosions in the distance, much too close for comfort.

I watched five-year-old children at a day care center learn how to play a game called Run, Rabbit, Run. They were too young to understand what they were doing, but they were being taught to jump in and out of trenches and hold their hands over their ears to protect them from bombs. A school nearby had been bombed. It was an incredible thing to watch little children trying to protect themselves against Contra attacks.

I met a lot of people and noticed that none of them had any hesitation criticizing the government and talking about what was wrong and what was right, hardly the sociology of a tyranny. I saw televised campaigns from the Communist Party complaining that the Sandinistas were "capitalistic and right wing." 60% of Nicaragua is privately owned. By contrast, in the U.S. less than 60% of the land is privately owned.

I went into a pharmacy and talked to the guy who owned it. I said, "Isn't this a Communist-run country?" He said it was news to him. He'd always owned the pharmacy and always would. At the time I was in Nicaragua, some 7,000 people had been killed in the war with the Contras, mostly women, children and teachers.

Upon my return, I decided to share the pictures and tape recordings with the public during an information-sharing forum at Boston City Hall on November 29th. The elections, as far as we could determine, were fair.

Reagan said that the Sandinistas had Soviet MIG jets. They did not exist. He condemned the elections which thousands of international observers praised for their openness. He railed against Soviet money for the Sandinistas but did not mention the money from France, Sweden and Japan. He mined Nicaragua's harbors. He supported terrorism abroad but lied about it to people here in the United States.

I remember speaking with then Speaker of the House Tip O'Neill about it, and he said, "I don't get it. Everywhere I go people like this guy." The era of spin was upon us, and the media became part of the cover-ups that characterized American policy under Republican regimes for decades. I gave a speech in 1985, one paragraph of which was:

> *You are too busy spending billions to protect the privileges of the unprincipled in Chile, the Contras in Nicaragua, the Duarte regime in El Salvador, and Botha's Reich in South Africa to pay attention to the needs of the poor and needy in America's cities and on America's farms.*

It astonished me that this gruesome and horrible president had blind followers like Councilor Jimmy Kelly who found him nothing but praiseworthy when in fact all of the nightmares brought by George Bush the second were conducted by the same cast of characters that Reagan had assembled in his foolish, destructive war to stop 'leftist' governments from rising around the world. A record deficit was his "balanced budget," U.S. financed terrorists were his "freedom fighters."

And he lied.

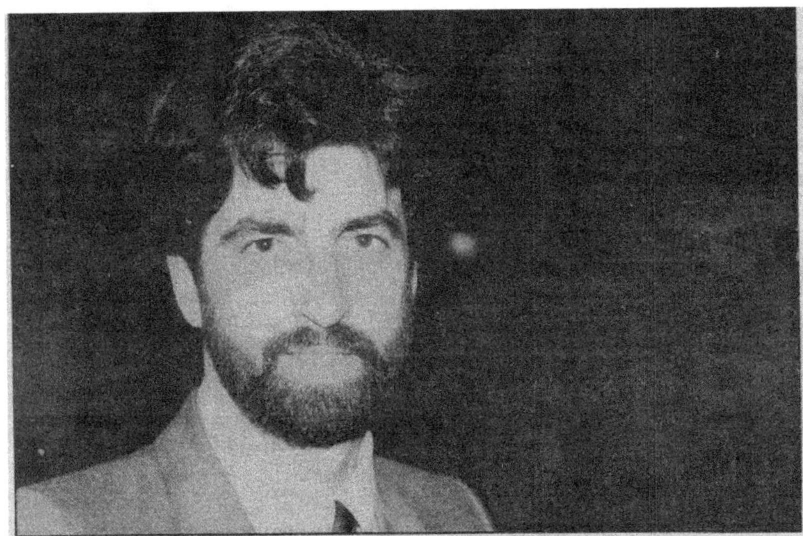

Scondras tells of Nicaragua

When District 8 Councilor David Scondras was in Nicaragua last week, he watched five-year-old children at a day care center learn how to play a game called Run, Rabbit, Run.

"They were really too young to understand what they were doing," Scondras said. "But they were being taught to jump in and out of trenches and hold their hands over their ears so they wouldn't blow up. A school nearby had been bombed—it's an incredible thing to watch little children trying to protect themselves against contra attacks."

During Scondras' week monitoring Nicaragua's local elections, he said that what he saw and what he heard "completely conflicted" with the Reagan Administration's descriptions of the Sandinista government and the Nicaraguan perception of US military forces.

"All the citizens I met with didn't seem hesistant at all to criticize the government and talk about what was wrong and what was right," Scondras said. "But it's obviously a very popular government. The elections were free and open."

Despite Reagan's claim that the Sandinistas are a dangerous communist regime, Scondras said that televised campaign advertisements by the communist party in Nicaragua complained that the Sandinistas were "capitalistic and right wing." He added that 60 percent of Nicaragua is privately owned.

"I went into a pharmacy there and talked to the man who owned it," Scondras recalled. "I said, 'Isn't this a communist-run country?' and he said it was news to him. He'd always owned the pharmacy and always would."

don't know is that 7000 people have been killed during this war—mostly women, children and teachers."

During his travels through the country with delegates from 35 other countries (unsupervised by the government), Scondras said he taped many of his conversations and took pictures. His observations will be open to the public during an "information sharing forum" at City Hall on Nov. 29.

"I'm concerned about this because many of my constituents are Hispanic and this is perceived as an attack on Hispanic people," Scondras said. ■
—S. Hutchison

I decided to ask about gay rights in Nicaragua under the Sandinistas. Tomás Borge, who was the Interior Minister, said that there was a serious problem with gay and lesbian people because gays were frightened of social opinion. He said the government went so far as to call up people who were gay in his ministry and assure them that they would be supported by the government and not be afraid to come out. I also met with Maria Luisa Vargas, legal counsel for the Council of State (the Sandinistas) who explained there were no laws against any consensual sexual activity including homosexual activity. But the culture itself was a machismo culture.

It would take many years before Daniel Ortega would become President of Nicaragua. For decades the Reagan efforts would put in place a right wing regime that reflected Reagan's horrid value system, and it remains to be seen if the initial promise of the Sandinistas will come to pass in Nicaragua.

As 1984 drew to a close and Christmas was fast approaching, the mayor gave each member of the city council a tie.

My colleague Mike McCormack held up his tie at a City Council meeting and said "I wonder how many polyesters had to give their lives for these ties."

McCormack started to note that a bloc of us on the council tended to support the actions that my office came up with. He began to refer to us as "The Scondrasistas."

68 /   Institutionalized Bullies

The experiences of my adult life do not define me. My identity is based on one fact: I am my mother's child. The whiteboard of my mind was written on long before the events that I write about. I am defined by one thing alone, that I am the child of Dorothea Coravos and Georgos Scondras. I am the boy mentored by Uncle Andy and Father John Sarantos, teachers and friends at schools, American and Greek — I am the lessons I learned as a child.

As an adult I refined the definition of who I am, and every issue, every event, every position, every action of my life was orchestrated by the teachings of those who made up my extended family in the Greek part of Lowell. Family was what mattered. Causing pain to others was intolerable. Everyone deserved fairness and food, fun and fantasy, love and pleasure. But also, I was infected with this fatal flaw: my need to be the chosen one, the good boy, the valedictorian, the Harvard scholar, the model citizen — the catastrophe of being gay.

As the conflict between approval and self-definition continued I grew instinctively to reach out to embrace all of those who had been marginalized by society, all of those who suffered, who did not share in the sense of belonging that was the birthright of those who were considered normal by the world. And soon 'normal' itself would come under the microscope of my analytic mind and slowly lost the reverence I had once held it in.

In general, I supported the weak over the powerful, equal access over special privileges, and an end to the ongoing culture wars that pitted one group of working poor against other groups of working poor.

This *factionalization* of people into competing groups was augmented by those in power, by feeding into the myths to gain power or keep it. Whether it was me personally or society in general, the struggle has been to become a people that make decisions based on facts, not myths, and we are far from that place.

One way that this conflict between reason and myth worked its way out was for some to bully others.

An institutional bully we hold onto, give power to, and pay a great deal for out of our myth that they "serve and protect us" are the police. It was 1985, an election year. I grew nervous as the campaign began again, but the issues of the powerful bullying the poor continued to dominate my agenda. The beginning of that year had me taking one action after another helping those who were weak against those who exploited their weakness. Specifically, the Boston Police Vice Squad.

In April 1985 in Boston, Lung Kwong Wong became one more example of that continuing disaster. Wong was charged with assault and battery on a police officer and soliciting sexual conduct for a fee. Since Wong spoke no English and the prostitute spoke no Chinese, it was unclear how this supposed arrangement was arrived at.

When the matter went to court, the judge postponed the case because Wong was too badly injured to go through a court procedure. Medical Center employees and other witnesses said the police officer, Frank Kelly, a vice squad detective, swung at Wong three times, hitting him in the nose and eye. Other employees said Kelly kept hitting him with a closed fist.

As is so often the case when police beat people up, Kelly charged Wong with assault and battery on a police officer. It is so common an event, the charges are regularly dismissed by judges and courts as fake. This fact, however, has not led to any reform whatsoever. It has become a fixture in the world of law enforcement. Kelly was 6 feet tall, weight close to 200 pounds and was in his early 30's. Wong was 56 years old, 5 foot 4 and weighed 125 pounds.

Numerous witnesses corroborated the sequence of events. The woman involved, Audrey A. Manns, got out of the car and yelled at Kelly "That's not the guy, that's the wrong guy!"

The Vice Squad

This type of bullying was nothing particularly new to me. In the Fenway, the police took prostitutes who worked the corner near my house into their wagon and got blowjobs, money, and drugs in exchange for not arresting them. I watched this in disbelief from my window, as the alley behind my house was a favorite spot to park their wagon.

The Boston Vice Squad patrolled the Fens late at night shining lights onto the gay men cruising, pushing them out of the public park calling them names and threatening them with arrest and beatings. I know because I was one of those men. I remember having one police bully take my head and smash it over and over against his car's hood after I questioned his right to harass guys in the Fens.

I was fed up with the bullies, appalled by the hypocrisy. I said publicly on the floor of the council, do we really need to have police arrest elderly men masturbating to a porn movie?

It was obvious to me that the Boston Vice Squad was a group of neopuritanical hypocrites who were the dregs of humanity and needed to be shut down. I remember one of them having to be restrained by another officer as he started turning red and saliva leaked from his mouth which was twisted in anger at me for having the nerve to tell him to get the hell out of Northeastern University's bathrooms which he patrolled to find gay people cruising. He wanted badly to beat me up.

I finally got the Vice Squad shut down, but not by trying to legislate them away. Our coalition, the "Scondrasistas," got enough power that I became the chairman of the budget committee, Ways and Means. I took the line item for the Vice Squad out of the budget. I said "I can't stop you from having a Vice Squad but I can make sure it can only use volunteers who are not paid." The law for Boston made it impossible for the mayor to put anything back into a budget that the council had rejected.

That put an end to this particular noxious brand of sexual abuse that the police and prosecutors had been engaged in for decades. They have never forgiven me.

I hated the police. They stood for everything that made me cringe. Bullies. Uniformed thugs whose alleged 'protection' of the public has no data supporting the theory that they in any way deter crime. Every criminal justice study I have seen shows that the number of police has nothing to do with the crime rates at all. Other sociological factors do, but not the police.

I know that people think the police are important and perform a vital public function. I think that they are wrong. "Community policing," the recent buzz word for flopping about looking for something socially justifiable for these gun-toting thugs to do, is about defining some new role for police. In some areas this has included such things as identifying broken windows for public action in light of their inability to prevent crime, or helping community organizations "fight crime" through neighborhood watches, or provide psychological relief for those who lived in fear after a serious crime was committed in a neighborhood.

An institution that does not deliver on its promise, costs money, diverts attention that could be paid to methods that might work, and engages in the very behaviors it was put in place to protect us all from, needs to be shut down.

I tried a series of reforms of the Boston Police Department, none of which got through. I tried to limit the number of police hired who had relatives in the department. I tried to mandate that a police officer had to have more than a high school education. (I wanted police to first have a degree from a college in criminal justice or law, sociology or psychology and cultural anthropology.) They were paid more than starting lawyers at city law firms, so why not have to have at least a little of the education lawyers are expected to have?

Some reforms ended up taking place as a result of a federal lawsuit ordering the Boston Police to hire on a one-to-one basis people who were other than white Irish relatives. It worked slowly, over time. Later I would join with President Nixon's former lawyer, James St. Clair, to reform the Boston Police Department — a rather amazing story I'll tell you about later [chapter 128, book iii].

Another kind of bully were the banks that found a way to steal legally from every homeowner by getting taxes paid to the city "escrowed" into their coffers (i.e. monthly contributions to the fund that would eventually be turned over to the city) which they then used until taxes were due . I took action against these bullies, and eventually won.

One of the more outrageous bullies in Boston were the landlords who really didn't care a lot about the life of their tenants. I am not being insensitive to the work done by landlords, as I have been one for much of my life by now.

I got one piece of very important legislation done to protect particularly weak tenants from the strong. I called it the "Grandparent Amendment." The *TAB* of April 30th, 1985 wrote, "The Boston City Council unanimously passed an amendment to the city's rent laws last week that extends protections to approximately 200 [elderly] tenants facing eviction due to condominium conversion." I got my colleagues to agree – even Dapper – that old folks should not be evicted to allow developers to make money on condo conversions.

I remembered Joannie Stowe, an elderly woman on St. Botolph Street, who was sitting in a chair while workers were tearing the ceiling down around her during a condo conversion. She was in shock. I had to do something. I raised hell.

I did not really understand sometimes how what I did affected others. I think that somehow I protected myself so much growing up by not allowing myself to feel, by playing with a poker face or maybe poker soul, that I got surprised to discover that I had made a difference in someone's life.

Joannie Stowe now could live in her apartment and no longer panicked about being evicted. She asked me to come see her. She gave me an amazing watch, one of those round timepieces that shut looking like a metal flying saucer made of silver, with a chain to hang on your belt.

"My father gave me this watch before he died," she said, "and I don't have children to give it to. So I want you to have it, David, to remember me by."

I still have Joannie's watch. It was in her family for many generations. And I consider it still is.

And as for fighting bullies — I still do.

69 / The 1985 election & grapes

My gay, Jewish, lawyer friend Fred Mandel was finally picked to be the head of the Human Rights Commission, which was established by the Human Rights bill I wrote and pushed through the Council. Fred was smart, short, smiled a lot, had a bit of a sarcastic flavor to his patter, and I liked him a lot. The Commission took forever to choose its members and for a long time people questioned whether the mayor would appoint a gay man. I pushed for Fred, and got Ray to pick the smartest lawyer with the biggest heart that we could find, who just happened to be a gay man.

Meanwhile my hectic, endless 18-hour days continued, day after day. Seeing the forest for the trees was a really hard thing to do with the confusion of so many things happening at the same time. But we tried hard to keep up. I wrote up a plan for the year broken out into the areas we wanted to influence, the agenda we wanted to push. And Jack Hall wrote out a detailed week-by-week re-election campaign plan that had to be integrated into the week-by-week city work that was, after all, my job.

We dealt with one issue after another that was thrown at us in addition to our own agenda.

Jails: Where do we put a new jail to replace the falling-down Charles Street Jail? I pushed for moving it into the South End near the old incinerator because by having more land we could allow for much bigger rooms and yards, and eventually I won. Eventually the old empty jail was transformed into the upscale "Liberty Hotel," with a hotel bar called "Alibi." (It's a place I won't go into given my memories of the monstrosity in which we caged people for so many years).

Lights: A lot of people, including us, fought to get the lights on Boston Common replaced so that you could actually see where you are going and who was in the darkness under the trees next to Beacon Hill.

The deficit: My eight point plan to raise some money for the city which got four of the points passed needed more pushing.

Federal actions destroying low income housing: The U.S. Department of Housing and Urban Development had a horrible rule concerning people who got loans years ago at ridiculously cheap rates to build apartment buildings. HUD changed one rule: to stop protecting and subsidizing housing that it acquires after private owners default on mortgages — in other words if you own a place, just don't pay your mortgage, and you'll get to convert the place to a building the rich can live in. By February 1985, 3,000 units in Massachusetts had already been sold and 4,000 more were on the market.

I fought hard to stop this destruction from happening. I warned that the very attractiveness of the Fenway and other parts of my district would lead to a change in who could live there as prices went up. The yuppification of the area would convert it from those genuinely committed to social change and growth to the yuppies and guppies (gay yuppies) that used both as decoration, as symbols of their political correctness, not believers but frauds. This eventually happened.

Grapes

In spite of the day to day whirlwind of issues that we dealt with, occasionally an issue came up that created a memorable moment, and this time it was about grapes.

Robert did many things in his life, one of which was to work harvesting asparagus in California. It was hard work in the hot sun, and he listened to a guy during a lunch break one day, a guy trying hard to organize farm workers to get them to get a better life. His name was César Chávez.

Few people in American history have been so important to the organization of migrant farm workers as this little brown man with the big smile. Chávez met Robert again in my office, remembering the tall skinny white kid in the asparagus. Chávez called for a new grape boycott. In person, at Boston City Hall.

I was able to find my "Viva la huegla; viva la causa" ("Long live the Strike; long live the Cause") button from the 1965 grape boycott which led to the first victories of the farm workers toward a decent working environment. On February 27th, 1985, I got a resolution endorsing the new Farm Worker's boycott of table grapes through the council. I made sure that it was introduced as a bill with 9 councilors names on it so that there was no question it would pass. Six thousand farm workers were owed over $72 million in back wages, and this precipitated the need for pressure on growers to get these wages out to the workers whose incomes were very low.

My resolution said "Resolved that the Boston City Council, in meeting assembled, does hereby endorse the farm worker's boycott of California table grapes and calls upon all citizens of Boston to support this boycott." It passed unanimously.

Dan Holmes owned a little restaurant called the 'Downtown Café' in the Combat Zone in Boston. We made arrangements for us to have César Chávez have lunch with us at Dan's, who was thrilled to have a famous man eating in the restaurant. We then went to the Fenway, to my home, and met up with Lou Diamond Phillips, a movie star whom I had seen act as Ritchie Valens in "La Bamba." He was not Latino but was concerned about how minorities were treated.

César Chávez, Lou Diamond Phillips and I walked over to the Stop and Shop in the West Fenway which sold a lot of grapes. We went into the store and started taking out the grapes, which had pesticide residue all over them. César particularly wanted to make sure that both workers in the fields and people who ate grapes did not end up eating carcinogens, which formed the powder on the surface of the grapes. We asked the manager to abide by our effort to end the sale of these kinds of grapes to the public, and we didn't get very far at first. But we stayed and talked to customers going in and out of the store until the manager decided that it was less trouble getting rid of the grapes than putting up with us.

Mayor Ray Flynn, and then the state legislature, endorsed the boycott. At a press conference I called, Chávez said the boycott would work if it got support from at least three million people. He pointed to me with my button from 1965 and said that the people his union had educated in past years have not disappeared. Massachusetts became the first state to endorse the boycott; Flynn became the first major mayor to do so.

BOSTON LEDGER MAR 13, 85

Cesar Chavez (standing), with Councilors David Scondras (center) and Charles Yancey, came to town to get the word out about a new grape [boy]cott.

Old causes never die

"Well, for one thing, it's easier. It's part of Americana, right?" —United Farm Workers Cesar Chavez, when asked why the UFW wanted people to boycott table grapes as opposed to another crop

In 1975, a Harris poll estimated that 17 million Americans had stopped eating grapes picked by non-union workers to support California farm workers' right to organize for better working conditions. Shortly afterwards, the United Farm Workers called off the boycott because the state established an Agricultural Labor Relations Board (ALRB) to protect that right. For seven years, UFW leaders say, the board functioned well.

But when George Deukmejian was elected California's governor in 1982, he began fulfilling a campaign promise to make the law "fair" to growers, picking someone sympathetic to the conglomerates to head the ALRB. According to the union, charges by farm workers have risen while the board has halved the number of complaints it filed against growers.

Union leaders also estimate that the growers owe $72 million in already litigated back pay cases and have also refused to sign several UFW contracts even though their workers voted to join. When the California legislature tried to clear up these backlogs by allocating $1 million to the ALRB budget, Deukmejian vetoed the appropriation.

In the face of the governor's actions, the UFW—still led by Cesar Chavez who first organized migrant farm workers in 1965—has again asked [cons]cientious people to stop buying non-union table grapes. And though [ti]mes have certainly changed (Ronald Reagan now represents Massachusetts, too) Chavez believes the grape boycott is enough a part of "Americana" to work again.

Judging from the reception he got in the Bay State this week—the Boston City Council, Mayor Raymond L. Flynn and the state legislature all endorsed the boycott—Chavez may be right.

At a press conference called by District 8 City Councilor David Scondras to announce the council resolution and later in an interview with the *Ledger*, Chavez said the boycott will work if it gets support from at least three million people. "We don't need to have the majority of the public support the boycott" to impact the growers, he said.

Chavez also pointed to people like Scondras—who wore his "Viva la huelga, viva la causa" button from 1965 at the press conference—Councilor Charles Yancey and others as proof that the people his union educated in past decades have not disappeared like so many soap bubbles. "You don't have to sell them anything. They know what [the boycott] is. You just have to get the word out," he said. "I'm very confident...it's just like the old days." Nine councilors co-sponsored the resolution.

Chavez acknowledged, however, that the UFW probably won't get as much support from young people as it did during the 1960's. Although he said many would support the boycott, he added: "I don't think we'll attract them to pickets and demonstrations unless a draft call went out."

Chavez agreed that in some ways Deukmejian's sabotage of the Agricultural Labor Relations Act paralleled President Reagan's treatment of programs he opposes. But Deukmejian, he said, has managed to outdo Reagan. "We anticipated [his neutralizing the ALRB] because, when Deukmejian was running for office, we were one of the controversial issues in the campaign. But we had no idea he would come in and be as vindictive as he has been," Chavez said. "Here we have a governor that's supposed to support the law breaking the law."

Has the situation improved for California's farm workers? "Where there was a union contract, definitely...but the others, no," he said, adding that the gap between union and non-union grape workers has widened. "We don't have collective bargaining rights in the United States and not until we get collective bargaining rights will the situation really change."

The Massachusetts legislature becomes the first state legislature to endorse the boycott; Flynn becomes the first major mayor to do so. The city council joins Detroit's in offering moral support to the effort.

One observation: New England has its own migrant agricultural workers, many of them Native Americans from Canada, who follow the cranberry, blueberry, apple and potato harvests. They face many of the same difficulties as their California counterparts. They, too, remain untouched by the National Labor Relations Act. Perhaps our elected officials can lobby their New England colleagues on their behalf.

—R.L.

A part of the effort was directed at getting people to avoid non-union grapes, and New England was not exempt from the politics of union-busting engaged in by Ronald Reagan, who neutralized the Agricultural Labor Relations Board. New England has its own migrant agricultural workers, many of them Native Americans from Canada who follow the cranberry, blueberry, apple, and potato harvests. They were all left out of protection by the labor relations boards which are supposed to protect workers rights to organize for better working conditions. including keeping toxic pesticides off grapes.

*Chávez speaking at a 1974 United Farm Workers rally i
n Delano, California*

My pattern of fighting with those who were underdogs trying to be treated fairly and respected continued in this labor arena, not the first or last time I would get involved in labor disputes. I continued to feel that a coalition of those who had been in one way or another left out of respect, as gays were, would eventually become a majority that would change America.

70 /   Gay Foster Parents

It was in every newspaper of any size in America. Don Babets and David Jean, a gay couple and friends of Robert's and mine, had been asked by the Massachusetts Department of Social Services to be foster parents to two children who had been treated very shabbily. Don was an Army intelligence officer from 1969 to 1977, then got a job at the Fair Housing Commission in Boston. David Jean was the manager of a private social service agency that worked with unwed teenaged mothers. *USA Today* quoted me as saying: "Gay foster parents are just like any other foster parents — gayness is not something you can catch."

But Don and David had been foster parents for only 15 days when the state took their two foster sons away.

The controversy had erupted when Ben Haith, whom I knew as a complete fake — a loudmouth looking for anything which would get him attention, especially in the context of his condemning someone for something — called the placement a "breakdown of the society and its values and morals" which the press lapped up. Ben Haith, a religious maniac who lived near the gay couple, complained to DSS claiming that "the neighborhood" was aghast at the placement. This was simply not true — the media gave this mentally deranged man a platform and credibility he certainly did not have among his own neighbors, most of whom stood up for Don and David.

On Tuesday May 9th, the boy's mother signed a statement saying she knew her sons were in foster care with gay men.

The leaders on the state level careened back and forth, making decisions based on reactions to the press rather than what would be in the interests of the children.

About 100 representatives of 50 Unitarian Churches expressed their support for the two gay men at a meeting on May 9th at the First Church in Roxbury. David Jean was the music director of the First Church.

The *Herald* quoted Dr. Joyce Brothers saying: "The only question is whether the men really care about the children." The May 10th article began with the sentence: "Leading child care experts yesterday said children raised by gay parents suffer no ill effects or sexual identity problems as long as the home is loving and supportive."

Of course Councilor Kelly agreed with the state decision to remove the children saying, "I don't think a gay couple is a family unit in the truest sense of the word and I don't think they should have custody of the children."

Don Babets blasted the state action saying, "There was a very angry three-year-old boy when I said goodbye to him. I said goodbye to the oldest boy and he kissed me and left. The youngest was scared and he cried."

By May 21st I had lost respect for Governor Dukakis. I begged him to change his mind. It was hopeless. Dukakis was really concerned about the political fallout from supporting gays. Both of us being Greek, I expected the governor should have paid more attention to what I had to say. He certainly knew I was gay.

Michael Dukakis was an interesting person. I met him originally on the MBTA Green Line, in a subway car, when he was going to work as a state representative. He is short, reserved, and smart in some ways, a bit of a policy wonk. He has the ability to remember names, which I lack. He also has a tendency to be a bit stingy or controlling.

In this case, he was making a mistake. He needed to base his decisions on rational criteria, not the whims of prejudiced people. From my point of view, to lead means also to teach, and few politicians are good at that. So either he felt that it was too politically costly to support gays, or he actually believed the nonsense he was spouting.

I was particularly upset that the governor was ignoring the law we had passed against discrimination in Boston. Dukakis ordered the foster children yanked from their home with gay foster parents, line-item vetoed AIDS funding two years in a row, arrested record number of gay men for gay "crimes" like "unnatural acts," had not hired a single openly gay or lesbian staff person in seven years.

On May 31st I wrote an article in *Bay Windows* that was widely circulated. It read in part:

> *The homophobic child-snatching has been absurd and insulting. Concerns about children becoming gay if raised by gay people have been expressed, showing that homophobes can be stupid as well as bigoted; bigoted because the implication is that there is something wrong with becoming gay, stupid because a moment's reflection on where gay people come from would dispel this simplistic notion of causality.*
>
> *Concerns about having only one sex as a role model have been raised, as if the 50% of children living in single parent households since 1978 have more than a single sex role model!*
>
> *Insidious remarks about child molesting being characteristic of gay men have been given implicit credence by the actions of the state, compounded by their ridiculous notion that some special study will be necessary to determine the fitness of gay people to raise kids. Of course, the vast majority of true child sex abuse cases involve older straight men molesting little girls. No study of this problem was suggested in the governor's "policy review."*
>
> *There will always be a rationalization to justify prejudice: we have heard researchers claim that blacks are genetically inferior to whites, that women are too emotional to do a man's job (whatever that means).*
>
> *For too long we have waited for our friends to help, only to be shown over and over again that we are in the back of the Democratic bus. In fact, the current administration seems to think that we should be content to walk behind the bus.*
>
> *We are the ones who need to stand up for the children.*
>
> *The worst form of child abuse is telling kids that they are no good, that those different religions or skin colors or sexual preferences are bad or inferior to others. Children who fall into one of these inferior categories are taught that they are not as good, somehow flawed and spend much of the rest of their lives compensating for a self-image created by people of prejudice.*

I went on to say that only the building of a coalition with other minorities powerful enough to unelect those who insult any of the groups is going to be powerful enough to change the society in any meaningful way.

I believe this is still true now.

And the losers are all the children who are denied parents who can love and care for them.

I once asked Charles Yancey to discuss with me his problem over the foster care issue in Massachusetts. Charles is a black city councilor, and he said he was worried about the effect on children of having gay parents. I was frustrated with him, and told him that there was a big difference between the black community and us. That if a person who was black came home to her parents having been made to feel ugly or hated or bad because she was black, her straight parents would put their arms around her and give her the love she needed but that if a gay person came home discouraged with being treated with negative worlds, and feeling so lonely she could die, there would be no arms around her. Charles said that that was sad and I said well that is the point, because the gay people who are parents would put their arms around both kids and love both of them and your community would not. So for all of the children, especially the children who are gay and lesbian, they are probably better off in a gay home, than in a home that ultimately rejects them.

It would take a very long time for any of this to be heard. In fact, because in large part of the disillusionment that this event was part of, the Democrats lost the governor's office by choosing a homophobe called John Silber to run for governor, leading gays to support the Republicans whose candidate William Weld and his successors were supported by gays for 16 years.

A story for a little later.

71 /   Coors

"He was a wise man who invented beer"
– Plato

"Beauty is in the eye of the beer holder.
– Kinky Friedman

One day in the early spring of 1985, we passed the Boston Common, using Charles Street to get to Cambridge Street on the way to the City Hall garage. The Common is a large park next to the Statehouse, whose gold dome dominates the park. The park was a long history of being the venue for speeches and parades, hot dogs and ice skating in the winter, ladies that fed huge flocks of pigeons (the inspiration for Tom Lehrer's song "Poisoning Pigeons in the Park"), and it was often the end point for many a Gay Pride day march — but it never had a ski slope.

Until that day.

It was early April, long after the snow had left. The sun was shining, it was a warm day, and there was this huge ski slope with lots of people playing in the snow — Coors was kicking off its expansion throughout New England with a ski slope. It bothered me that they used public property for their private benefit.

We didn't know much about Coors in those days, except for a gay guy named Howard Wallace from the West Coast who was a labor activist who kept the national strike against Coors beer alive. He was a kind of leading expert on the Coors boycott, which didn't mean much to us because Coors wasn't in New England or New York at that time.

I knew that Harvey Milk had been involved with a Coors boycott, so I asked Gary Dotterman to call the union and see if the boycott was still on. I thought it would strengthen my relationship with labor, with unions.

Yes, the Coors boycott was still on. We spent months digesting a ton of conflicting information about Coors. I never really wanted to know much about Golden, Colorado, but there was no helping it. We became experts on hiring, beer manufacturing, the union gripes about Coors, polygraph tests given before you could get hired, etc., and the more we read the more upset we got. But, for a long time, we didn't actually do anything besides learn about Coors.

No one seemed to care what we were up to until the Friday night before the 1985 Gay Pride parade. We got a mad, panicked call from Pat Lyons. The Lyons brothers owned a bunch of properties on Lansdowne Street, clubs that had gay nights and they made their money by selling booze to students. Pat Lyons called with Ray Tye, the owner and president of United Liquors, the largest distributor of alcohol in the Boston area, a distributor for Coors.

Pat and Ray and Ray's son Michael Tye came into City Hall, to ask could we please "call it off, the big demonstration you are planning at Gay Pride tomorrow against Coors and give us a chance to make our case." Because there was no demonstration planned at the parade against Coors it was easy and politically smart to "call it off," but it made us look powerful to agree to do so and at the same time gave us chits to play later. We said, "Well, you know, there has been a lot of work put into that demonstration, but I will do what I can as a favor to Pat Lyons." The next day, at the Gay Pride parade, there was nothing except one guy with a Coors sign on, so it appeared we kept our word and squelched the big demonstration.

Michael Tye then made an appointment to sit down with us with a representative of Coors so that we could talk out what we were concerned about. They figured that this fight with Coors was a political thing, so they brought us a stack of material to read which countered everything that the California labor activist Howard Wallace had said.

But the more we learned about various members of the Coors family, the more upset we were getting. We found out that in 1984 William Coors, at a talk in Denver, attributed the economic problems of black-governed African nations to a "lack of intellectual capacity." In a speech to minority business owners in Denver, Coors called America the "Land of Opportunity" saying: "One of the best things they (slave traders) did for you is to drag your ancestors over here in chains." Later, when we pressed this issue, Peter Coors said that his uncle William was "misinterpreted."

We found out that Coors was administering polygraph tests as a prescreening for jobs with Coors including questions about the sexual preference of the applicant (a spokesmen from Coors said the test was initially used after the kidnapping and killing of Adolph Coors III).

Coors by the late summer of 1985 had perhaps 20% of the Boston beer market. Vincent Howell, a person of color who worked in our office, conducted a study of Coors including sales and concluded that weekly sales by the end of the summer were somewhere between $10,000 and $18,000 per week. Vincent had decided to take on the Coors issue, representing State Representative Byron Rushing and us.

Everyone on the city council got an invitation to meet with Peter Coors at the Parker House hotel. When the Coors staff got wind that there would be a union demonstration they changed the location. So of course we told the unions and they showed up at the new site. We gave Vincent the invitation, and he poured beer over Peter Coors, which became the news story.

In the meantime, Arthur Osborne got lots of credit at national AFL-CIO for making the Coors boycott take off. Vincent, according to the press, had become the 'leader' of the local boycott. Together with others, we got 25 businesses to throw out Coors by August of 1985. I met with all the gay bar managers, sent a formal letter to each as well, and after those meetings and letters, Coors was thrown out of gay bars in Boston. As the bar managers talk with each other, and the AFL-CIO started organizing and talking to the bars, about 200 bars in the city publicly declared they would no longer carry Coors.

It is so difficult to get to the truth when people like Mike Wallace, a famous and well respected national media figure who was one of the anchors of "60 Minutes," said Coors was being unfairly accused of things. Peter Coors, the tall, thin, slightly graying brewer, denied that the company had been accused of discriminatory practices: "We've never had a cleaner record. We've never been convicted of discrimination." Now if he had said "we've changed," I might have listened.

Vincent, who had worked for me for a long time, was not a lightweight in the research department. He said, "That's an outright gross lie. The Colorado branch of the NAACP charged them with discrimination.

The Civil Rights Commission in Colorado found them guilty of discrimination in several cases that they litigated." In the 1970's the company was accused by the Equal Employment Opportunities Commission of unlawful employment practices and was put on probation as well as forced to pay and rehire minority and female workers.

I got a bill cosponsored by Maura Hennigan and Tommy Menino through the City Council. The choice of cosponsors is critical in this case because Hennigan and Menino were considered the most 'moderate' and anything with their names on it would be viewed as 'safe' by most people. I introduced the bill on January 15th, 1986 and it read:

> ***Whereas*** *the Coors Brewery has a long history of violating federal labor laws and union busting, breaking 19 unions in the past 20 years and being ordered by federal courts to reinstate employees whose jobs were lost because of violations and*
>
> ***Whereas*** *Brewery Workers Local 366 were forced to strike the Coors Brewery over human dignity issues such as forced lie detector tests and search and seizure of personal property and*
>
> ***Whereas*** *the organized labor movement across the United States including the Massachusetts AFL-CIO continues its support of the longstanding Coors boycott;*
>
> ***Be it therefore Resolved***, *that the Boston City Council does hereby establish a Council policy discouraging official city participation in any event involving the promotion of Coors beer or other Coors products so long as the national organized labor boycott endorsed by the AFL-CIO shall continue and be it further*
>
> ***Resolved*** *that from this time hence, and until the national Coors boycott is lifted, city staff shall avoid even informal involvement during the performance of their city duties in any future events involving the promotion of Coors beer.*

I got this resolution passed unanimously by the City Council that same day for the reason that I had worked for a long time with many unions all present at the time over another issue involving a meat packing plant, and the conservative members of the City Council were not about to undercut my effort to help unions in front of them so we decided to do the Coors boycott piece at the same time as the meat packing plant issue.

For Arthur Osborne and the AFL-CIO, the big target was the Boston Red Sox. One day I got a phone call from Domenic Bozzotto (the president of the Hotel Workers union) and he invited me to come with him and Osborne to go to the Red Sox ballpark and talk with the Italian guy who handled the concessions at the ball park.

It turned out that the Italian guy, named Ricco, was the owner of the company that did the concessions at the Fenway Ballpark like "Fenway Franks" and we sat with him for an hour. But this was a seriously frustrating meeting: Ricco wasn't gonna budge.

Getting up to leave, I said, "This is an official policy of the City of Boston to boycott Coors, and I could move to have your liquor license revoked. And I would win votes because the neighborhood really hates having beer served at the ball park. It wouldn't make me popular with ball fans, but the people that vote for me would build me a statue if I got beer out of the ballpark for good. They hate the drunk Red Sox fans and their beer cans all over the place." What I didn't know was that he was in front of the liquor licensing board right at that time.

All of a sudden he says to come back and sit down. He said, "Let me tell you, I am under contract. I will disperse Coors this year because I am bound by a contract. Next year I will not renew the contract with Coors, will that satisfy you? If you will go along with this deal then I will pull Coors out of every ballpark and venue that we serve."

Well, that was a nice deal, we agreed to it; AFL-CIO agreed; everybody agreed. And of course we got back to City Hall and we wrote up a nice press release. What I didn't realize was Ricco's company, besides serving the concessions at Fenway ballpark, also handled it at Yankee Stadium and the Meadowlands, the three most important ballparks in baseball. A game I didn't know how to play.

I really didn't realize what a big deal it was until national news went on and on saying "the Red Sox are boycotting Coor's," not accurate of course, but hey, that's the media.

Coors now had to do something.

So Coors sent Ray Tye to my office again. We met and they used Elaine Noble as the intermediary. We had 3 or 4 meetings at the Bostonian Hotel. The final deal was Coors would put up $50,000 – $25,000 from the national and $25,000 from the distributor – into a Human Rights Foundation which I created with Elaine's help. Ray Tye put up his $25,000 – In typical lack of style, Coors never paid their $25,000.

Eventually, the foundation would become Boston Human Rights Institute which did business as *Search For A Cure* and among many other things helped get a grant of $190 million to fight AIDS for the poorest countries in Africa [see chapter 132, book IV].

Harvey Milk, the City official I was most often compared with, worked successfully to get gay bars to boycott Coors throughout California in the 1970's. (He also worked on the 'majority of minorities' concept long before I started talking about it).

Allan Baird; photo by Strange de Jim

Above is a photo taken in 2003 of Allan Baird. In the 1970s he was the Teamster official in charge of the Coors boycott. He approached Harvey about getting gay bars to boycott Coors and was impressed when Harvey asked for nothing in return except that gay people be given jobs as truck drivers. Harvey got Coors banned in gay bars throughout California. Allan kept his word and hired gay drivers. With Allan's help, Harvey, amazingly, became the first openly gay candidate to be endorsed by the Teamsters, firefighters and construction workers unions.

Below is a photo from the birthday party at the Harvey Milk Gay Democratic Club Annual dinner May 22, 1980. (after Harvey Milk was assassinated, the Gay Democratic Club changed its name to honor Harvey in 1978.) From left to right are Harvey's successor Supervisor Harry Britt, Jane Fonda, Tom Hayden, and Bill Kraus (Congressman Phil Burton's aide). They led the attendees in singing "Happy Birthday" to the late Harvey. Teamster leader Allan Baird took Ms. Fonda to task for drinking a Coors in her latest movie, heedless of the boycott. She apologized.

Harvey Milk Gay Democratic Club Annual dinner: photo by Daniel Nicoletta

1985: The Little Things That Matter

"It's the little details that are vital. Little things make big things happen."
– John Wooden

The 1985 political agenda was made up of a lot of little brick-like political actions that we cemented together into a coherent structure — society's house, to our perhaps grandiose way of thinking. We put together a team that could handle the hundreds of little things that mattered to people and still move forward on our policy agenda that would impact large numbers of people at the same time.

On September 23rd, 1985, some thirteen years since the first gay rights bill had been introduced, the Massachusetts House crushed the bill, 88 to 65, with the Roman Catholic Church opposing the bill as did Christian Scientists from the "mother church" in my neighborhood. Think about the idea of "separation of Church and State" for a moment, and how often we twist the common sense meanings of our system to accommodate those with power.

Governor Dukakis made some effort but after the foster care debacle it is not clear that anyone really believed his sincerity. AIDS may have killed the bill this year as the House minority leader William G. Robinson was quoted by the *Boston Globe* as saying he would ask that the bill be sent to the House Ways and Means Committee for a study of its impact on AIDS. He was a key vote for the bill. He had voted for it in 1983 but apparently AIDS changed his mind. He said "tell me with absolute certainty that a parallel cannot be drawn between the public health issue and the gay rights issue."

Mark Roosevelt, who had become the John F. Kennedy Library manager, worked out with me a scheme to have high school kids have a mock election for city council and school committee before the real one.

The results would be posted before the real election so that candidates would go through the public schools and listen to kids and teachers. I figured this 'straw poll' idea could actually get a lot of people to pay attention to the school system. We got the election department to agree to put real voting machines in the public school and to have kids actually vote in the mock elections.

On June 13th over 200 demonstrators were dragged out of the JFK Federal Building protesting additional aid to the Contras. They were part of a crowd of 3,000 that were outside the building. Similar protests were held in several cities. 24 people were arrested in Greenfield, in western Massachusetts, when they refused to leave the IRS office. In Chicopee, 62 people were carried or dragged to a bus when they tried to block the gate to Westover Air Force Base. In a *Herald* article, I was quoted saying at a mock trial of the U.S. government that "I was in Nicaragua when their election was taking place. It would be the envy of this city in terms of fairness and openness." This protest was about a vote of the Congress on giving the Contras $27 million to help them overthrow the elected government of Nicaragua because it was "leftist."

I convinced the Police Commissioner for the City of Boston, Francis "Mickey" Roache, to come a Dignity event, the organization of gay Catholics. He came with his wife, and spoke to them in an address, which was followed by a Sunday worship service. "Gays and lesbians have a right to be treated with respect and dignity and every policeman in the city of Boston must respect that right," he said, which made the *Advocate*, the gay national magazine. Mickey was genuinely surprised and said, "They just want to be respected," over and over to me. It was a beginning to a complicated and lengthy set of negotiations between the police and me over putting an end to the unofficial war between gays and police.

The Boston Housing Court ruled in May that my old nemesis Norman Levenson, a large landlord in the west Fenway who required his low income tenants to find a co-signer in order to renew their leases, was both discriminatory and illegal. Levenson was slapped with an injunction prohibiting him from continuing this practice. Levenson owned nearly 1,000 apartments and managed 500 condominiums, which were becoming more and more a problem as condo owners pushed out tenants. Levenson was actually using a twist in the rent laws put in by Jim Kelly to figure out a way around rent control so he could make more money. He was making sure that people who rented had to earn, as a group, more than $25,000 per year, so that he could up rents 12.5% every year instead of the maximum being about 4% or the consumer price index, which the city law required for tenants who, as a group, made below that amount. Making more money would require he get rid of poor folks which in the case of the Fenway pretty much meant 'black folks.'

On Mission Hill another drama was unfolding. A three-story brick town house on Wigglesworth Street, a really nice-looking building, was slated for being torn down to make room for a convenience store. The company that bought the building wanted to build a 7-Eleven store on the site. Despite requests from Mayor Flynn and the local state rep Kevin Fitzgerald, the company refused to meet with the neighborhood.

So we got some press on the situation, including a *Boston Globe* editorial headlined "Arrogance on Mission Hill," and I met with the landlord, Southland. I convinced them that we were trying to respect their need to make money while also getting what we needed as a neighborhood, and that collaborating would end up easier, because our city's permitting process can be unbelievably slow when it gets bogged down by controversies. They said okay to making new apartments in the existing building. An article in the *Phoenix* called 'David and Goliath,' said:

> *City Councilor David Scondras calls it 'an amazing compromise'*
> *and, you know, he's right. How often does a neighborhood*
> *association succeed in talking sense to a major corporation with*
> *designs on some local property especially when the*
> *neighborhood association is in Boston and the giant corporation*
> *is headquartered in Dallas. Scondras and Southland agreed to*
> *preserve the building.*

Across the country there were few gay elected officials. I met Steven Shulte, who was a former Colt model (a cool porn magazine that featured Steven a few times), and we decided to host the first meeting of what became known as the 'Gay Officials Conference.' In those days we called it the Gay Elected and Appointed Officials Conference and invited anyone appointed to anything to join us, or we would have had only 15 people or so at our convention because there were so few elected officials.

The saga of the boats in which people lived in Boston Harbor continued from previous years. There was a 1932 Tringali fishing trawler owned by a man named Sam Osokow that was sunk on February 3rd to the bottom of Fort Point Channel. Police divers found that a 4-inch hole had been cut in the hull of the 43-foot houseboat. Sam was not rich, the boat was not insured, and he was ruined. He had been one of the folks fighting together to stop the owners of the *Chelsea*, a former New York City ferry that was converted to offices. Osokow and other owners nearby complained to the marina management that the *Chelsea* was not properly secured and endangered their homes, their houseboats. The fight between the big man and the little guys, the big boat and the little ones continued with my friend Judge George Daher in the middle of it all, as he had ruled that the big company could not evict or harass the little boat owners.

On February 15th, I joined with Ray Flynn to announce a grant I got him to make to the AIDS Action Committee for $150,000 to do their work helping educate, counsel and support people with AIDS.

It is important to understand that although the virus had been identified in 1983, a test for it had yet to be licensed by the FDA. So there was no way to tell who did and did not have the virus that causes AIDS.

Irrationality continued to dominate public actions about AIDS. For example, in New Hampshire a bill was put forward which would have made it a felony for a "homosexual" to donate blood. This included lesbians who were at the least risk for contracting AIDS from sexual behavior than any other demographic.

I gave a speech to the Democratic National Committee Fairness Commission in Faneuil Hall near City Hall. The committee was holding hearings about the subtle transformation of the commitment of the party to the needs and rights of minorities and to the re-interpretation of the call for those rights as pleas of "special interests" for "special treatment."

Beneath this was the desire by political party thinkers to move the party toward the 'center' and away from its natural base in labor, blacks, gays, etc. in order to get a bigger percentage of independent voters. It was not clear to those running the party that such a move might benefit the party in the short run, but that the gains would be illusory as the failure to engage those who had lost hope that government could help by moving away from them would force the party to become increasingly one that resembled the Republicans.

My speech was cut up and used across the country. The August 28th headline in *Your Paper,* a San Jose newspaper, read "Scondras warns Democrats: "Reject Us and We'll Walk."

Every state had a paper with some variation of this article in it — many dozens of news outlets would carry my speech. The *Mirror* said I had "chastised" the Democratic Party and called the National Committee "Hopelessly Lost." *Bay Windows* covered the speech. *Metra*, the Midwest's leading gay paper, printed my whole speech. The *San Diego Gazette* headlined it as "Scondras warns Demos: ignoring us means defeat." The *Philadelphia Gay News* headlined its August 22 edition with "Scondras scolds Democrats." In Portland, Oregon a paper called *Just Out* put out an article making similar points. *Frontline* in Connecticut headlined an article "Scondras warns: 'Reject us and we'll walk.'"

Interesting how news outlets began using just my name in headlines across the country, without explaining who I was. I had apparently accumulated some notoriety. The Baltimore paper, similar to all the others, read in part:

Openly Gay Boston City Councilor David Scondras, testifying before the Democratic National Committee's first Fairness Commission Hearing in Boston on August 3rd warned Party leaders that to ignore justice for Gay and Lesbian people is to ensure defeat at the polls. "Justice is not a peripheral issue," Scondras said, "It is the soul of our party. Justice is not political baggage; it is the best way to achieve real power and the only way to keep it."...Wild applause and cheering briefly halted the hearing when Scondras told the Commission "As Gay people, we are sick and tired of 'leaders' who want our time, our money, our creativity, our commitment, our work and our votes, but reject us.

A more nuanced way of saying, as Ginny Apuzzo did, "No more free fucks!"

The two years 1984 and 1985 were packed with many different events — yet through it all a thread of continuity emerged. Trying to make systems treat everyone with fairness and dignity, compassion and sharing. Given our society's primitive economic and social structures built on myths, there were unending opportunities to try to make a difference in people's lives just by telling the truth to whoever would listen. And what I found particularly interesting was how many people within the systems we created understood that they were broken and knew a lot about how to fix them. They just felt afraid to speak up and not powerful enough to take action.

73 /   Back Bay Sinking

Boston's Back Bay was once actually a bay, a tidal estuary with salty water into which sewage and garbage were dumped. Eventually, this created a smell so bad there was a cry to clean it up. The smell, combined with the allure of profits that could be made by growing the city larger, reshaped Boston by filling in the bay and other sections of the city.

It was 1857 when the 30-year project to fill in the Back Bay began. Thirty-five car trains were used 24 hours a day to haul dirt from Needham, which was dumped onto the peat of the tidal flats.

They took tall spruce trees, stripped them of branches, turned the resultant giant toothpicks upside down and rammed them into the ground deep enough to get the tops into the solid blue clay far below, and these "piles" served as the giant sticks on which big stones were put to make foundations for the thousands of beautiful town houses that make up the Back Bay, now a section of Boston rather than a marsh.

The reason these piles were necessary is that the fill, the sand and mud above the solid clay, could never hold up a building of stone and brick. So like the Swiss lake-dwellers of pre modern times, the Victorians of Boston lived in platforms held up by sticks into the deep earth.

But there was a problem. The wood that the piles are made out of is fine so long as they are under water. Otherwise the wood rots.

The builders were not afraid because with the sea all around Boston and the fill being just sand and gravel, the water level would be higher than the piles.

But they didn't know about subway tunnels and expanding sewer lines, one acting like dams the other likes drains, so the water level in many places fell below the tops of the wooden piles. They began to rot.

In 1929 cracks appeared in the walls of the Boston Public Library. When city workers tried to figure out what was going on, they found that a nearby sewer drained enough water from the ground to have the piles exposed to oxygen and the fungus and bacteria did the rest. By the late

1930's a groundwater monitoring program started, putting in 700 small observation wells, and pipes into the ground used to measure the water level. But over the years, many of them were paved over and lost.

Over 15,000 homes were built before 1940 in the Back Bay and the flats of Beacon Hill which could be affected by the water levels.

And the crisis hit while I was in my first term.

Bob Beal

The old Custom House tower in Boston was owned by Robert Beal, and tied up in a gigantic red bow. I kept thinking it must have been for Christmas or something, like a present, but to whom? Robert Beal certainly had enough money to buy it.

Bob, it turns out, was gay, and so was his brother John. Bob spoke in low, carefully measured, dulcet tones — a man of words chosen to remove ambiguity without diluting complexities. He contacted me because the house he lived in on Brimmer Street was sinking, and it would cost a fortune to fix. I was astonished Bob could speak so calmly and rationally about a crisis so personal and so serious. He loved his house.

I got myself a crash course on subterranean aquifers, water tables, wood rot, the way buildings were built and stabilized and decided to hold public hearings on the crisis. It appeared that a lot of the city of Boston might end up in a hole. But it was a wealthy part of Boston.

As we started to work on the project, the *Boston Globe*, the *TAB*, *Ledger* and *Herald* started articles on the sinking of buildings until they reached *USA Today* and the *New York Times*. Something about rich people losing their homes tickled the *hoi polloi*.

By July 23rd, 1985 the city had declared 16 buildings along Brimmer Street "unsafe and dangerous" as a result of the foundations collapsing. "Beacon Hill is Sinking" yelled some media on steroids; the *TAB* headlined it "Piles of Trouble," the *International Herald Tribune* called it "In Boston, Real Downer."

PHOTO BY SARAH HOOD, INSET PHOTO BY RICHARD FELDMAN
Boston City Councillor David Scondras is calling on the city and the state to tackle the water table problem in Beacon Hill, the Back Bay, the South End and the Fenway.

Concerns over costly water table damage aired at hearing

By Jonathan Wells

Property owners and city and state officials packed the city council chambers at Boston City Hall last week to discuss the extent and cost of rotting wood foundations caused by the lowering of the water table beneath the flat of Beacon Hill.

A top city official also made several recommendations to the mayor last week designed to determine the extent of the problem.

An array of local officials and engineering experts told the crowd of concerned homeowners at the July 15 city council hearing that a serious water table problem exists at the foot of Beacon Hill, but officials could not say whether similar problems may be developing in the residential neighborhoods of the Back Bay, the South End or the Fenway.

The Tab reported last month that 16 buildings in the Brimmer Street area have been declared "unsafe and dangerous" by the city's inspectional services department (ISD) in the past six weeks see **Damage**, page 19

Because the repairs would cost millions, buildings in many parts of the city might be involved, and many people would have limited means to make them, I asked Michael Dukakis to declare the sections of the city involved a disaster area so we could apply for federal funds to help out. A lot of people felt this was cheeky — the rich asking for money from the taxpayers who weren't. A reporter from *USA Today* wrote: "Beacon Hill's City Councilor David Scondras said 'In the worst case, every building could come down.'"

    I got Mayor Ray Flynn to put together a meeting at the Parkman House, the mansion owned by the city on Beacon Hill, to present our findings to the neighborhood and share a suggested course of action. Ray and I knew that our paying attention to this problem would be helpful with a group of very well-to-do folks who ordinarily might not like us, who might help fund our campaigns, and would help shape our image as concerned with everyone, not just the poor. Besides, a lot of poor would be affected by the water table crisis, and if we could get some rich folks to kick in some money, we might be able to help those of limited means through building a coalition with the rich.

    I kept trying to get the rich guys away from their lawyers who were focused on trying to figure out who to blame and sue them. That would lead to years of litigation and lots of defensiveness among city and state agencies from whom we would need cooperation to solve the problem. Unless I could change the dynamic we would end up with rich lawyers and sinking houses.

My staff put together a giant map of Boston and colored it in where there were problems with the ground water. We used it at a council meeting where it towered ten feet tall, to help show people in graphic detail how much of the city was in trouble.

I called for the creation of a water table trust — an agency that would monitor the groundwater on an ongoing basis that would allow us to take action quickly to restore water levels and make sure construction or anything else that changed water tables would be done in ways that did not lower the water level. Ray was happy to have me take the lead on this as I had studied and understood the technicalities of the ground water issue.

On July 2nd, 1986, after nearly a year of work, I got the Boston Ground Water Trust established by city ordinance with powers to open old wells, measure water levels, and intervene to stabilize the water table. And I got Galen Gilbert, my neighbor, lawyer, friend, and someone I greatly admired for his tenacity, to be a member (he became its treasurer.) He served the city as a trustee until 2013. So the groundwater monitoring program system put in place in the 1930's finally got a push to get it working in the 1980's.

74 / 1986: Being an Activist Elected Official

"Appreciation is a wonderful thing:
it makes what is excellent in others belong to us as well."
- Voltaire

Being a political person for me meant juggling a matrix of personalities and issues, responding to requests for help and acting as surrogate authority, the voice or presence of the city at public events and affairs, and from time to time maybe even its conscience. It was a chaotic blend of interactions through which ran the threads of our agendas, This effort was supported by many institutions, which we guided and infused with the cultural predispositions of our constituents and ourselves. I want to give you a sense of the people, and the feeling of the juggling of time and circumstances, that made up my life during those years. 1986 is a good year to pick to help frame what it was like to be an activist elected official.

The Characters In The Game

Over the years I learned a little more about the people with whom I got elected.

Ray Flynn, Mayor of Boston — Tall, ran a lot, lived in a modest house in South Boston. Had a bunch of kids, a great wife. Ray seemed to care about two things: people and the Pope, or at least God. He once said to me in the middle of a fight with Jerry Rappaport, a big landlord opposed to rent control, "People like that must go right to hell." He meant the real place that God sends unrepentant sinners. Ray liked me, he said, because I cared about poor people and sick people, taking care of people in need. I did. Ray was unusual in that he knew what he didn't know and was not afraid to have people a lot smarter than him around him. He treated intelligence the way a carpenter treats tools — something to use to help you built the house you want.

Albert "Dapper" O'Neil — City councilor for many, many years. He ran for office many times before becoming a city councilor. He knew that he was a cartoon. He would say "watch this" to me, winking, and then say something to a crowd that he knew would bring it to its feet cheering, and then he would turn his back to the crowd, smile and roll his eyes so I knew that he knew he was the puppet master of the stupid. He was fat and tall, white haired with blue eyes and a huge nose. People thought he drank a lot but I don't think he did. He was full of contradictions. I think he was a gay guy who could never actually deal with being a gay guy.

Bob Travaglini — The Italian councilor from East Boston, I think he was the protégé of Gus Serra or maybe his enemy – all these things get mixed up in memory — but he was a handsome, single guy who took care of his looks and prayed on Sunday. He was a Catholic. He was also really practical and liked to pontificate when he was a little insecure. He was a good guy — and the only one on the City Council that Robert thought was as good as me. After the City Council he get elected as State Senator and went on to become President of the Massachusetts Senate.

Tommy Menino — The guy that started his career as Senator Joe Timilty's driver. He worked in Joe Timilty's office for years before running for office, and he managed to occupy the 'center' of the political spectrum. He was a nice guy on many levels but very touchy. He was always the last on the council to decide which way to vote, and always strategic. He played it safe. He went on to become Mayor for many years.

Bruce Bolling — Smart, from a family with several elected officials, a father who was a State Senator and a brother, Royal Bolling Jr., who was a State Representative, the Bollings were a power to be reckoned with in the community of color. Bruce tried to see everything logically, reduce everything to reasoned discourse. At times he used reason to justify what he emotionally wanted to do. He was smart, kind, and a nice person. Oh, he was black too. He became the first black President of the Boston City Council.

Charles Yancey — Ran for council several times before getting there. He was a thoughtful person, not afraid to be 'out there,' tended to have an ethical system informed by religion. He was somewhat assimilated into American social norms when it came to family life and into revolutionary norms when it came to economic and social policy that impacted people's ability to share in the common wealth.

Jimmy Byrne — Then there was Byrne, the lawyer type, quiet, right wing, not particularly talkative, held his opinions to himself, spent a lot of time working out of his law office. He was a puppet of landlords — I remember once negotiating with Jerry Rappaport whom we called the '14th councilor' because he really did control votes on that body, and he sent a wording of a change that he could accept in the rent laws to me by way of his runner, Jimmy Byrne. It was odd to have a colleague on the council act as a mailman for a landlord not elected to anything.

Mike McCormack — Began his life in public housing, became a lawyer, was smart, left behind his roots in poverty, eventually married and moved to the rich suburb Wellesley. He was liberalish, logical, a capitalist in general and loved the soap opera of politics. I think that his wife really wanted him to leave it all and eventually he did. He was very ambitious but also very clear about his limits.

Maura Hennigan — The lady of the council. She was connected to powerful people in her family and had a lot of power being one of the only women on the council at the time. The only other woman I remember on the council was the earlier famous Louisa Day Hicks, the anti-busing, one time congresswoman whose seat was taken over by Joe Moakley when she lost her second bid for the job. Maura supported the death penalty, was opposed to abortion, but tended to take positions that were politically 'safe' and you could never rule her out as a potential ally. Folks did not treat her with respect, which is sad because she deserved it.

Joe Tierney — A practical lawyer with a good sense of humor whose city council tenure was characterized by his playing politics as the game it is for most who are in it. He was a real politician and enjoyed the fight. He was amazingly conservative in every sense of the word, but also practical. He would not stay on the council for long, running for Mayor as a way to exit.

Brian McLaughlin — Always a sweet guy who lived with his mom and pop. We all thought that he was the lover of his chief staff aide — but if he was gay he was in the deep freeze. He was a tenant advocate and in general supported progressive positions on the council. He came from a part of the city that elected Tom Gallagher as their state rep who was a smart, terrific, man who endorsed me at a time endorsing a gay guy was politically dangerous. Brian came very close to losing his election a couple of times and it was clear that he hated running for office as much as I did.

Jimmy Kelly — Dangerous because besides being a product of violence, doing a stint for carrying a gun without a license, and an alcoholic with the self-righteousness that only reformed sinners can achieve, he had a brain. He did what he said and he said what he would do. He was not a dissembling man, and I respected his honesty and his clarity but found his thinking alarming because it reflected in many ways the concatenation of mythology and meanness that defines to this day what an "American" means to many.

Chris Iannella — Finally there was the old man of the council, Chris Iannella and his sons who followed him around. Chris was the Italian "listen to everyone, try to persuade" person. He ran his law practice pretty much out of his city council office. I will never forget one day him coming over to my office sitting me on the couch in the waiting room outside the west wing offices and saying something like: "What are you trying to do" to me, aghast at my activities. "You're supposed to listen and care, not try to change anything. You do too much. Take a vacation. Every time you do something someone ends up hating you and eventually you're going to lose an election! You're supposed to sound like you care, not change anything!" Chris was old, not stupid, liberalish as most of the Italians tended to be on the council, and had lived in City Hall for a good part of his life.

Bob Kaven — Iannella's aide Bob Kaven was a gay man that I never met sober. He was a functioning drunk. He invited me to gay party-orgies on Mission Hill that were a part of gay life in the 80's. Robert and I went to one, but didn't think it lived up to its billing.

There were a lot of people in this game called politics and the players played hard, fast, smart, not so smart, and often in very complicated ways. Makes football seem awfully tame to me.

1986, the beginning of my second term, was an incredible year. It began with figuring out how to get Bruce Bolling the votes to be the first black president of the Boston City Council in history. Eventually the lure of being president overcame his earlier commitment to vote for Joe Tierney. We appealed to him on our collective desire to move Boston in a more progressive direction. We argued with him about his previous hasty agreement to support Tierney and pointed out that all commitments are based on the assumption that circumstances do not radically alter — we were not asking him to change his vote for an event on the same scale as supporting some other councilor, but on the basis of becoming president himself and, by so doing, change history. Our arguments won out.

A few weeks later at the dinner that Tommy Menino held after every selection of a council president, the councilors trash each other, make jokes in that odd style we call a roast. That particular night, Joe Tierney who was supposed to be voted in as President got up to make a toast, and said "Bruce told me he was with me to the end — this is the end." Those dinners were not exactly comfortable but they were entertaining. Menino was bidding to become the "leader of the pack" through this annual dinner coupled with other actions focused on having him become the social cohesion between city workers, unions, etc. He was already planning to become mayor.

We would be dealing with many issues simultaneously. One of the realities of life among those whose lives had not yet calcified into repetitive reruns of yesterday's ideas, is the difficulty of seeing the forest for the trees. The forest did not change in all the years I was in office, or for that matter all the years after it. It was dominated by an underlying struggle, which explains both the politics of the age, and the reasons so many of us fear for the survival of our species. Class war was a part of that underlying struggle, but in fact was itself another in the long list of symptoms we characterize incorrectly as the problem itself.

Letters

Every day people wrote asking for help, thank me, advising us on what to do. Here is a flavor from the many thousands of letters we received over ten years. They do not include the hate mail, which has its own section [see chapter 83 below].

Dona Sommers sent me a note thanking me for my active support for the Boston Shakespeare Company during a crisis that threatened its existence. I passed a resolution to Congress putting Boston on record opposing actions that would tax non-profit artist groups. I met with the Shakespeare Company, visited the building, and made a public issue of this extraordinary resource being destroyed to facilitate the greed of a landlord who wanted to cash in on the condo conversion craze.

May 9th from the Beantown Softball League: "Thanks for coming out to the opening day ceremony of the Softball League," Gary Hills, 1986. It seems only the gay softball league had their cars towed while others coming and parking for other types of games did not. The Beantown League is the gay league, which grew out of the decision by area gay bars to create and fund a league. It played each year and beat the police league over and over. The verbal exchanges with the police were not polite and the police just towed cars instead of warning people to move.

The union representing workers at City Hospital wrote a note on May 5th saying, "We would like to thank you from the bottom of our hearts for your participation in April 16th's hearing on the rebuilding of the hospital. It's made a difference already. You helped us remind folks that the hospital produces services to those that no other hospital can or will and without us many would not receive care at all. We have noticed an immediate improvement in our negotiations with the hospital ."

I got this letter from someone named Robert from Lewiston, Maine dated March 1st, 1986: It began:

I got a hand printed note on April 27th which said thank you for "all the help that was given to my family and me during the time of the malfunctioning of the sewage pipes in my building."

I got an April 8th letter from Herbert Berman from Brooklyn who was on the New York City Council that begins: "Your letter arrived in the nick of time. It was indeed a welcome respite in the avalanche of pressure that followed the vote..." [New York's Gay Rights vote]

I got a Feb 10th note from Betty Woodberry, which brought back memories. During the struggle against the war in Vietnam, this amazing family of Quakers put me up in their Newton house where I lived for awhile. They cared for me, listened to my rambling and pain, the confusion of being gay and living in a society torn by war. She closed the letter with, "You're still extended family, ya know." I wish that I could feel what love was directed toward me, but the defenses that protected me all my life also kept out the praise and love and caring. It was a safe but lonely place that hate brought me, the hate toward me for being queer that I had internalized.

One of the issues in 1986 was condo conversion. I got a letter in February of 1986 from Rochelle Glickman saying, "Your courage in not buckling under pressure from Real Estate interests deeply impressed me. Even though I do not live in your district, if you ever run for another office, I will definitely vote for you."

Brian Clague, a wonderful violinist whom I have known for almost 30 years now, sent me a note on June 11, 1986 at a time he was representing the Buckminster Tenants against Ed Shamsi, who would be the bane of my existence and ultimately get me unelected. The note read:

*Your appearance and strong speech gave a huge morale boost
to all of our members. Between fighting a scumbag with pots
full of money and the exhausting legal and bureaucratic battles,
our people can get easily discouraged.*

Everything is not about big stuff but it is all-important. Judith Lynch sent me a note on April 8th regarding the status of cable TV in the Back Bay, "You have continued to update us as new information became available and we appreciate it. It is rare and wonderful to see such an example of good service."

On December 24th I got a note from Dan Kenary who was starting a new small brewery in Boston that would brew a new beer "Harpoon Ale," "Thank you for your help," he wrote, "I look forward to meeting you at our brewery opening."

Mary Corcoran said, "Thank you for your help in our housing crisis…without your help I'm afraid we would be in pretty dire circumstances, especially since the Berkeley Residence is one of the very few affordable places left for single women…" November 1986.

From Stephen Baierwick November 12th, 1986 from the Long Island Shelter:

"Who is the city rep for the homeless if anyone? I hope it is you...I've been at Long Island Shelter since October 10. Holding down a full time job while staying here is nearly impossible. The number one problem is the lack of protection for Long Island guests waiting in the line on Mass Ave. There are many line cutters. If you object...you are threatened or even assaulted. One day someone was stabbed, another day someone else was robbed. Women have been intimidated and sexually harassed...I hope that you and other council members will visit Long Island Shelter some afternoon. Maybe you could even get all the plumbing and windows repaired for us."

We did.

AIDS Action Council in Washington DC sent me a note on March 28th telling me that my visit to the assistant secretary of the U.S. Department of Health and Human Services caused the secretary to send them a letter regarding the delegation of city officials, one of whom was myself. Part of the letter from the U.S. Public Health Service said:

Mr. Scondras from Boston has been led to believe that compound S (now called azidothymidine or AZT) will be locked up in bureaucratic red tape for 17 months. I hope the attached notice will satisfy him that this drug is on a very fast track....
— Donald Ian Macdonald, M.D.
Acting Assistant Secretary for Health, March 12th 1986.

This was interesting as a group of us invaded Dr. Tony Fauci's office after Reagan appointed him to deal with AIDS. I remember being somewhat impolite... well, frankly, I was standing on his table to make sure he remembered me pointing out that Rock Hudson had to go to France to get AZT which had been invented at the NIH in 1965 and used in many people over the years for transplant therapy and yet Americans couldn't get it.

A copy of a letter sent to Ray Flynn said: "If you will bear with a superannuated septuagenarian of 32 years on Temple Street I cannot improve upon David Scondras' warning: 'Notwithstanding anyone's best intentions, it would be unfortunate for us all for a McDonald's to open on Temple Street.' Amen. Yours, Martha Hawkins, Sept 12th, 1986."

A handwritten thank you note from John Crabtree of August 28[th.] We made sure John Crabtree would continue to teach an evening course in the college of continuing education at Wentworth. John was gay. Wentworth was not.

Ruth Bateson sent a note to us on August 26th thanking us for intervening with the building department on her behalf, "I wish to thank Councilor Scondras for the kind of office he maintains where his people try to be helpful and show concern for those who need advice." She had been treated shabbily by a probably overworked city worker.

From Henry D. Messer, MD, a long note. It said:

Fan letters are not my usual style, but this one is definitely a fan letter. I was so impressed by your presentation at the MOHR meeting in Grand Rapids that I feel that I just must let you know it...Like you, I believe that POWER is indeed the way we have to go. How often we talk to police or to the politicians and they may speak nicely to us, but then nothing much changes. You are absolutely right that running a gay candidate for office would bring out a great deal of support...It was a delight to learn that you have eliminated the vice squad in Boston...Detroit has a very busy and homophobic one. The state police are very active against gays along the state highways too. Most of our lawyers fight it in the courts which mean that they win a few and lose a few but the arrests go on. I believe that the only way to stop it is political power...We somehow have to motivate our community to get out there and oppose what is wrong with the way our governments treat us. .
— Yours for justice, Henry D. Messer.

From all the organizers of Local 26th, the hotel workers union, a letter thanking me for standing with them at their first membership meeting at the Back Bay Hilton on October 9th. Dated October 21st.

From Jean Michaels, a note on November 23[rd,] "My neighbor, Ms. Millie Rothstein, reported to me that you were supportive of our opposition to the garage next door…I am very grateful for your personal help in this matter."

"Warmest regards from the Superintendent of the Suffolk County House of Corrections for attending the awards ceremony thanking those who tried to help make Human Services a better and bigger part of jail."

In the midst of this chaotic life, responding to everyone with a request, we also took on issues that broke new ground in appearance but was consistent with the underlying effort: bringing power to those who need it to increase their quality of life. The problem we ran into over and over was exemplified by tenants' inability, notwithstanding their great numbers, to overcome the political clout of landlords. The real reason behind this is what Robert and I called "the landlord inside the tenant." Every time we tried to help tenants, many voted and pushed to protect the landlords they hoped someday they would become themselves. In general, if you make decisions based upon what you wish you were but aren't, the decisions will hurt you not help you. But a fundamental problem with democracy is that people vote not for who they are but for who they want to be.

The job we carved out for ourselves was to help people and institutions learn who they were, what their interests were, and who would serve those interests. And to organize to get the power to make this happen. The letters helped us keep in touch with the day to day crises of everyday life in our society.

75 /   Hot Dogs and the Boss

*"I have spent my life judging the distance between American reality,
and the American Dream"*
— Bruce Springsteen

Mel King used to say that there were two struggles, one for the mind and one for the land, and both occurred simultaneously. This was particularly true when it came to the fight over Fenway Franks. Hot dogs. The most famous hot dogs in Boston made in Boston by the Colonial meat packing plant. A company in Chicago wanted to buy the plant, fire the hundreds of workers, and move the name *Colonial* to its Chicago plant which led to a fight between the owner and workers.

The AFL-CIO union included 600 meatpackers at the Colonial Provision Company. The guy that owned the place got city money to help keep the company alive, as well as millions of dollars worth of givebacks agreed upon by the union. But in spite of this, the plant was losing money and he wanted to sell it to Thorn Apple Valley, Inc. Thorn was interested in the Colonial name which was a significant asset as even I knew about the quality of Colonial hams — they were great. And, maybe even more importantly for name recognition, the plant was contracted to make the hot dogs used at Fenway Park, home of the Red Sox. Thorn was headquartered in Michigan, nowhere near Boston, and if they bought Colonial they would close the Boston plant and some 600 people would lose their jobs.

Arthur Obsborne, the president of the Massachusetts AFL-CIO said that the union would launch a regional boycott of Colonial if Thorn fired everyone and expected New Englanders to still eat Colonial Ham. Osborne said, "If they leave, I won't eat another Colonial ham in my life," and Joel Dorfman, the buyer of Colonial, replied that he couldn't care less.

The big plant was on Massachusetts Avenue — I had passed it many times. This was an unusual issue that pretty much all the local officials were on the same side, but not all.

Dapper Interrupts Ham Fight with Gay Fight

Troublemakers know no sleep and the early days of 1986 were full of trouble. Lyndon LaRouche, a true fascist whose followers reminded me of born again Christians, put together a document called "The Memorial Bill to Stop AIDS" which Albert L. "Dapper" O'Neil submitted to the city council. The bill called for mandatory screening of people for HIV through blood tests of all food handlers, workers in service occupations like barbers and eye doctors, elementary and secondary school teachers etc., and those who tested positive would be interviewed to figure out who their sex partners were since AIDS is "a national security risk" and O'Neil also called for mandatory isolation of people with AIDS.

Maybe Dapper thought the food handler restriction might make his bill relevant to the Colonial meatpacker fight. Maybe he thought union people were anti-gay and he could get their support. Maybe he just liked another opportunity to attack gays.

When I got a copy of the bill, AIDS Action Committee and I made sure hundreds of people would show up at the council the next day with signs that read "Cut the crap, Dap" and "Quarantine the virus not people". When Dapper saw the "Cut the crap Dap" sign, he went crazy, screamed and yelled, called for security.

Meanwhile the Fight Over Hot Dogs Went On

The guy who sold Colonial to Thorn had another offer in the wings by a company that would keep the workers, but he wanted more money. I felt terrible about the nightmare closing the Colonial Meat Packing Plant would create for the many workers who were really not going to be able to get 'retrained' for some other job that no one would hire them for anyway. The company had grossed $75 million the previous year — it was not a hopeless case. Joel Dorfman who ran Thorn Apple got letters begging him in the name of the governor, mayor, and God (priests wrote letters). To no avail.

The city offered carrots and sticks galore. Mayor Flynn's policy director, informed the current owners that the bonds the city gave them (cheap, tax free) could not be given to a buyer that eliminates jobs. I suggested Boston could forgive bills like a $70,000 water bill, and provide tax breaks. Nothing worked.

A *Globe* article of January 14th summarizes the plight of the folks who worked at Colonial:

> *After nearly 30 years at the plant, Mary A. Baughns earns $9 an hour as a packer in sliced meats. A frail woman who refused to give her age, Baughns has completed a data entry course. But would rather stay at Colonial. She said she likes everything about her job but the cool temperature in the plant. "This is such a shock. One minute someone's buying us. The next they're maybe closing the doors," she said.*

I was livid. It became increasingly clear that the decisions being made about people's lives were about making the most money possible, period. And that this worked only because most of us were not connected enough to each other to know that the 15-cent difference in the price of a ham meant Mary Baughns would lose her job.

I noticed that there was a huge fuss among the company bosses when I said we should just seize the company by eminent domain and sell it to the alternative buyers who would protect the workers' jobs. I didn't care who made out on owning the plant, I cared about the hundreds of families that depended on the jobs for their lives.

So I held a huge hearing that was mobbed at City Hall the week of January 13th. Over 300 workers and families showed up along with union officials, and state and city officials. The city council gallery was overflowing. I said that in the past Boston used eminent domain to refurbish Quincy Market. I said we should "decide for once to use that power for the working people of this city." The mayor made it clear that this was a serious possibility by ordering the city's lawyer to check out the legal issues.

Not surprisingly, people were a little confused about eminent domain – they thought I meant steal the land — so I explained, "We're not talking about taking someone's property. We're talking about buying it and then turning it over to a responsible owner."

So many unions were on board that my colleagues included Dapper and Jim Kelly who depended on union votes to win elections. To them, the term 'union' meant hetero macho man – hence Dapper and Jim's comfort level with them – but that had been changing lately, as seen in the "Cut the crap Dap" incident above.

The president of the company in Michigan apparently had been paying attention to my hearing. He screamed loudly enough to make it into every paper in the country the day after. The *Herald* of January 21 had an article titled "Buyer rips Hub takeover plan."

"I didn't know we were in Nicaragua," he said.

Yup. I got his attention.

Samuel Guynn, an employee of Colonial Provision Company, sits with his son David, 5, yesterday during City Hall hearing on the closing of the plant. GLOBE STAFF PHOTO BY TED DULLY

I had the votes to go to court, and I knew that it didn't matter who won or lost because our court system is one more piece in the game we call politics even if it thinks it's about something else. I said, "Does Dorfman (the guy that ran Thorn) have the money to be tied up in court for the next two years not able to do anything at all with Colonial? Because we do. If he's prepared to do that, we are prepared to fight."

I knew that Dorfman, when he cooled off, would be told by his lawyers that he didn't want to do this because it would bankrupt him and Thorn already had a lot of money trouble.

Soon enough my spies told me that Dorfman was negotiating quietly with the city on what the city would do for him and what he would do for the folks who worked at Colonial. But he was stubborn, full of himself and not too interested in the folks who worked at the plant. The deals he suggested were just nowhere near enough.

DAILY WORLD

20¢

CONTINUING THE DAILY WORKER, FOUNDED 1924

Vol. XVIII No. 145 — New York, N.Y. — Wednesday, February 19, 1986 — Daily except Sun., Mon. and major holidays

Precedent setting decision

BOSTON VOTES TO TAKE OVER PLANT

Boston votes plant takeover

Special to the Daily World

BOSTON — The City Council and the mayor have agreed to a public takeover of the Colonial Provision Company's meatpacking plant here in order to save 600 jobs, if the owners insist on closing the plant.

By a 12-1 vote, the council made its decision February 10 in a gallery packed with 200 unionists a week after 300 workers demonstrated at council hearings.

The lone dissenter in the vote was former City Council President Joseph Tierney, who said that "eminent domain is justifiable only if there is a public purpose to the seizure." Political observers here noted that apparently the preservation of 600 jobs does not serve Tierney's "public purpose."

Members of United Food and Commercial Workers Local 616 were elated with the outcome of the council's vote and Mayor Raymond Flynn's agreement with the decision.

Brian Lang, chief shop steward remarked, "The Economic Development and Industrial Corporation (EDIC) has maintained that Colonial, because of its high regional recognition, can be a profitable enterprise. Several buyers, including a grouping from within the present management, have expressed interest in purchasing the plant and keeping it open.

The problem at Colonial is entirely one of gross mismanagement."

Curtis-Burns of Rochester, New York, purchased the Colonial meatpacking concern in 1983. Despite the overall sales of $630 million in 1985, Curtis Burns contends that they have been unable to make a profit. Workers were forced to concede over $4 million in benefits and wages in the past five years, including a recent wage cut of $2.16, all under the threat of losing their jobs. In December, Curtis Burns announced the impending sale of Colonial to Thorn Apple Valley, Inc. of Michigan.

Thorn Apple refused to commit themselves to keeping Colonial open, and later admitted that they sought to purchase the Colonial trademark and formulas, close operations in Boston and produce the Colonial brand in the Midwest for sale back in New England. Under tremendous pressure from the union and after the formation of the Community-Labor Coalition to save Colonial Jobs, the Boston Cty Council held the series of hearings to consider the question of eminent domain.

City Councilor David Scondras, in introducing the bill to proceed with seizing the plant, noted that the precedent had been set by the city long ago. During the period of "urban renewal" in the 1950s and 60s, entire workingclass neighborhoods were razed to make room for high-rise office and luxury housing developments. "In the last 10 years alone, the city has used eminent domain 5,516 times to award sites to developers. Finally, this right must be exercised for the city's people, said Scondras."

By February 4th, Thorn Apple agreed to reconsider shutting the Colonial plant. We began the negotiations but Ray would chicken out of the plant seizing because they got the owner of Atlantic Brands in Newmarket Square to agree to buy Colonial and hire back the workers. The city eventually came up with a variety of loans to make it all work and it would begin with 100 of the 600 laid off workers, hire an additional 300 within 12 months and the rest depending on the success of the venture.

Just in case, in the meantime, on February 5th, my law was voted on by the city council, which read in part:

> ***Whereas*** *there is no means other than the potential for taking Colonial Provision by eminent domain that the city can leverage the out-of-state corporations, Thorne Apple Valley, Inc. and Curtice Burns, Inc. to negotiate in good faith with the city to maintain the plant with the current workforce in Boston therefore be it*

> ***Ordered*** *that the Economic Development and Industrial Corporation of the City of Boston begin proceedings to purchase the Colonial Provision Company pork processing plant at 1100 Massachusetts Avenue by using its eminent domain powers and further Ordered the EDIC is ordered to begin this process by holding a public hearing on an economic development plan for the New Market area.*

The bill to save Colonial was passed to the cheers of an audience by 12 to 1. Joe Tierney alone was recorded as negative on this order.

Needless to say, having a city seize a company because it was mismanaged was seen as something new. It is hard after a time when President Obama seized a car company to explain how extraordinary this action was in 1986. At the time I took action to seize the meat plant, Reagan was president for God's sake.

The *Lowell Sun* AP article was a reaction to the council vote. It began:

> *In an unprecedented last-ditch effort to save 600 jobs, city officials have started eminent domain proceedings that could allow them to take over the hot dog factory that has long supplied frankfurters to Boston Red Sox fans at Fenway Park.*

> *"This company is part of the fabric of the city," Councilor David Scondras said. "We're not going to throw it out."*

> *The action marks an unprecedented attempt by any city or state to use eminent domain to save jobs.*

> *Colonial, which has made Fenway Franks as well as bacon and ham for 50 years is scheduled to close March 7th after its*

*trademark is sold to Thorn Apple Valley, Inc. But the city hopes
to step in after the sale forcibly buy Colonial and then run the
company until it can find an owner who promises to keep the
Boston plant alive.*

*"We don't intend to be in the meat business We intend to hold it
for as short a time as possible," said the EDIC. "We've never
done this kind of thing before but we think Colonial can be
profitable. We think we can make this work."*

*The City Council's 12-1 vote Wednesday that instructed the EDIC
to begin eminent domain proceedings followed months of
lobbying by the union...Scondras said, "There is a moral
responsibility on the part of the city to maintain and support
those kinds of business activities which allow for quality of life
to be maintained and in this case means keeping a number of
blue collar jobs."*

By February 8th the *Boston Globe* editorialized that while the city should not be in the meat packing business, the companies gave it no choice and that the moral obligation I referred to should have been borne by the company. But increasingly companies have lost all thinking except how much money is to be made. And this is another of the symptoms of the disease beneath our troubles.

I felt pretty good about it all. When you think about it, all this fuss and effort to focus on the human side of corporate activity is another symptom of our disease: the inability to distinguish between the goal of making money and the purpose of economic activity to improve our collective quality of life. Companies are not the purpose of society. Helping society is the purpose of companies and when they fail in this they need to be seized or sold or shut down.

76 /   The Death of the Lion

"The work goes on, the cause endures,
the hope still lives and the dream shall never die."
– Edward Kennedy

These words are out of chronological order, but then death is always out of order, even when expected it is never the right time.

The coffee table wobbled in the basement of our house at 34 Edgerly Road in the Fenway, upon which stood U.S. Senator Edward Kennedy, shaking hands with everyone in the room. I stood behind him, holding him from falling as he stepped toward the edge, me holding the ceiling with one hand and him with the other. My mother stared at him, a little surprised at how short Kennedy was.

He looked out over the crowd that filled our room, which hung over the edges of the staircase in the corner and peered through the windows and the open door to our left. "Rooms and rooms," he said. He remembered me that way. "You're the one with all the rooms filled with people," he would say when he met me from time to time. He was running for re-election to the Senate, this time against William Weld, and the crowd that came to my house filled all the floors of our four-story townhouse. He moved through the crowd beginning upstairs where people crowded on that staircase as well and in each of the rooms on that floor on the way to the wobbly basement coffee table shaking hands and saying "good to see you" to each person.

I was a city councilor but the Senator was a lion. The lion died on August 25th, 2009, but the dream will never die, for it is what we all dream — to make a difference.

I looked at the picture of me with him in Washington at a meeting of local officials, where I spoke with him about AIDS. At the bottom of the picture was a message to me thanking me for coming to meet with him at the Capitol.

I remember the mastery he had and his filling of his offices with men and women of surpassing intelligence so that where he might not know the details he had those who had spent their lives defining them.

I listened as the senator spoke to the crowd in my house, with energy and enthusiasm, pushing for more than votes, pushing for a commitment to continue to work for change. There was little room to move, but his words echoed from our brick walls and you could hear this man vibrating the emotions of those who came to hear the legend speak common sense with eloquence about health care and ending wars, about fighting for justice and compassion.

He jumped up and down and after he finished, he wished everyone well, thanked everyone for his or her time, and walked through the crowd with me. I felt honored. His staff told me that our gathering was the most enthusiastic of the day. Our whole Fenway neighborhood turned up, perhaps 200 people crowded into our small home's spaces.

I met him many times over the years, each with a request, and each request responded to with clarity and intelligence.

I spent time with his nephew Joe Kennedy and Joe's political man, Jim Spencer. I wonder how they feel today. I feel sad for them, but glad that our country had such a man.

The lion is dead. A Catholic who respected gay men and women's right to choose is dead.

But his roar goes on.

Kennedy was a gift to us all, with more intelligence and compassion, determination and grit, seasoning and wisdom than any politician I have ever known.

I called Gary who was on his way to Revere to sit and watch the ocean and think about the man he advanced for so many years. Gary got a letter from Ted dated July 24th 2009, just a few weeks ago, a letter of recommendation helping Gary become a resident of Brazil to be with his lover in his lover's country. We spoke of the obvious — would Joe Kennedy run for his uncle's vacant Senate seat?

I remember Joe Kennedy running for Congress, listening to him say again and again "We are all here because we want to make a difference" years later, echoing the words of the patriarch of the Senate and the Kennedy family.

It was stunning to me that the funeral where Barack Obama would give the eulogy and where past presidents Clinton, Carter, Bush the older and Bush the younger, and Vice President Joe Biden, would be present was to be at the Mission Hill Church I had spent so much time at, sometimes dealing with issues about the surrounding neighborhood of people of color, the Irish homeowners, Latinos, a rainbow of different people. It was a basilica in which Ted Kennedy found solace several times before and chose for his funeral instead of a fancy place. A church that was for the common man that was in many ways where Kennedy's heart was.

I feel a loss. I feel my chest heave a little, remembering the speeches of his brothers, knowing that the most eloquent of the men of America have all now died. Fearing a future without their guidance and courage. Hoping for a future that has room for such people. Glad to have known them and sad to lose opportunities to be with them one more time.

Goodbye. I wish I knew you better, had more time with you, and spent more energy trying to emulate you.

We need more men like Edward Moore Kennedy. Ted. The youngest of the clan that captured America and redefined Camelot.

I will cultivate my roar. And teach others how to make that sound.

77 /   1986

"The rich will do anything for the poor but get off their backs."
– Karl Marx

Real Estate speculator Ed Shamsi was amoral, a liar, and a pain in the ass. Besides giving me a headache by rent-gouging poor people on Mission Hill, he began a war against tenants at the Buckminster, a grand old hotel converted to a lodging house in Kenmore Square. Many of the folks who lived there didn't have a lot of money.

Brian Clague became the spokesperson for the tenants who lived in the Buckminster. He was so attractive it was distracting, but had a girlfriend so I assumed he was not "one of the family." But I learned this need not be true — there really are bisexuals. He smiled at me, said something nice, and my heart melted.

I know that readers might think, "Gee, are you cheating on your lover Robert?" which would make sense if Robert and I had a relationship that mimicked the ones that we watched on "Leave it to Beaver" or other television shows, but practically nobody really has these relationships. Everyone pretends to, and feels like a guilty fake. I loved Robert and he loved me. But as we struggled toward making ourselves happy, it became clear that no one person could satisfy all our needs. Eating carrots did not reduce our interest in potatoes. Over time we developed an open relationship as Robert discovered he wanted more experiences as a top and, because I am a total top, I couldn't be his bottom. We shared our money, our time, our caring, our love, our thoughts and vacations, our movies and our ideas. We were family, not owners of each other. So it was comfortable for me to notice Brian and to like him.

By June the tenants at the Buckminster had had it with Shamsi. His building was falling apart, his rents were shooting up, his treatment of his tenants was irresponsible and they got pushed out of the building, one of the last rooming houses in Boston. As a city we could not continue to condone the brutality of the man.

An article in the June 17th *TAB* said:

> *"The time has come for immediate and decisive action," said*
> *BTA (Buckminster Tenants Association) spokesman Brian*
> *Clague. The tenants filed 47 grievances with the Boston Rent*
> *Equity Board (a board that my housing law gave more powers*
> *to over the years).*

Of the 168 units in the building, 98 were vacant — a clear indication that Shamsi was trying to get rid of tenants to make room for richer sorts of people, like owners of condos or out of town renters.

I went through the building with City Councilor Maura Hennigan who was so totally upset she joined me in telling Shamsi he had to fix the problems with his slum building and stop harassing tenants. There were ceilings which leaked, windows through which air blew, walls in disrepair, lights that did not work. We asked Shamsi and the mayor to take action to sell the building to a non-profit that would protect tenants.

Maura was particularly pissed off because she had met with Shamsi, gotten him to agree to make it all better, was double crossed after she put her ego on the line by telling tenants that a deal had been struck, and she was determined to get back at him for the insult. It was great for me because I needed Maura to get my housing bills through, and there really is nothing like a woman scorned, especially one with a lot of power.

Shamsi ended up being the biggest single reason we got reforms in housing laws through the City Council.

AIDS

Crises often bring to light underlying facts about our behavior we would not be proud to look at. On Sunday, June 9th, an article in the *Times-Picayune* reflected upon a speech I gave at the 11th annual Southeastern Conference for Lesbian and Gay Men at Tulane University. At this point there were 23 openly gay elected officials in a country with at least 13 million gay people. Openly gay elected officials were the smallest group of elected officials representing such a large group of citizens.

I said that the AIDS crisis was a unifying force among gays causing people to rise above factions and "put the rest of the political system on trial." AIDS taught gay people many things, I said —

It has taught us about bigots — no attempt was made to deal with AIDS though it was known to be killing people in Africa in the 70's because they were Africans who were black and far away.

It has taught us about sexism — it's called the gay plague though it does not affect one half of gay people but they're women, so they're not counted.

It has taught us how anti-erotic this culture is — this country would rather let people die than teach them about safe sex.

And it has taught us how homophobic this society is — if this disease affected mainly straight couples this society would be declaring war on it.

— June 9th Times-Picayune *article by Joan Kent*

The AIDS crisis deepened daily, with no end in sight, no cure on the horizon, no treatment that worked, no vaccine that protected and no Manhattan Project to focus science on finding a way to end the epidemic. It became clear to me that millions would die unless billions were spent to find medicines that worked.

I remember feeling sad that whatever joy from sex could be gleaned from our neo-puritanical culture was being replaced with fear and fundamentalist condemnation. A new killer was in town and nobody wanted to confront it.

Hardwick vs. Bowers

On June 30th, the newspapers printed one of the Supreme Court's darkest decisions. It all began in 1982 in Atlanta, Georgia.

Michael Hardwick was a bartender who worked at night a lot. A police officer in Atlanta went to his house because he had not paid a fine for "public drunkenness." The cop arrived at the apartment around noon, and when he was let in by a roommate, Hardwick, still in bed which was typical for a person working until early morning hours, had his bedroom invaded by this bully who showed no sense of propriety about people's privacy. Hardwick was having sex with another man, and instead of excusing himself and waiting outside Hardwick's bedroom, the cop arrested Hardwick and his friend. They were charged with sodomy, an offense punishable in Georgia at the time by up to 20 years in prison.

Hardwick and his lawyers challenged the constitutionality of the Georgia statute. Four years and hundreds of thousands of dollars later, the decision in the *Hardwick vs. Bowers* case was announced: the Supreme Court said Georgia had the right to arrest and try Hardwick and friend for what they were doing in the privacy of his own bedroom.

Justice White said that "proscriptions against that conduct have ancient roots," and Warren Burger cited Roman and English laws from the past (even though the Roman empire ended over 1,500 years ago and England decriminalized sodomy many years earlier) saying that "Condemnation of those practices is firmly rooted in Judeo-Christian moral and ethical standards" (as was slavery, denying women the right to vote, and eating pork).

I was quoted in papers across the country saying "the decision underlines the need we have to get more aggressive in our civil rights struggle. If people didn't know it, they should know it now. We're not even legal."

The decision was a bald intrusion of some types of religious belief into the world of government, ignored issues of the right to privacy, and re-iterated the right of the state to punish gay people for being gay. It was a horrible decision.

Robert, having grown up Methodist, said that most American religions are suspicious that "somewhere someone might be having a good time."

It was, however, dissenting Justice Harry Blackmun's finest hour. He took the unusual step of reading aloud from his dissenting opinion. Quoting Oliver Wendell Holmes he said, "It is revolting to have no better reason for a rule of law than that it was laid down in the time of Henry IV. It is still more revolting if the grounds upon which it was laid down have vanished long since, and the rule simply persists from blind imitation of the past." Blackmun said the majority had an "almost obsessive focus on homosexual activity," adding, "The legitimacy of secular legislation depends on whether the State can advance some justification beyond its conformity to religious doctrine."

I was furious. I said, "The gay and lesbian community needs to gear up and fight. Hiding doesn't help, it only weakens you."

Gay men and women took to the streets: In New York protesters blocked traffic. In Boston we put together "Sodomize Democracy" stickers and marched on Beacon Hill. We held a "Kiss-In" on the steps of the State House. I said, "We are not going away. Get used to us." We decided to go to Washington to the steps of the Supreme Court and get arrested.

The blue sky framed the white of the Supreme Court looking austere and solid in the air of Washington, D.C. I was with Robert, Gary Dotterman, and Chris Norris, along with thousands of demonstrators who were delivering a message to the court — that judges and the judiciary were not the purveyors of justice but its guardian, and a failure to guard more seriously undermines the justice it serves more than any other single act of any other institution.

I struggled with my staff because I felt there was a need to be arrested, to make a statement that could not be misunderstood or underestimated. But Robert, Gary and Chris and the others who protected my future felt I had been arrested enough, that I would gain another *Herald* headline saying "Scondras Arrested" and I had been arrested often enough that I might end up in jail if I got arrested again.

I pulled at the hands holding me back as arrests began, feeling that I had let down the people who I had helped get the courage to come here. But in the end I decided to hold back, feeling that my staff might have had a point.

I saw a really handsome man on the left side of the steps, alone for the moment, and asked Gary who the blond was over there. "Hardwick," he said.

Oh my God. I would not pass up this one chance. I walked over to him and whispered in his ear. He smiled at me, a wonderful impish smile, and bent toward me, put his arms around me and we walked up the steps of the Supreme Court.

We kissed on those steps, and I felt vindicated on some level. "See," I said to myself, "We will be what we are wherever we are." I kissed him in part because he was beautiful but mostly because he was a hero, a man of courage, and together we were continuing the battle to overcome the bigotry of the bullies. We said "get used to us" in the best way we could say it.

I left and he left, looking back at each other for the last time we would ever see each other. I felt so good.

I got back to Boston and the *Herald*, the newspaper of rumor and rightwing rage, had a headline that said, "Scondras not arrested in D.C."

They just had to have my name and arrested in the same sentence and I said to Gary, "See, I told you so. They were gonna do it either way, Gary."

But they didn't get a picture of the kiss. I have it still today, locked in my memory where it will stay.

The Hardwick decision took twenty years to get overturned by the Supreme Court, which reversed it, and is taught today to would-be lawyers as a pointed example of particularly laughably bad decision-making by a particularly bigoted group of jurists.

A Maniac in the Reeds

A maniac was killing and maiming gay men by bludgeoning them in the Fens with a hammer. I spoke with some of the guys who had spent time at local hospitals being repaired.

At first it was not clear that the crime wave was the result of one person's insanity. I spoke with Police Commissioner Francis Roache, who made two plainclothes police available to my office. We decided to go through the Fens at night with them.

The setting is everything in understanding what happened. The Victory Garden area of the Fens is a horseshoe shaped set of plots of land, edged by tall reeds which hides whoever is there, surrounded on all but one side by water, the Muddy River, and on the last side by a large, well-trafficked, well-lit road. There is no reason whatsoever to be in the area at night unless you are cruising because it is not 'on the way' to anywhere in particular. You have to go out of your way to get there and if you are in the area at night it is because you want to be there. It was a place gay men cruised and had sex with each other out of sight of the erotophobes.

This is relevant as an endless amount of nonsense was written and said about the Fens that a moment's reflection makes you realize was prejudice, not analysis.

For example, the folks who pointed to crime as an excuse to cut the reeds were just looking for a good excuse to shut down one more way gay men got together. The Boston Police arrested people using the park at night. It made no difference that the state Supreme Judicial Court had made it clear that what people do in the parks consensually was none of the police's business. At least, while I was an elected official, the police had to be on somewhat better behavior.

The two plainclothes cops assigned by Commissioner Roache arrived at my house. I took a look and laughed. I couldn't believe it. They were wearing outfits that made them look like American tourists in the Caribbean. They only lacked cameras and bags. Clearly the police thought on some level that this polyester parade would be mistaken for two gay men — maybe, just maybe a couple of aging queens parodying straight culture's picture of gays but, geez, didn't they ever check out GQ?

Anyway, the August 21 1986 article in *Bay Windows* by C.L. Van Auken said under the headline "Scondras takes to the Bushes."

> *City Counselor David Scondras toured the bushes in the Fens Friday night, talking with people about the problem of gay bashing. Two undercover police officers visited the Fens from 10 to 11 pm on August 15th.*

> *Rumors describing several groups of gay bashers were shared with the investigators and the undercover policemen confiscated a "Rambo" knife from a 16-year-old in a group similar to one of the groups described by the men in the Fens. The youth reportedly told the police that he carried the knife to protect himself from "fags" in the Fens.*

In reality, more than two police officers eventually started helping out, they stayed a lot longer than an hour, and they put an end to the gay bashing. They did it in a way that was brave and unexpected. People in our office figured out that everyone who was attacked was attacked in the same exact way. This led us to think that the gangs of kids who were gay-bashing were not the reason for the series of men whose head had been bashed with a piece of metal, clearly intended to kill.

Turns out a man who had previously attacked gay men in the same way had been recently released from prison and returned to the Fens to finish his work. An Asian police officer acted as a decoy in the Fens and was actually attacked by the maniac, and the group of plains clothed cops caught him.

After he was removed from the scene, the series of horrible events ended. The crime wave was over. And for ten years I protected the reeds [see chapter 114 for more on the reeds].

Richmond Virginia

The Richmond *Times-Dispatch* reported that 725 area gays and lesbians came out of the closet to rally for human rights. The Virginia gay paper *The Throttle* began its big article with:

I was in Richmond and I remember how the police had to hold back protestors who held angry signs against us. Whatever anger against gay people was part of life in Massachusetts, multiply it by ten for Virginia. And I was fired up.

RICHMOND, VA. TIMES - DISPATCH

Staff photo by Bob Brown

725 area gays and lesbians came out of the closet to rally for human rights

I spoke in front of a big log cabin. I took the mike and I said, looking at the crowd and talking to them as well as the flag-wavers far behind the police lines:

When we were invisible and kept to our closets, you never heard a word out of them.

We have listened for too long to these polyester patriots that have the nerve to pretend that America is about their bigotry and their narrow-mindedness and their hatred of everything and everyone except themselves.

They know nothing about America.

Over 200 years ago a 32-year-old Virginian took pen in hand and wrote these words —

"We hold these truths to be self evident, that all people are created equal, that they are endowed by their creator with certain inalienable rights, that among these are life, liberty and the pursuit of happiness"

And these words ignited a revolution we continue by saying we are people and we demand our liberty and the right to pursue happiness in our own way!

It's going to take more than flag-waving to make us forget the words of Thomas Jefferson. We are the freedom fighters of this generation and people like us have been fighting for over two hundred years to make "We the People" mean all of the people.

When our constitution was written it only included white men who owned a lot of property, and the first battles in our history was fought by progressives to include small farmers and tenants of the land who gave their labor to create the beginning of our great wealth, and we won that fight.

Then our people, who captured the spirit of America, fought to include those who sought God in their own ways, the Catholics and Jews, and even those who could not find a God and we won that fight for freedom of thought and religion and speech.

Then we fought to include as part of the "we" in "we the people" black people held in slavery, an economic institution we found despicable and we won that fight to abolish slavery. And in recent times we went further to say that freedom belongs to all of us regardless of the color of our skin and that fight continues through today, for the old ideas of exclusion die hard.

We, the freedom fighters, fought and won women's right to vote and the fight for women's equality continues through today.

Now we approach the celebration of our constitution and the same people who have always said there should be one religion in our country tell us...

By the same people who have always said that blacks should live as inferiors to the rest of humanity...

By the same people who have always fought against women's rights, by the same people who are apologists for apartheid in South Africa, by the Falwells and the LaRouches and Anita Bryants and Pat Robertsons of this world who fight freedom every step of the way

We are told that gay and lesbian people must not be included as part of the 'We' in 'We the People.' Well, we must tell these people with their old and tired ideas that America is about the right to be different, that we stand by our brothers and sisters of color, that we stand by the struggles of women for parity and meaningful equality, that we gay and lesbian Americans are part of the "we" in "We the people" and that hose people who keep telling American gays and lesbian and women and blacks and any other American who is different from their idea of who is fit that we should be satisfied with something less that freedom and equality, we are telling these new Reich bigots that America is all of us, gay and straight, Jew and gentile, old and young, men and woman, Love it or Leave it!

There are those who tell us, this is not the right time. And we answer: it is never the right time. If not now, when? There are those who tell us they fear rocking the boat. And we answer: you should only be afraid of rocking the boat when you are in the boat and won't let us aboard.

Next fall, Mr. Reagan, we are coming, hundreds of thousands of us to Washington and we won't take no for an answer.

- *There must be an end to children thrown off bridges because they are gay*

- *There must be an end to the fear of holding hands with a person*

- *There must be the day when anyone can dance anywhere with anyone without fearing violence against them*

- *There must be a day when those who have lived for the past 200 years and died lives of quiet desperation in closets of fear can feel safe to come out*

- *There must come a day for us when children are taught that the capacity to love is never sinful or abnormal or sick*

- *There must be the day when we are free to be who we are, proud and free from fear. And it is up to us to get to that day.*

We are the freedom fighters of this generation. Our people have
paid their dues. We know that freedom is worth fighting for.
And that no change will happen unless we fight for it
And if you understand that we all die in the end
And the question is whether our life is lived in freedom or fear
Then you will fight for it,
Not accept the back of the bus
Understand that there is no fight more precious
No cause more real
No victory more deserving,
No time more urgent,
No wealth more liberating
Than our fight, our cause, our victory, our time, our freedom.

We are the freedom fighters of this generation
Facing the Dred Scott decision of this generation
Suffering the disease of this generation
With the accumulated oppression of two centuries
And we are ready to march together until the day comes
that we can say, loudly and proudly,
Free,
We are all free,
All of us,
Free at last.

Across the country my speeches became a rallying cry that would result in the largest march on Washington of gay and lesbian people in its history. Just as injustice anywhere demeans all of us, does not a burst of freedom anywhere liberate all of us?

78 /   Movie Critics

Among other things, Robert and I were for awhile the movie critics for the Fenway News. We would sneak off to movies where we were handed little press packets from the movie folks. We got to see a lot of movies and became new kind of celebrities as a lot of people wrote us about our opinions on movies.

It reinforced an idea I had had for a long time: people like to know what public figures do and think about the kinds of things that everyone does — movies and soap, clothes and eye shadow, exercise and pets. We were the Ebert and Siskel of the Fenway. But the paper sometimes got Robert's last name wrong which he seemed to take in stride.

AT THE MOVIES

Boy's reverie sweet but empty

by Robert Krebb

by David Scondras

Stand By Me is a film which succeeds in evoking that peculiar nostalgia of childhood. Its superb and sensitive acting combined with photography designed to enhance the feeling of "remembrance of times past" makes you feel a sense of recognition, gives you that special feeling that this is a true memory of being a young adolescent bonding with other young special friends come to life.

The simple and compelling theme, four boys who decide to set out to find the body of a missing youth, creates a context in which the sense of adventure in explorations of a world still new are recreated.

It is a kind of rediscovery of the wonder we felt, of the fear of the unknown, of the safety and security in bonding together as a group to

I agree with Bob that the film is worth seeing in the sense that it leaves on with a pleasant sense of nostalgic wistfulness. But I object to the artifice behind that success.

The movie succeeds because it hits upon a series of commonly experienced events: the bullies who push around the little kids; the train that chases you and you get out of the way just in the nick of time; the discovery that people really die; the fear of being alone in the dark; and the safety of clinging to each other emotionally when we are scared, etc. etc.

However, the characters are not developed. In fact, the time frame leaves no room for development, and to tell what happens and leave it to the audience to provide their own analysis

continued on page 8

Four friends on a body hunt in Stand by Me.

79 /   1986: Condo Conversions

"More ways may be found than one to kill a witch that will not drown"
– Elijah Fenton, 1712

On October 29, 1986, Stuart Johnson, Boston's Rental Housing Association President was quoted in the *Herald* as saying, "This is our Alamo." He was talking about the tougher law I proposed in response to the courts throwing out my earlier weaker law protecting tenants from condo conversion. The courts ruled the law I passed the previous year was not constitutional, that we could not stop apartments from being converted into condominiums. But I realized that this did not stop us from passing a law that restricted owners from evicting tenants from those apartments no matter what they chose to call them, condos or barns, and I used this fact to fashion a law that would in fact stop rental housing from being turned into condominiums. I was determined to kill the witch.

Boston had reached a point where people were buying up apartment buildings, kicking out people who lived in them for many years, slapping on a coat of paint, and then selling them as condos, mostly to speculators who in turn waited awhile, maybe did some more cheap cosmetic stuff to the apartment and then sold it again, often to a speculator or somebody who wanted it as a kind of savings bond that grew in value more rapidly than the ones issued by Uncle Sam.

I saw clearly the danger in allowing a necessity of life, housing, which had limited supply, being turned into another stock gambled in the same casino as pork belly futures. This drove prices up, tore apart neighborhoods, fomented a housing bubble that eventually had to burst, turned housing into retirement funds, and did not increase the amount of housing at all.

I put a law together that said you could not evict anyone for a condo conversion unless the buyer was going to live in the apartment and even then you had to give a tenant three years to find another apartment. I said, "my message to the real estate industry is this: if you want to make money, build housing." I did not restrict anything in new housing, so I felt my law would take all that ambition and greed to make money and turn it into more housing which would slow down the price hikes that were out of control and which were more the result of gambling on price hikes in the future than reflecting a normal price increase connected to increased demand and costs of construction.

Yeah, I know this stuff is a bit technical, but I was, after all, a housing economist with an MA in economics from Northeastern so I felt pretty cocky about it. And I was right. By 2008 the nonsense around housing would bring the entire financial system to its knees. But I was determined to do whatever I could in 1986 to tame the casino, and it worked until a state referendum threw out all controls altogether.

The state referendum, financed by the real estate industry, was an effort to get rid of rent control, in the exact same way that under Reagan and later Bush the financial industries worked successfully to get rid of controls on financing the housing bubble by making bad bets on losing propositions.

Anyway, my new law would cap rent hikes to 12.5% per year (don't ask me where we got that ridiculous number), to make sure that the squeeze in housing didn't end up making lots of money for squeezers without any new housing for the city. The city had already lost most of its rooming houses converted into apartment buildings, condos, and hotels. These rooming houses were where mostly elderly singles lived, a far better alternative to the assisted housing that ultimately replaced some of them at extraordinarily higher prices.

I remembered my days at the Boston Center for Older Americans [see book I, chapter 21]. So I brought Dapper O'Neil from building to building in which elderly women told him that without help from the city they would lose their homes and have to go to shelters. Dapper was actually moved to co-sponsor a housing bill of mine to protect the elderly, much to the shock of real estate barons. It was obvious that for many landlords "get whatever you can get and to hell with the lives of the people you affect," was a legitimate operating premise.

All of our sanitary and building codes were developed in response to landlords shoving people into buildings that were structurally unsound, or fire traps, or overcrowded and under-lit — make no mistake about it. The huge number of code requirements reflect the extent to which greed replaced all other incentives, including self-respect, in what real estate and its flock of parasites laughingly called 'free enterprise'.

On October 28th, 1986, I held hearings at City Hall and tenants from across the city showed up. I know that most people thought primarily of the class issue, that I was supporting people of limited means against forces beyond their control, but it was more than that. I was also trying to protect communities which, in areas of the city where most people lived in rental housing and did not own their homes, meant making sure housing would not become another commodity exchanged like stocks in the marketplace casino that the housing market had become. If a neighborhood suffered forced migration, the myriad connections between people that created what we call community would be destroyed.

Where exactly did those who wanted people to wash their dishes, drive their cabs, cut their lawns, empty their bedpans, cook their food, wait on their tables, and clean their hospitals think that these workers would live? In a suburb even though they could not afford a car, driving in and out of the city taking 2-3 hours a day out of their life, and who and how exactly would their children be taken care of?

In Lowell during the 1830's, the mill companies built housing for mill workers close to work. In Boston the city forced the universities to build housing for students to take pressure off of the prices of places workers lived. It was not 'radical' or 'socialist' to try to stabilize communities, yet the anger directed at me by those who speculated on housing was astonishingly vituperative.

Ray Flynn got us to pass a home-rule petition to the legislature, which would enable us to stop condo conversion directly. We passed the petition, but such laws have to go to the state legislature, be passed by both the House and the Senate, be signed into law by the governor, and only after all that would Boston be given the right to stop condo conversions. That meant another law would have to be written to do this which might or might not actually get passed by the council.

Our team decided to go after the impact of condo conversion directly, and the real estate industry saw clearly that I was aiming at their roulette wheels and did everything that they could to stop us.

You can get a flavor of the debate, which would go on for years by checking out the magazine Banker and Tradesman, December 10, 1986. It begins:

> The bell for round 200 of the condominium battle in Boston has
> sounded and both sides have come out swinging...
>
> Councilor David Scondras has already submitted a three-part
> affordable housing plan, the first part of which deals specifically
> with "stabilizing" the city's rental housing market.

Meanwhile the home rule petition we submitted to the legislature looked like it was going to pass. The Rental Housing Association, with Stuart Johnson speaking for it, said that, "Anyone reading the language carefully should shiver at the extent of the power it grants to the city government."

I decided to get a bit more detailed in my concerns, trying to reach out to the rational.

I said that more than a quarter of the people who work in Boston now pay more than 50% of their income toward rent. As a result: Those workers either have to demand higher wages, which negatively affects city businesses, or leave the area in search of lower housing costs. I said new business ventures or expansions are not occurring in Boston because people are leaving because of the high cost of housing. [In 1980 12% of tenants paid over 50% of their income in rents. By 1985 that went up to 21%. And it continued to escalate over the years].

> What that means, I said, it that the share of the city's economic
> boom going to the real estate industry is being subsidized by the
> other sectors of the business community.

I was determined to get people to understand that allowing housing to become a rollercoaster, another chit in the casino economy that the banks, real estate brokers, owners and speculators were turning housing into would lead to serious economic problems for the society.

A society that allowed any sector, any activity to be inflated in prices without commensurate increases in supply, with the primary driving force behind price increases the desire of people to capitalize on the rapid price rise driven by speculation, was doomed to reap a financial cataclysm when that bubble, that huge portfolio of loans backed by assets whose real value could not keep up with the prices demanded by speculation, finally defaulted, collapsing further investments in buying homes and robbing money from people who would otherwise use it to support all the other sectors of the economy. This is exactly what happened in 1929 and then in 2008 — paper backed by loans that could not be paid back led to financial ruin.

The real estate industry kept telling lies, which drove me to distraction. They claimed my laws would dry up new construction of new housing. In point of fact there was a construction boom at the time. The problem was developers saw a lot more profit in recycling existing apartments as condos than building new housing, the latter of which we purposefully kept from having any regulations on at all so that we would encourage the investors to build new housing instead of dumping out tenants, putting on cute awnings, and charging a fortune to speculators for the end result.

I said, "I'm tired of hearing the whining from an industry that has made more money in the last 15 years than any other, particularly while the problem of homelessness and the affordable housing situation is getting worse."

Maura Hennigan, with whom I worked to get Shamsi under some control, tried to work with me to come up with a compromise set of rules that would protect tenants while not giving the real estate guys that funded election campaigns an apoplectic fit.

It was clear that the war, which was essentially a class struggle, would get worse until we reached some mutually acceptable treaty.

Even the YWCA got involved, as lawyer Laura Monroe, a holocaust survivor, fought successfully to get the rooms the Y rented to women covered by the rent board, to control escalating rents and stop evictions of tenants. Laura was sweet, full of energy but ultimately her age and the pains of age ended her status as a soldier for justice. Robert and I found her to be an amazing example of a life full of crises that she managed to convert into compassion.

We would take some interim steps to protect tenants and be beaten back over and over by the real estate folks who replaced their eyeballs with dollars signs.

It would take us until 1988 to get my 'Tenant Protection Act' passed with many amendments and changes needed to get something through the council. It would help a lot of people but ultimately was not the breakthrough needed to end the war between those who needed their homes protected from greed and those whose dreams of wealth made from cashing in on the housing bubble outvoted their sense of fairness and compassion.

The difficulty of getting laws past to regulate housing was directly related to the fact that the landlords funded much of the election campaigns in Boston. They were the biggest donors and they had clout.

Those of us who loved our communities saw a danger in the price hikes that spelled the end of sitting in the evening on stoops gossiping with neighbors or sharing a beer. The end of people talking with each other and the beginning of locked doors and front desks.

I felt that slowly our cities were becoming gigantic hotels where nobody knew each other, everyone paid too much for too little, security was everywhere, freedom was gone, making money was the only human activity and the notion of community was a romantic episode in our history.

It would turn out in practice that the treaty would be postponed until the war was put on hold by the economic meltdown of the entire financial system in the year 2008 caused by the financial ruin the speculative bubble created. And even now as I write this note, until a revamp of the entire housing market is undertaken, it is only a matter of time before the crises inevitable when housing is continued as a commodity in the casino that runs Wall Street and once again undermines all of our economic activities. Most housing in the 21st century is being bought by speculators once again driving up costs and prices.

"I travel all over the country making speeches for people I believe in."
– Ann Richards (Texas State Treasurer and later Governor)

I gave 22 speeches in 16 states, many in the South, rallying gay people to the cause of freedom, part of the social movement that continues to today to free this most-hated, least-loved group of Americans to demand equality. Some representative excerpts follow.

Houston, Texas

I was the keynote speaker at the Houston Gay Political Caucus. Houston's city council had had the guts to pass gay rights, but it went to the ballot and lost. The people of the fair city did not like queers. I pointed out that whites in Houston voted overwhelmingly to overturn gay rights, but that blacks, in spite of preachings from the pulpit to overturn the gay rights law, voted 50/50 — a pattern I would notice across the USA. Minorities tended to be uncomfortable overturning civil rights for others.

Before the dinner, Robert and I went to a reception hosted by a well-to-do activist in the Caucus. His house was classically modern, perfect for the works of art displayed on the white walls, most of which had a nautical theme. The owner of the house was gentle spoken but Robert got his attention rather dramatically. Robert was looking at a painting and got really excited. He told our host, "You have a picture of the Olympic!" (Robert was a Titanic buff, knew everything there was to know about that ill-fated ship). The host was impressed, and said, "You are the first man who ever knew the difference!" The Olympic was the sister ship of the Titanic. You could tell because one deck was not enclosed, unlike Titanic. The slight differences caught Robert's eye immediately.

I was relegated to being Robert's companion for that night. It was a pleasant change from being the object of curiosity and interaction, allowing me to wander around and helped me understand a bit more how Robert usually felt when we went places together. I gave a stump speech that was well received in Houston, and remarked how simultaneously polite and full of fun Southerners seemed to be. Their politics were often retrograde, but their way of making you feel at home and their penchant for a good time was a relief from the more Puritanical strains of New England.

Atlanta, Georgia

I spoke on February 2nd to the Atlanta Business and Professional Guild. It was warm and humid even though it was winter. Gays assembled to greet our plane (a plane that seemed to be a gay one, with pink and grey décor, plus real knives and forks), and as the plane stopped a limousine pulled up. We wondered who the celebrity was on the plane when it turned out it was us. We were ushered off the plane as if we were visiting royalty.

I have a plaque from Andrew Young, then Mayor of Atlanta, giving me the 'Keys to the City,' and was transported to the speech by the limousine complete with complimentary champagne. I said to the crowd that assembled to hear me:

> *We are the future. Coming from a past in which we have been taught to feel as outcasts, we have come together in every state to say: We have paid our fare. We will not be left to walk behind the bus. And when we get on, we will not be told where to sit.*

> *When I visited the Houston Gay Political Caucus, an Atlanta native got kidded about her accent, claiming she sounded like came from the 'regressive South.' She paused and then quietly pointed out that the two southern presidents of this generation compare quite favorably on human rights issues: Johnson signed civil rights legislation; Carter invited gay and lesbian people to the White House to discuss their concerns. Southerners have had a proud role in the struggle to make America American.*

> *We live in two Americas — one represented by a coalition of the greedy, the bigoted and the ignorant who have taken the American flag that I wear [which Robert had convinced me to put on and own] and turned it into a symbol of intolerance, arrogance and stupidity. Just a few months ago, one element of this America wrote a fundraising letter intercepted by my office*

offering a color photo of Nancy Reagan for a ten dollar contribution to the Young Americans for Freedom: who are in a bitter national struggle to stop the "conspiracy of homosexuals and communists from overthrowing this administration."

The struggle against the other America, which has the gall to call itself patriotic, is not a new one.

From those who fought successfully from 1836 to 1844 to rescind the gag rule that prohibited public debate on the abolition of slavery; to those who fought just a year ago for the rights of teachers to talk about homosexuality; Americans are people who believe in free speech.

From those who fought against the Caribbean jingoism of the 1890's when McKinley criticized anti-imperialists as short-sighted isolationists to those today who stand up for freedom in central America only to be tarred with the century old isolationist brush from an equally undistinguished president. Those are our freedom fighters.

Those who found to end slavery. Those who marched with that great Atlantan, Martin Luther King, Jr. Those who call for an end to our support for apartheid. Those are our people.

Those lesbian mothers who fought for custody of their own children; those battling against a homophobic governor for the right to share their love and care with needy foster children — those are our parents.

The days of talking up every cause and flying every banner except our own are over.

Alone among the groups in our society, gays must also deal with racism for some of us are black; we must confront anti-Semitism for some of us are Jewish; we must challenge sexism for we are both men and women; we must be concerned about access for some of us are disabled; we must deal with issues affecting the elderly, the young, the working, and the poor for we are all of those things. We cannot unite within ourselves without addressing these concerns.

We are the key to a coalition of minorities, which is our best hope for the power we must get.

We are one of two Americas and we are in a great struggle for freedom.

We are at the right time; the right place and we are the right people.

I felt sad those years ago about a boy from Atlanta who was my friend as a freshman named Craig. He called me from Atlanta as he went through hell trying to deal with his gayness. While at Harvard he had a girlfriend, but he was also my friend. When I cried I would not tell him what was eating at me, that I was gay, and I was stunned that he cried too, discouraged that I did not trust him. It was perhaps too late to tell him that I had changed, that I finally understood that he was reaching out to comfort me. That I didn't have to be so alone in my heart all those years at Harvard.

So I felt that my speech in Atlanta was a kind of saying "thank you" to him.

He now attends the Harvard Gay Alumni dinners sometimes and I saw him once again recently. He seemed a lot more together, and seemed to have forgotten the turmoil of the past. I was not the center of his universe. But he was part of the constellation that made up mine.

Bangor, Maine

I went to the Maine Alliance in February of '86 and met Dale McCormick. (After my speech I encouraged her to run for office as an open lesbian, which she did, and won).

Maine is beautiful and cold, and close enough to Boston that I had to take a little propeller plane instead of a jumbo jet, like I was used to. I started off with that story, and how Robert had to hold my hand on the little plane. Then I told the story of the election, still a new event to most of the world, and people loved the anecdotes.

I had begun to have a theme, a central premise, an idea, a belief that came from my past and has lasted through today. You have a new world to build, different from the past, based upon the principle that all people have a right to whatever society can give them to ensure each person can grow into the most complete human being possible — and that means access to resources which are material as well as the condition of respect, and I believe you will be instrumental in bringing about this new world.

> *I see a world in which we can go fishing with our children in waters that are clean, whose people live without fear of nuclear holocaust, in which diseases are fought, in which children are not raised learning to hate themselves because they are gay or lesbian or black or brown or different, in which women are not taught their horizons are limited, in which the quality of life is not measured in terms of the quantity of children but the quality of children's lives, in which economic activity is subject to the needs of people not the other way around...*

I tried to think through why it had taken us so long to get our act together.

I said, "I looked within my life and I want to share with you the obstacles I found there which you must overcome." I knew from bitter experience that I could not do it, at least not yet — I kept a lot back. Even as I write these words I marvel at the life I have led and have not felt, the love that rained on me without getting me wet, the robbery of feeling that was what being closeted is all about. One of the prices we all pay for lying, for the pretense of being what we are not out of our necessity to protect ourselves from the violence directed at our kind, is the inability to feel or believe the kindnesses and respect showered on us by those who are truly kind and caring. We protect ourselves with a wall of invisibility that does not allow respect and caring through it...we don't feel them or perhaps don't believe they are genuine.

So I listed for the crowd the obstacles to our success at organizing a freedom movement: The first [obstacle] is self hate. When I first realized I was a gay person I went for help to Harvard's health facilities. It was in 1964. They told me that there was hope for me to become normal and I was grateful. I tried hard but it didn't work. I couldn't become normal because I already was, but I didn't know that. One obstacle we must overcome is the running away that our brothers and sisters do because they have been taught to hate themselves, whether that running away is in the form of alcoholism or whether it's in denial. We must fight our addictions, including drugs, alcohol and conceptual addictions.

Hm. Conceptual addictions. I had begun to understand that the mythologies that ruled our lives were addictive because they managed our fear. A second obstacle I have found is my need to have approval:

> *My need for approval comes from the doctors and lawyers with their laws about sodomy, from the expectations of mom and dad which can never be fulfilled, from television which only talks about the problems of the Waltons and straight couples like Olivia and John, never about David and Robert, nor about Sheila and Margaret. Those kinds of couples never had enough approval growing up. Not for being gay.*
>
> *Approval-seeking is a killer. The reason is we often look for approval from others who cannot give it. Ultimately only we can give ourselves approval. So when your parents get upset if they do, as they will, tell them to get a counselor cause they need it, not you.*

New York City

In February I gave a speech in New York City. I began calling for a March on Washington early and often, and eventually in 1987 it would become the largest march gay people and their friends ever held. At the speech in New York, I said:

> *As Washington's response to the AIDS crisis makes tragically clear, we need the power that can be born out of a coalition. We need the political clout to demand adequate funding from the outset, not five years into the epidemic. We need the power to be able to dictate that life-saving education will for forward and anti-erotic handwringers be damned. We need the ability to be able to direct medical research that meets our needs...health concerns in parts of the world where the populations affected are people of color can no longer conveniently be ignored by white people on the other side of the globe. Young people in our community can no longer think of sickness and infirmity as only older people's concern. And rich people denied health insurance*

*because of who they are, who despite their wealth cannot
afford today's staggering health care costs, can no longer
pretend our disgraceful system of medical care for those who
can afford it is just.*

*...Just as coming out helps one deal with personal self-hatred,
AIDS has forced us to deal with its political counterpart, apathy,
by forcing us to become political.*

*...If this crisis can focus us on the need for coalition politics, and
the need to give each other the approval and affirmation we
merit, we will emerge the test stronger people ready to show
others the way out of the darkness."*

New Orleans, Louisiana

New Orleans is a beautiful city. I love it. The French Quarter is a fantasyland of bars and boutiques, jazz and dancing, sex and fun. The city is just amazing. I got to the microphone, aware that I was delivering a message but also providing a way for our community to have unity and direction. It was a cool speech appropriate to the cool of Cajun country in the far South. I referred to the many ferries and dikes in the city:

"I want you to know how honored I am to be in a city serviced by fairies and protected by dykes!" The audience broke into cheers and laughter.

I continued with the speech that became a mantra, we are the freedom fighters; we are united with those who are left behind, the majority of minorities. I taught again that a victory without a new deal, a new sharing of resources was an empty victory. That in a fundamental way needing someone to blame required having a condition that needed something to blame and I was determined to get rid of that condition which I felt was the feeling of unfair powerless, lack of resources, and contingent respect that so many felt so much of the time.

Underneath the prejudices that could occupy many books full of complicated words about the sociology and psychology of hate was something a lot simpler: people need freedom and food, which ultimately means respect for who they are and a share of the resources they need. Everything bad that happens including bigotry happens because people do not have that freedom and that food.

I finished the speech in New Orleans with a call for that new kind of freedom:

> *"We're the freedom fighters on the road to victory — united with those who feel left out, united with those left behind in the land of plenty to suffer alone hunger and disease, united with people of color who have fought for centuries without losing their appetite for an equal share to life, united with all of those women who marched before us for the respect and equality they deserved, united together — nothing's going to stop us until we can say once and for all, and for all of us — freedom, freedom, freedom.*

The applause was deafening and lasted a very long time.

I could tell that I was not going to be a popular guy among the folks who liked being on top of the ladder.

81 /   Gay Liberation

*"All I'm trying to do is survive and make good out of the
dirty, nasty, unbelievable lifestyle that they gave me."*
– Tupac Shakur

*"[Scondras] has been speaking far and wide, addressing gay
groups and collegiate homophobia workshops from University
of Massachusetts to the West Coast. In addition to running an
AIDS workshop at the national convention of gay and lesbian
elected officials in November, Scondras took a night out of the
three-day weekend in Washington to fly to Allentown,
Pennsylvania and address the Lehigh Valley Gay and Lesbian
Association. In connection with the conference in New York City,
held to start organizing next year's March on Washington,
Scondras traveled to Grand Rapids, Michigan, and spoke to the
state wide Michigan Organization for Human Rights. Altogether
Scondras had had some 22 speaking engagements in 16
different states outside of Massachusetts."*
— Bay Windows, December 11, 1986

As across the country the gay liberation movement gathered steam, a large group of gays continued to feel safer closeted or occupying roles as gatekeepers to power, rather than seeking power themselves (I call them "assimilationists"). This was not a surprise, and besides speaking to the liberationists, I had to address in many different ways and forums those who chose to continue the marginal existence of our community in the shadows of American life.

I tried every parable I could think of to energize those who were part of our army and vaccinate them against the lure of false assimilation — invisibility.

In speaking out for the March on Washington to gay activists, I tried out an Old Testament version of my call to action speech where I thought it might do some good. Like the Jews in the wilderness are gay and lesbian people today. We are confronted with enormous challenges, hardships, discomforts and even death.

*We are lured by false ideals — our condos and comfortable
ghettos becoming our golden calves.*

*And there are those among us who urge accommodation with
the powers that be instead of true liberation, those who urge a
return to the pharaoh's Egypt where their own power is based
on our oppression.*

*But like the Jews in the wilderness, we are not going back — we
have our eyes on the Promised Land.*

*This October there will be a March on Washington, a march by
hundreds of thousands of lesbians and gay men to demand the
rights we deserve, the resources we need and the respect we
merit. By being there you will move us all closer to the promised
land.*

In other rallies I spoke to all of the minority groups to come
together at our time in the capitol. It is a test. Will we be the political
force for justice carrying the banner of human rights forward to the end of
the century, or will we fade again into our straitjackets? Will we demand
the government teach safer sex to children or allow ourselves to be
herded into quarantine camps? The march is an opportunity for the
progressive black leadership to join us in exposing the enemy we share in
a homophobic court and racist administration. The women's movement
has an opportunity to march with us and fight our common fight for
respect and equality.

*I know we are surrounded by the profound realization of our
mortality but that has made us remember that we all die in the
end anyway.*

*The only real issue is whether we live our life in freedom fighting
our oppression or in fear; as ourselves or as they would have us
live.*

*Come to Washington! Spend October 11th with hundreds of
thousands of your real family and friends fighting for you!!*

*We need you, for we are a people with a destiny! We need you
in Washington to show the candidates of both parties that
although we many not yet have the strength to decide who will
be President, we do have the numbers and commitment to
dictate who will not!*

In Los Angeles at the Municipal Elections Committee in November, I said:

> *We live in two Americas: One America of polyester patriots who wear flags, condemn sodomy, apologize for apartheid, raise bigotry to the status of religion, and who are and always have been opposed to freedom; and our America which has for 209 years stood up for justice and freedom, for human rights, the suffrage movement, the abolition movement, the civil rights movement, the gay rights movement, the anti-apartheid movement and many more.*

> *We have a real challenge right now in AIDS. As much as we feel we have done, the other America is using AIDS to insure that its anti-erotic, homophobic, and racist worldview is furthered through the agony of this disease.*

> *When the Center for Disease Control appropriated $1.4 million for educational purposes among AIDS groups, a member of the White House staff confiscated the entire amount saying that they didn't want it to go to those groups because the material being produced was too pro-gay. There is open talk of quarantine across the country in virtually every state in one form or another. The CDC has, as of a few weeks ago, refused to continue any studies of safe sex because research into safe sex implies teaching people how to continue to be gay.*

> *The bottom line: 14,000 have contracted AIDS, half of whom are dead. This government spent more in six weeks to deal with the handful of people with Legionnaires' disease than what was spent in the first four years of the AIDS crisis.*

> *For for the friends I have who are dying, I will propose at our convention tomorrow a March on Washington next year, a march for life, a Gay Pride year in which we can take our struggle to the man in charge and get the justice we deserve, a year in which we do what we have to do to protect all of us.*

> *We have to act now, for our own sake, for our self-respect. Believe me, for the next century the question that will be asked about every person in this room is "What did you do during the epidemic and the witch hunt that followed it?"*

82 /   Gay Bashing

"Being gay is natural. Hating gay is a lifestyle choice."
— John Fugelsang

"The Bible contains six admonishments to homosexuals and 362 admonishments to heterosexuals That doesn't mean that God doesn't love heterosexuals. It's just that they need more supervision."
— Lynn Lavner

In every major city in the USA, statistics I got from several sources on anti-gay violence was printed. The February 12th edition of *Bay Windows* begins:

> *An eight foot board with the words "Anti-Gay and Lesbian Violence in Boston" positioned across the street from the fire station at Boylston and Hereford Streets was the object of media attention last week. The sign displayed the statistics released at a press conference held there Thursday, February 5th, by representatives of the Public Safety Community of the Alliance, Fenway Community Health Center, and City Councilor David Scondras' office."*

There were on that chart for the year 1986, 135 documented cases of violence against gays in Boston. 33% were threats of violence, 42% involved a physical assault, 17% involved being chased, followed or spat at, 1% involved vandalism, 1% were bomb threats, 4% were police abuse and 2% were murders.

I demanded the hiring of openly gay police, with recruitment ads placed in gay papers, with tours of gay and lesbian bars and meeting with gay and lesbian leadership by representatives of the police department.

Part of the reason for all this was to push people to understand that one of the many excuses for not doing anything for gays, that "sexual orientation is a private matter" was bankrupt. I said, "Homophobia is a public reality, not a private matter."

It would eventually be seen, as slowly across the country states were forced by the gay community to keep statistics, that hate crimes against gays, a smaller minority than blacks, were larger in number.

I testified before a Congressional subcommittee on criminal justice, pushing them to make hate crimes against gays something that would be reported to the FBI on a regular basis. Eventually this would happen.

I said, "Violence is the symptom of a disease called homophobia. Until now society has not been willing to confront homophobia directly by showing gay and lesbian people on television, the teaching respect for gay and lesbian people in our schools, by including gay and lesbian people in all levels of our government, and by acknowledging God's love for gay and lesbian people in our churches."

This was not going to sit well with the immoral majority. And the culture war was far from over.

At about 9:45 PM one night two women and one man were walking past a fire station on Boylston Street when they were attacked by three men shouting, "queers" and "faggots." One of the women was taken to the hospital for an injury to her forearm. The two police who were present at the event did not file a complaint. The three who attacked the gays were Boston Firefighters. The three victims were kicked during the attack.

I called for the immediate transfer of the firemen to another station to protect the large minority and gay population living near the fire station. I also called for a full time liaison between the Boston City Police Department and the lesbian and gay community.

It was believed from surveys made at the time that 80% of assaults against gays are never reported, for somewhat obvious reasons.

On April 16th, fifty people came to City Hall to testify at my hearing. The *Bay Windows* article about the hearing said, "They winced, grimaced and hung their heads as they listened to account after account of street violence, police brutality, and the resulting feelings of isolation."

They had not heard the worst.

A black man wearing blue jeans and a sweatshirt, built like a football player sat down in front of the microphone. "My name is Robert Jackson. I am a City of Boston firefighter. I'm gay. The things these guys got, I have been getting for 11 years. I've got virtually no self-respect left on the job." Robert Jackson, the first member of any of Boston's uniformed services to come out publicly, spoke of the discrimination he has had to endure, "every day, 365 days a year, for the past 11 years." Each question asked by the councilors present at the hearing led to more accounting of the nightmare that has been Bob Jackson's professional life, the story Jackson knew opened him up to even more humiliation and danger as soon as he returned to his firehouse.

Bob Jackson saw his co-workers physically threaten an obviously gay man. He saw firefighters deface gay people's homes. He overheard his co-workers discussing a plan to knock him out at the scene of the next fire and leave him to die in the fire and smoke. He watched white firefighters deliberately inflict damage to houses in black neighborhoods. He was hit by debris intentionally thrown by white firefighters at the scene of a fire. He was written up for not cleaning up coffee cups or being late three minutes because he was on the sidewalk outside a firehouse instead of inside it.

After ten years with the department, he was not allowed to eat with other firefighters, not been promoted, been told by other firefighters that "no one wants to be in a firehouse where there is a gay," and more recently that they wish he'd get AIDS and die.

Bob Jackson was a brave man. I was so proud of him. He was a real hero. He got onto the fire department as a result of the federal court order of U.S. District Court Jude Freedman to stop using racially discriminatory exams and to hire white and black firefighters on a one to one ratio. The fire department, according to our studies, had 72% of its workforce related to another person working for the City of Boston.

The Fire Department was not the only department of the City of Boston under a federal court order to clean up its act.

I was determined to make this problem better. I met secretly for months with a member of the department who agreed to become an openly gay firefighter liaison to my office and to the gay community. It did not last; he could not take the punishment.

83 /   1987: Hate Mail

If you make change there are those who hate you and those who love you: few people have no opinion of your life. It is a price for being an agent of change.

The letters we got reflected this. 1987 was still in the age of hand-written letters. Our office received hundreds of them every week, some typed, most of them handwritten; all of them kept and categorized. It would be impossible to put them all into this short history. But some stand out as rather instructive.

May 7th, 1987

From D L, 555 Mass Avenue in Boston

While sitting on a courtroom bench near room 701 at the new court house, I overheard someone talking very loudly and exclaim "...and I threw the dyke out of my office." Then I overheard loud comments such as "...and then she brought her fag friend with her" and "I said 'I don't speak to fags or dykes. They should all be shot."

When it was getting too loud for comfort, I approached the group and said, "Excuse me, but I'm gay and I find your loud prejudices objectionable." I was then told to "mind your fucking business, buddy, and get your fucking gay ass over to that bench." I then asked this person what his name was and he said, "You fags all know who I am, you're all frightened of me." He then gave his name but I didn't catch it. He then started making obviously overt gay gestures such as making his wrist go limp and saying "Nice to meet you, ma'am" and "Aren't you a sweet boy?" speaking all of the above with a lisp. I explained to him that I wasn't trying to get into an argument with him and that I was there to pay a parking ticket and he was very loudly making prejudiced comments. He then said, "Get your fucking fag ass over to that bench and pay your ticket like everybody else," I walked away from him and he said, "Here faggot would you like my card?" He then handed me his 'councilor at large' business card. [Attached to the letter to me.]

My City Council colleague Dapper, the fat man with the red nose and the blue eyes, lips twisted with snide snickering, continued afterwards to make fun of me at City Council meetings. The members of the press and audience in attendance all commented upon it for years.

My office sent a note to Mr. D L telling him that perhaps speaking with *Bay Windows* and *Gay Community News* would be useful (all papers targeting the gay community).

I mention this story to you not because it is about gay people — it is actually about how people who are different are treated in our society. And about how those people in turn have a different take on that society, a view from which we can learn a great deal. I kept explaining to people that I was not focusing on gay issues, I was the lightning rod for them and it was the issues that were focusing on me. More precisely, if gays and I were not the continual subject of attacks for being gay then we would not spend five minutes discussing, working on or talking about gay anything except perhaps the cute guy we met at a bar the other night.

It is often said that gay rights, the rights of women, people of color, immigrants or others who have been victims of systematic abuse by our society are "special interests." But one of the key facts of life is this: until everybody makes fairness toward everyone else their personal business and concern, there will be no peace or real prosperity on this planet of ours.

Martin Luther King was first to articulate this principle and my interpretation goes like this: gay stuff is not for gays, it's for straights. An analysis of what goes wrong toward women is for men. An understanding of what happens to people of color is for the understanding and actions that whites need to take. Understanding and taking action to fix what is broken in countries that are poverty stricken is the agenda for rich countries. And to think that these things are "special interests" or boring or not directly impacting your life is to continue to live in the dream world that is bringing us international conflagrations, melting our economies, ruining our planet, and nurturing hate toward our society that will continue to isolate it as an object of fear and loathing by billions of people.

Far from being a small, incidental set of issues, human rights — fairness, honesty, sharing all resources and caring for all people, respect for diversity and protecting the weak from exploitation from the strong — are the prerequisites to our survival.

This book is about a lot more than being gay, just like the Holocaust was about a lot more than being Jewish.

Anyway, many, many of my letters were positive — I don't want you to get the idea that I got only 'crazy' mail. [See "Letters" in chapter 74 above]. However, there was an endless stream of crazy mail that helped me understand how some folks felt about my community and about me.

For example, take this note from March 10th, 1987. It contained a pamphlet that advised me:

> *There are concerned people who know what you're going through and know how to help. Many of them have been set free from homosexuality themselves and would love to help you in any way they could. If you or someone you love is struggling with homosexuality, you can receive helpful literature or counseling. Just write one of the groups listed below. We love you!*

These types of letters sounded sweeter but in fact they were more insidious because they attempted to twist the knives that taught people that they were sick and could get help from what nature dictates they must be. I still suffer from the wounds of those knives. I got lots of these kinds of letters.

And I got other more explicit kinds of letters. I suggested to Police Commissioner Mickey Roache that we get some gay cops to at least come out so that there were people who could relate to that part of our community. From the NYE Evergreen Farm, 1386 Pleasant Street in Athol, Massachusetts on May 26th of 1987 I got a hand written letter from Harold L. Nye that said:

It would be a mistake to assume the only mail I got was about gay stuff. For example on November 1st, 1987, as I continued to fight for a rational housing plan, I got this note from a landlord:

*I own a building and have wealthy tenants, Doctors, Executives,
Millionaires, etc..... I think you need your head examined to
freeze their rent...the College students arrive in BMW's and go
to Europe for Christmas. They don't even vote!! The Universities
make enough money out of them. Let them worry about
housing...There are "slum lords," but I am not. I don't wish to be
labeled a "pig" and have my rich tenants get a free ride from
you.*

Thank you,
[Illegible signature]

It is important to note here that at no time had anyone suggested freezing anything, that rent control allowed for automatic 12.5% yearly increases in rent and with submission of cost information, increases beyond that [see chapter 79 above]. New construction was never under any controls as we believed that it would lead to more housing being built, and the vast majority of people who rented in older, decaying housing in the city were not rich by any means.

Our efforts to help tenants resulted in hundreds of letters. In general people tend to place their "bigger more important agendas" ahead of those of smaller, weaker people. I never liked that because for those affected the importance of an agenda is connected to how it affects their lives. And it is not always 'bad' people that do 'bad' things. This is another myth upon which much harm is based. For example, take the following letter:

> *My Dear Councilor,*
> *This is to thank you so very much for the helping hand, which*
> *you have lent us tenants of 491, 497, and 499 Huntington*
> *Avenue during the weeks and months of our controversy with*
> *the Museum of Fine Arts. [The Museum wanted them out.]*
>
> *It is no exaggeration to say that without your help, we would*
> *not have gotten even half as far as we did. I beg you to accept*
> *my deeply felt gratitude.*
>
> *Very respectfully yours,*
> *Henry W. Cohen*

The Boston Museum of Fine Arts is not 'evil' — it was just was caught in a conflict of interest which needed mediation.

I spent time every week on a myriad of issues and found that there is room for everyone to help our society in ways big and small, which in the aggregate creates a home for us all.

I mention these letters to underline the diversity of efforts our staff and the flock of students who worked with us were able to undertake in 1987.

84 /   Censorship

Censorship, like charity, should begin at home,
but, unlike charity, it should end there.
– Clare Boothe Luce

Censorship takes many forms. Gay people experienced it as being made invisible. Sometimes when I spoke, gatekeepers tried to stop me from being heard. This was the social ostracism which gay people shared with blacks and everyone else not part of the old boy network — that ladder stretching up to the bosses from us field hands.

I got a letter about being censored from James R. Przeslawski, Ann Arbor, Michigan, on April 7[th,] regarding a speech I had given earlier in Grand Rapids which had been taped and shown on some cable television shows in the area.

My speech was banned on mainstream T.V. across Michigan. Speaking about gay rights was not popular. In one city in Michigan the mayor banned the show vowing that only a court order would make him budge. Most cable companies did not ban the show but they worked the existing rules to keep the show from being seen, such as submitting the show to "committees of approval" that would, in reality, never meet.

In James' letter I was told, "Some [local cable television stations] have taken to making their own copies. Here in Ann Arbor they've been averaging ten calls a week to view the program. I would hazard a guess that you're a face that will be familiar to lots of folks here in Michigan."

Censorship in its many forms was a kind of violence I had to deal with for decades. It was and is part of the selective perception that keeps us ignorant of what is actually happening in the world.

85 / Lawns and political power

I have a theory on how lawns got started, and why lawnmowers invaded unbelievably large amounts of land around houses in suburbs across the world. I admit it is a fantasy, but I suspect there is a bit of truth in this perhaps apocryphal tale.

It begins with the observation that from architectural styles to clothing styles to the design of sinks and faucets you do not see a proliferation of the most functional, but rather imitations of what is imagined to clothe and clean the bodies of the wealthy.

There was a time not long ago when white powder was used to make white-skinned workers appear whiter, not to avoid looking negroid but because prior to the Industrial revolution, a tan meant you were lower class – a field hand – and this was seen as ugly, while the upper class were light white. Hence the sale of white powder to lighten skin.

After the Industrial revolution, tanning salons, beach wear to maximize sun exposure, and sun tan lotion became popular because having a tan came to mean good-looking and wealthy. Note that during the same period of time, working-class Caucasian people were light white because they were devoid of sun, working in large factories or offices and the leisure class basked in sunshine.

I think that what happened around lawns is a similar kind of event, and it is a parable for how working people, tenants, the poor and others of limited means support the rules, habits, lifestyles and economic systems that enrich the elite whom workers hope someday to be. It is the emulation of what one is not. It also helps explain the cultural battle within the gay community between assimilationism and liberation, and within communities of color between black power and accommodation, cooptation and assimilation.

Once upon a time there were feudal baronies with huge castles around which herds of cattle, sheep, goats and other grass munchers stayed close to the castle walls. This was to protect flocks from thieves and it was practical as well. For this reason, the first travelers from the new mercantile class that went from town to town spread the idea from observation that not only is a man's home his castle, but a castle required a lawn. It was what the newly transformed peasants of the middle ages associated with wealth and power.

And to this day suburbanites buy lawnmowers and cut the grass in lieu of sheep doing it for them, continuing to assume the trappings of power and wealth as interpreted by the peasants of a thousand years ago.

This theory is consistent with my experiences in trying to get tenants rights passed (tenants voted often for landlord rights); to get gay people to support their liberation struggles (they fight for the status of hetero-lite, complete with marriage and military service); and to improve teaching methods and curriculum in our public schools which imitated for a long time the education given to the children of English nobility.

This theory permeated everything I did as a politician for some 3,653 days, even to my clothing with the somewhat modernized suits of country gentlemen of the 19th century.

It was clear to me that the politics of class continues to dominate our public discourse, although in forms not always recognizable as such. I mention all of this because we have forgotten or do not acknowledge the key role of class in our lives and politics — as a central fact of our social order which determines an astonishing amount of how people vote, think, feel and act.

86 /   Dukakis, the water table, and his run for President

"Like a good general, I treated everyone who wasn't with me as against me."
– Michael Dukakis

By March of 1987 it became clear that Massachusetts Governor Michael Dukakis, by then running for president of the United States, was going to ignore my request to get federal money to help people fix their homes damaged by the falling water table in Beacon Hill, the Back Bay, and Chinatown[see chapter 73, "Back Bay Sinking;" failing levels of water tables caused underground pilings to rot]. Gary Dotterman said in the *Boston Herald* of March 29th, "To this day the governor has not even confirmed receiving the letter, never mind applying for the funds." I suggested five specific sections under the Federal Emergency Disaster Relief Act under which residents might qualify for money but there was silence from the governor.

I continued to raise money for my Boston Ground Water Trust to monitor ground water levels (for example $40,000 from the Four Seasons Hotel in Park Square). The main causes of lowering water was the city and state's underground construction of subway walls, their altering of the water levels to accommodate big new construction, and the poor performance of the dam and pumps that were supposed to keep the level steady. I thought it was outrageous for the state, city and feds to pass the buck for the damage they created to its victims.

The governor's office said through James Simon, spokesman for the Executive Office of Environmental Affairs, "If you buy property over a spongy area, you know you run the risk of water table problems."

I suppose we should cancel everyone's health insurance who smokes, doesn't exercise, eats saturated fats, or has babies all of which costs us a fortune and you ought to know that you run the risk of expensive medical care if you fornicate or eat cheese. And let's not forget the risk of having babies!

I mention this because it was another in a long list of issues that made me not very happy with Michael Dukakis — he was in many ways a man best characterized by an aggressive search at the airport for the quarter he thought his wife Kitty lost in the car. A stingy sort of soul. It made it clear to me that being smart and analytical does not mean you will be generous, compassionate, kind or caring.

I think that he has a lot of love for people but he had internalized a lot of our Greek culture's teachings about "waste not, want not" and interpreted that as requiring rejection of what are perceived of as defects of character, like eating too much or high caloric foods. And he was familiar with extended Greek families that took care of each other instead of the more dispersed family structure of today. That led him to ask me, as he slashed welfare, "Why don't they get their families to help?" He didn't appreciate how few had any families at all, much less ones that could help.

87 /   1987: Rosaria decides to run for City Council

"JFK used to say the bishops and the cardinals were all Republicans,
but the nuns were Democrats! I sort of believe that too."
– Kitty Kelley

Rosaria Salerno was part of the Northeastern University Campus Ministry. She was a beautiful woman, and a nun. At least until she left the order. We all felt that this was because she was in love with Father Robert Case. Rosaria and Bob were an important part of organizing the Fenway into one of the most activist, community-building places in Boston.

Rosaria lived in the first housing coop in the Fenway on Mass Avenue across from the Berklee College of Music. She sang beautifully, cared about us all, was kind and sensible.

One day, around March 1987, she came to see me. She asked me to run citywide this time for City Council because she wanted to run for city council and felt that she could win the district seat and that I could run citywide consistent with my ambitions to be mayor of Boston.

She might have been right, I don't know. But I was afraid. I remember feeling rather tortured by the request. For some reason, perhaps because I felt that at long last I had gotten some of that approval from folks that I needed, having been deprived of it as a gay guy for so so long, that I didn't want to risk losing it. Frankly, I was chicken.

We talked it out, and eventually it was decided that Rosaria would run citywide. She chose as her symbol the rose, a beautiful idea.

I still don't know how my life would have been different if I had decided to do what she proposed originally and run citywide for city council — a big step toward becoming mayor of Boston.

I got a letter in March telling me that Rosaria had decided to run in the fall and asked me to be an "integral part of her campaign" which Robert and I would become. [Rosaria won; see chapter 118 in book iii].

88 /   Larry Kramer and ACT UP

*"I don't consider myself an artist. I consider myself a very opinionated man
who uses words as fighting tools."*
– Larry Kramer

I was on the docket with Larry Kramer who got to talk before me at the 4th Annual North East Lesbian and Gay Student Union Conference held at Columbia University across the weekend of March 27th, 1987. Larry, a noted gay playwright, is credited for starting "ACT UP," the group of AIDS activists pushing for the government to have a Manhattan Project to find a cure for AIDS. And he was on a tear.

The audience was made up of representatives from over 150 student organizations — it was astonishing how fast gay groups were forming across the nation. They were to a large extent young gay men, full of idealism and passion, ready to take on the brutalization of gays.

Larry told them all to stand up. Look to the right and to the left. One of you will be dead in a few years, he said. You're on a death trip.

I looked over the downcast audience and went in the opposite direction, fired them up, rallied their sense of justice and told them we could do it. I told them that we had invented safer sex. That AIDS would not destroy us, it would teach us how to fight even harder, to adjust our behavior to protect each other and to protect the millions that no one cared about, the drug addicts and the poor, the people of other countries who died silently as the epidemic mowed down a generation.

I felt that you had to get people excited about winning, not afraid of losing, believing in themselves, not like the novels of Theodore Drieser which taught that no matter what they did that they would die miserably.

Larry might be a good playwright but I would hate to have him as a team coach. These young men and women were the future of our movement and the way the leadership was shaping it, through coalitions with other groups, perhaps the future of the country and the world.

I pushed for the March on Washington, warned about assimilationism as our greatest danger, gave people hope for their future, told them that they would be the first generation to meet gay kids not full of self-hate, doubt and pain about who they were, and I hoped to be the last to remember what that was like.

I warned that in spite of everything, the way the world works is to divide people against each other to keep control and that this was our enemy. That beneath our effort to form coalitions was an agenda of making resources available to everyone on our planet so that we could all benefit from the dreams of all the people on our small world. I recast our movement as a fight to end poverty and disease, discrimination and narrow mindedness of all kinds.

I explained that there was more of a danger in losing the real point of what we were after than losing the game of power — we would win the power game but could easily lose the whole point if we did not stick to our principles, to our understanding of how oppressions work, to our decision to free the world from its pain. I said that the movement's great danger was that we would eliminate a ladder of power whose lower positions on the steps were occupied by people of color, gays, and others who were devalued (the risk was that gays would take a step up the ladder without others n the coalition). Instead, we needed to make a new kind of ladder altogether, and that would make coalitions and learn why the class hierarchies existed in the first place and how to get rid of them.

I do not know how many folks "got it" but a lot did. Many of them came up to me to thank me for encouraging them during this difficult fight. Unfortunately many or most were destined to die long before they could complete their mission.

Later, Robert and I went to the Saint, a gay club that helped pay for this huge conference. It was in a huge, old movie theater that had all the seats taken out and a big dance area with a perforated dome and a planetarium projector. It was a lot of fun. As Robert and I danced, I felt a sense of wonder that I could dance beneath a canopy of stars and lights in a space that made me feel like flying.

Then the magic was over and the next morning we got on Amtrak and went back to Boston to the 18-hour-a-day schedule.

89 /   Coors Continues

I was trashed daily for my participation in the national Coors beer boycott.

While *USA Today* documented gay bashing as an AIDS backlash (it was not, just a new rationale to continue doing what they had never stopped) I was being bashed by media critics of my policies regarding a bottle of carbonated hops. This is because while the Coors boycott among gays actually happened a year earlier, Harry Stevens kept his word and yanked the beer from Fenway Park. It made national news. It did not get attention when gays did it, but it sure got attention when the Red Sox did it. Often it is not what is said but who is saying it that matters.

On March 24th, without actually doing any real checking, as was its custom, the *Boston Herald* dressed up its totally right-wing position:

> *Now City Councilor David Scondras has decided that imbibing the wrong brew means "subsidizing a terrorist war in Central America." Scondras has browbeaten the Red Sox management into banning the sale of Coors beer at Fenway this coming season. The war on Coors has been a staple of the left for more than a decade, ever since the AFL-CIO lost a union election there and declared a boycott (so much for democracy). The Coors family does indeed support freedom and Democratic capitalism worldwide with its contributions, which, of course leads to the usual charges that Coors is racist, etc., etc. Instead of Scondras-style censorship, we say let the fans decide. If they don't like the politics of the Coors family, then they don't have to partake of the product. As for the Red Sox Management, instead of standing up to the Scondrasistas, they apparently saved all their spine for dealing with Roger Clemens.*

How cute. The media really needs a fact-checker to review its scribbles, or at least a public readership whose crap detectors are not on the blink. For example, note the dismissing of the ban on Coors as a 'staple of the left,' as if it's a tired old thing not worthy of any time or thought. Imagine in 1860 someone saying, "railing against the Dred Scott decision and hiding runaway slaves, a staple of the Abolitionists for more than a decade" as if fighting slavery were a kind of banjo Abolitionists kept around the house for entertainment. This is a typical example of mediocracy — the dictatorship of the mind by those well off enough to buy media and use it to twist truth.

The closest the *Herald* got to truth was that the Coors family does support worldwide efforts at capitalism. This is rightwing code meaning support for making money. It did not, of course, spell out exactly what these efforts actually were that included funding hundreds of right wing groups from neo-Nazi organizations to anti-environmental think tanks.

The bashing did not stop with one little article. Here is another, direct from the owner of the *Boston Ledger* on March 28th:

> *Who the hell do you think you are, David Scondras? I have the feeling your so-called position of power has gone to your head and I think you have lost either your senses or your sense of direction! Perhaps Coors beer is not your "cup of tea" for a number of personal reasons, but Councilor Scondras, when you start telling me, or anyone, that just because Coors is not a "blast" with you it has to be a no-no for me, you are wrong, David, dead wrong! This country was founded on the premise of freedom — freedom of choice — and if I choose not to partake or purchase a product because of personal preference, so be it, but I have absolutely no right to pass judgment on it for the rest of the world. It's a free country, Councilor, a country founded on free enterprise and in case you haven't noticed, it works!*
>
> *Let Coors beer come to bat in Boston, Councilor Scondras, otherwise it's one, two, three strikes and you're out in my ballgame.*
>
> *— Frederic N. Phinney, Publisher*

Wow, the publisher! I pissed off the guy with the cash!! I wonder if he has any money invested with Coors? How much you want to bet? And I take strenuous exception to the notion that free enterprise is working for any one who is not in the wealthiest 1%, its minions, or its wannabees.

I will leave aside the irrelevant sidesteps like the "not your cup of tea" line as if the issue were about some personal preference of mine about something as trivial as a brand of tea (or beer for that matter), but what is particularly interesting is the use of "freedom of choice," and the painting of me as a powerful tyrant who would deprive others of their choices. You would never know that we were talking about one little stand out of twelve at the ball park, that Coors was sold across the street from the ballpark and in virtually every bar that surrounded the ballpark for miles, or that Coors was the fastest growing beer in New England. I clearly could not stop anyone from drinking Coors and that's not what Phinney was really worried about. It made national news that the Red Sox was opposed to Coors and a lot of people would be asking 'why' and people like Phinney did not want that questions to start forming in the minds of working people across the country because the answers to *THAT* question in *THOSE* minds could spell more serious trouble than David Scondras could ever dream of for Coors and other companies that behaved like them.

The company sent PR teams, letters, calls, local distributors, the companies' owners, lawyers, and now media maggots all to stop anyone from asking the questions I was asking. "The lady doth protest too much, methinks," said Shakespeare.

By April, the guns were blasting as papers in many states across the USA got into the act. The *Herald* changed its stance, putting my boycott as the lead on its 'Business' page, not that there is much in the *Herald* that could pass the sniff test for economic accuracies.

The special edition of the paper had me with a can of Coors in my hand and Peter Coors. The caption has me saying "stop funding right-wing hate organizations" meaning all of them, and Coors replies that he isn't anti-gay. Translation: marginalize the issue whenever you can. Make it about gay stuff when it's about a lot more because many people will see it as trivial when it's about gay stuff. Peter kept trying to separate what the company 'Coors' does from what the family that makes the money from the company does with that money. I said, "In political terms, there is no difference between a product and the people who manage a company which produces the product." But Peter Coors defended his family's contributions, careful to state how much it gave but not clear on where exactly the money went. In the *Herald* article he says "none of those organizations (which got $24.5 million from Coors) have as their charter or primary purpose the elimination of gay rights."

In fact none of these groups had as their *PRIMARY* purpose the elimination of gay rights. Well, Peter ought to know. Coors brewery did not have the elimination of gay rights as its primary purpose — making and selling beer was. Or more precisely keeping the Coors family rich was. Screening out gay candidates for jobs from its breweries was more a secondary kind of concern of the company.

By April 4th the *Globe* caved in and attacked through a pathetic article by Will McDonough called "Silly Boycott is brewing." I thought at first it was about coffee. I don't care one way of another about Coors beer. What bothers me in this instance is that because of the Sox' decision to surrender to the Scondras threat, which is what the club considers it, Scondras is taking money out of the pocket of Ray Tye, one of the best guys ever to walk the streets of this city.

McDonough forgets to mention that Ray Tye gave me money to run for office, that Ray Tye owned United Liquors and was a multimillionaire, that the son Ray Tye loved a great deal was gay and died of AIDS — my actions about Coors didn't affect Ray Tye's cash reserve ten cents. My pushing for AIDS funding, research and gay rights was what mattered to Ray Tye.

In April, slowly, the material that we used to make our decision to fight Coors came out in articles across the country, usually in the gay press. From the April edition of "Just Out":

> *Just in case you're buying Coors, Killian's Irish Red, Herman Joseph beers or Colorado Cooler, we thought you might like to know where your money goes. It has been ascertained in Congressional hearings that the John Birch Society receives an annual donation from Joseph Coors, according to the New York Native. Also, contributions have been made to Jerry Falwell's Liberty Foundation. America's Future as well as other right wing organizations, which funnel millions of dollars to Nicaraguan Contras. The Coors family also sits on various boards, including the council for National Policy where Holly and Joseph Coors*

*serve on the Board of Governors with Falwell, Jesse Helms,
Herbert and Nelson Hunt, Richard Viguerie, Pat Robertson and
Phyllis Schlafly; Morality in Media which lists Joseph Coors on
the National Planning Board; Pat Roberton's CBN University
which lists Holly Coors on its Board of Regents; and the Heritage
Foundation, the Washington think tank which came up with the
anti-gay "Family Protection Act"*

On April 8th the *Mirror* published an article titled "Coors Excludes Same Sex Couples from Race" and reads in part:

*In another of its continuing attacks on the Lesbian and Gay
community, Adolph Coors Company specifically excluded same
sex couples from entering the Coors Couples Run on Valentine's
Day in Portland, Oregon. The race was held to benefit the
American Heart Association. Catherine Crooker, Special Events
Coordinator for the Heart Association explained that the
sponsoring firm prepared the events entire design and
promotion.*

*When the race brochure was printed stating seven times that
same sex couples could not participate, Mr. Crooker questioned
the policy. She was told that the set up of the race was not
adaptable to same sex runners because two men or two women
would not be equal to a mixed couple in running strength.*

But I have to say the best letter I saw printed was because it defended me directly. I loved it. It was from Rick Jasany in the Back Bay. Perhaps I was hasty in judging the Back Bay as too conservative for me. He was answering an April 4th article by Will McDonough in the *Boston Globe* headlined "Silly Boycott is brewing." Part of the letter:

*You deliver the ultimate judgment that David Scondras is "a
zero," an absurdity. On what facts do you base this assessment?
On the fact that Scondras is gay? And does this mean that all
gay people are categorically zeroes? Or is it just David Scondras
who's a zero? And if so why is it important to mention that he's
gay? I'd like to think that rather than yielding to pressure, the
Red Sox got a little education and decided that carrying Coors
was not in the spirit of compassionate community relations.
However, if Scondras does have the 'the muscle' to twist arms, I
guess he's not the wimp your article implies, or the 'zero' you've
labeled him.*

I wish I had met Rick Jasany. It made me feel so good to read what I really could not say for myself.

It is an irony that in the end, it is what others say of you that most persuasively teaches you and others who you are. For this reason it is important to neither ignore those who dislike you nor fawn over those who approve of your every move. One of the protections from the indoctrinations we laughingly call 'news' in America is the people we find who have good crap detectors and common sense and who use them to help you see what is actually happening.

1987 was getting to be a year of explosive events and it was just beginning. An election for President was coming; and I would end up traveling many thousands of miles and being trashed many thousands of times.

But I was alive.

I remember my friend, the chairman of Harvard's Philosophy Department, Rogers Albritton once saying something like: "Even if I were offered something" like what Tim Leary was pushing, LSD or some such, "that could make you happy just by taking it, I would not take it, because happiness is not the point. Being engaged in life is the point."

I think he was right.

So I can't say I was always happy.

But I was never bored.

*"I don't think politics has anything to do with left, right or center.
It has to do with trying to do right by people."*
—Paul Wellstone

Across the country the gay movement was building up steam. While I was a city councilor in Boston, I was a gay leader in the United States. On April 6th Robert and I got a note that said:

> *I want to thank you and Robert for taking a weekend to spend time with us here in Birmingham [Alabama]…We are already setting in motion plans to run an openly gay person for Council this year. Thank you for being the guest speaker at PROPAC's spring banquet. Good luck in your election this year.*
>
> *– Tim Davis of the Privacy Rights Organization,*
> *Political Action Committee of Birmingham.*

We received similar notes from dozens of cities in many states. Without realizing it, we had become noted figures in the gay community, appearing in some 400 publications across the country. So it should not have been a surprise to us that eventually this would lead to involvement in national politics.

My staff aide French Wall was excited. He said, "We can get T shirts, 'Run, Ginny, Run' on them," as he pushed for us to get Ginny Apuzzo, the ex-nun who had become a major Democratic party activist, to run for President. She worked in Democratic Governor of New York Cuomo's administration. It says a good deal about Cuomo that he supported her in spite of the political difficulty of supporting an openly lesbian member of his administration who spoke out so often, so loudly, and so eloquently about gay issues. Ginny had an extraordinarily reasonable, charismatic way of talking — she could convince an Eskimo to buy snow. Anyway, I decided it was a good idea, and called on her to run as an openly gay presidential candidate to send a message to the Democratic Party to stop taking us for granted.

Ironically, people who never ran for anything or made any change anywhere anytime kept lambasting my idea, suggesting it was too early, it will piss off party officials, cause a backlash, or would take energy away from all the important stuff they were doing (God knows what it was), etc.

I know and knew that in the world of change, the mobilization of a critical mass of people with an agenda is the single most important step in making that change possible.

Without gay power there would be no gay rights. It would not be a gift from a magnanimous Democratic Party. It was a political calculation on how to get and keep power that would move the party — and that included of course how to minimize alienation from members of the party that hated us.

So I asked Ginny to run. I called her on the phone and tried to persuade her to do it. She said she'd think about it and give her some time.

So I wrote articles requesting Ginny to run and it became a topic in our community for a long time. The call to action that I liked best was reprinted and got Ginny to publically talk about the movement to get her to run; it said:

I agree with Reverend Pat Robertson. His gun-toting, bible-thumping television 'ministry' warns us that America is in desperate need of salvation, and I agree.

But we are talking about saving two different America's — his one of polyester patriots who sees conformity as an index of righteousness and who fear the responsibility freedom brings.

His political vision of this country is the one I want to save our country from.

But Reverend Robertson is ahead in the battle. As a presidential candidate he understands that though his views represent only a small minority of people in this country he can exercise disproportionate political influence because he has organized, vocalized and energized his followers.

*The gay and lesbian community can learn a lot from Reverend
Robertson.*

*And the number one lesson is that we should run an openly gay
or lesbian candidate for President….*

*The national Democratic party has repeatedly slammed its door
in our face, willing to take our resources, votes and energy but
unwilling to stand up for us except with hushed mouth lip
service.*

*The time has come to push open the door, to announce that it
will be easier to include us than to take us for granted.*

*Pat Robertson is running for President and understands he is
fighting a war with homosexuals over America's salvation.*

*I know which side I'm on. And I know I need a lesbian or gay
presidential candidate.*

Ginny was genuinely flattered, and did not rule out becoming a candidate.

Ginny, who was Deputy Executive Director of the New York State Consumer Protection Board, said:

*"David suggests that a gay or lesbian candidate would be a
valid way of raising our issue in the context of the national
dialogue. I think it is an intelligent and politically astute
strategy…. I think David is putting out a strategy that it's
incumbent upon the leadership of the community to consider."*

In our office we got wildly enthusiastic letters pushing Ginny to run from New Hampshire, Texas, California, Illinois, Pennsylvania, Missouri, Florida, Massachusetts, Maryland, Rhode Island and Indiana.

Ginny Apuzzo for President

Spring, 1987

We Need a Gay or Lesbian Presidential Candidate

Run, Ginny, Run

by Boston City Councillor David Scondras

I agree with Reverend Pat Robertson.

His gun-toting, bible-thumping "ministry" warns us that America is in desperate need of salvation, and I agree.

But we are talking about saving two different Americas--his being one of polyester patriots who see conformity as an index of rightousness and fear the responsibility that freedom brings.

His political vision of this country is precisely the one I want to save our America from.

But Reverend Robertson is ahead in the battle. As a presidential candidate he understands though his views represent only a small minority of people in this country he can exercise disproportionate political influence because he has organized, vocalized, and energized his followers.

The gay and lesbian community can learn a lot from Reverend Robertson.

And the number one lesson is that we should run an openly lesbian or gay person for president.

To such a race we bring limited, but enormously useful and powerful, resources. We are natural coalition builders for we are male and female, black and white, young and old, urban and rural, comprised of every nationality, religion, and economic background.

And we are everywhere. Our hundreds of newspapers, thousands of bars, community centers, health clinics, churches, organizations, and millions of brothers and sisters coupled with our compassion, energy, and creativity are ripe with national political potential.

Imagine this scenario: someone with the skill, persuasiveness, and appeal of Ginny Apuzzo enters the New Hampshire primary.

Hundreds of students from New England stream into New

Ginny Apuzzo

Hampshire joining activists there to tell voters of Ginny's vision, her commitment to a broad range of issues, and her courage in fighting to liberate us all from

(continued on page 3)

Five Steps to Victory

1) Contact Ginny and let her know of your support-- tell her why it would make a difference to you if she ran:

Ginny Apuzzo
99 Washington Avenue
Room 1020
Albany, NY 12210

2) Register to vote as a Democrat and organize to become a delegate to the 1988 Democratic Convention as an Apuzzo delegate, an uncommited delegate, or a "delegate of conscience" pledged to another candidate-- for more information on how to become a delegate call the National Association of Gay and Lesbian Democratic Clubs at (202) 543-0298 or the Democratic National Committee (202) 863-8000.

3) Get involved in your local lesbian and gay political groups and excite them about the Apuzzo Campaign-- make them realize the tremendous organizing potential the campaign holds for them.

4) Write gay and lesbian, progressive, and Democratic-Party-politics newspapers about the power of an Apuzzo Campaign and be aware of opportunities to use non-gay and lesbian media-- the idea of an openly lesbian woman running for President is novel and newsworthy.

5) Order "Apuzzo for President" buttons from page three of this newsletter and be sure to wear a button all the time to provoke discussion of the Apuzzo Campaign-- all button orders help support this newsletter.

do some simple little program for two months that's not going to attract any attention at all."

While Stanford criticized the legislative committee for holding up the grant, he observed that the controversy and the media attention it generated resulted in much-needed enlightenment in Arkansas about AIDS issues: "Inadvertently, we have forced the legislature and the governor to articulate a very progressive position. They've articulated that this is a very serious and urgent problem, and that the general public is at risk. It's kind of nice to see them on record as saying all these sensible things."

— **Dave Walter**

Scondras Calls on Apuzzo To Run As Openly Gay Presidential Candidate

In a proposal entitled "Run, Ginny, Run: We Need a Gay or Lesbian Presidential Candidate," openly gay Boston Councillor David Scondras has urged gay activist Virginia Apuzzo to seek the Democratic nomination for President.

Apuzzo, former executive director of the National Gay and Lesbian Task Force (NGLTF) and now deputy director of the New York State Consumer Protection Board, did not immediately rule out becoming a candidate.

"David suggests that a gay or lesbian candidate would be a valid way of raising our issue in the context of the national dialogue," Apuzzo declared. "I think it is an intelligent and politically astute strategy. The extent to which I would be the most appropriate candidate, or would consider being a candidate, is jumping the gun. I think that David is putting out a strategy that it's incumbent on the leadership of the community to consider."

One national gay leader, Vic Basile, executive director of the Human Rights Campaign Fund, which contributes to progay candidates for federal office, threw cold water on the idea, asserting that it would be a waste of resources.

"We're just beginning to look seriously at electing openly gay people to city councils and state legislatures and the U.S. Congress," Basile said. "We need to focus our attention and energy on solidifying a political base — we need to be realistic about where we put our limited resources. Devoting considerable energies to electing someone as President serves very little political purpose."

Jeff Levi, NGLTF's current executive director, commented that a gay candidate "certainly gains us visibility," but added, "I don't know in substantive terms how much it will accomplish." Nevertheless, Levi stated that he would "await with anticipation the decision of the potential candidate."

In Boston, where Scondras' views are sometimes controversial in the gay community, one prominent activist called his proposal "absurd" and "off the wall." But two members of the Houston Gay Political Caucus expressed enthusiasm for the idea.

In his proposal, Scondras wrote, "Imagine this scenario: Someone with the skill, persuasiveness and appeal of Ginny Apuzzo enters the New Hampshire primary."

He envisioned "hundreds of students from New England" streaming into New Hampshire to work on her campaign, and said Democratic candidates such as Gary Hart and Rep. Richard Gephardt (D-Mo.) would be "forced to deal with lesbian and gay issues, to hear our demands as presented by an articulate, personable woman."

Scondras asserted that "how many delegates she wins, how many primaries she manages to run in, is not as important as the fact of her conducting a campaign."

"The national Democratic Party has repeatedly slammed its

Apuzzo for President: "flattering," "politically astute" or "off the wall"?

door in our face, willing to take our resources, votes and energy, but unwilling to stand up for us except with mush-mouth lip service. The time has come to push open the door, to announce that it will be easier to include us than to take us for granted."

Apuzzo, a long-time Democratic activist who ran unsuccessfully for the New York State legislature in 1978, said she was "flattered" by Scondras' proposal. But she emphasized that any gay candidacy would require "some degree of consensus" among gay leaders, "a good deal of planning" and an evaluation of its impact on gay activism at the local level.

— **Peter Freiberg**

APRIL 14, '87

91 /   Frank Sinatra

"May you live to be 100 and may the last voice you hear be mine."
– Frank Sinatra

Through a process I don't quite remember, Robert and I were given tickets to a concert of Sinatra's at Symphony Hall. When Robert found out that Rosaria Salerno loved Sinatra's music, he gave his ticket to her. So Rosaria, who was running for City Council in the fall elections, went with me to hear him at Boston Symphony Hall on Sunday, April 26th.

We were feeling rather special, having been given $5,000 tickets to sit in the front row seats and hear "Old Blue Eyes" sing some songs to raise money for the Boston Youth Partnership.

Rosaria was elegant, I wore my usual bland tuxedo. The evening was enchanting, and Sinatra came on the stage, large, mellow, and sang in a voice that echoed the persuasive melodies of a half a century.

I was surprised to notice that he was looking at a little machine on the floor on the stage — a teleprompter that made sure he remembered the words. It amuses me to think that people are annoyed at Obama using teleprompters nowadays when so many who are so great made sure that they got it right. It is in fact an act of respect toward the audience.

"When I was 17, it was a very good year," he sang, and I thought of all the times I had heard this man, an icon of my parent's generation, a man whose life was long complex and full of music that made millions feel special, and now he used his voice to raise money for the poor.

I still have that ticket to his concert. I put it on the wall at City Hall, where I put hundreds of special things that people saw when they came to see me, from presents from Russian delegations to the book of poetry given to me by the vice president of Nicaragua.

Rosaria was beaming that night. I played the role of 'City Councilor,' my new first name, and Ray Flynn played the role of 'His Honor.' Around us were the movers and shakers of the city, and for the first time in Boston's history an openly gay man was one of them.

92 /   Light Bulbs

"I am on until I am dead, like a light bulb."
– Henry Rollins

I went with Gary Dotterman from bulb to bulb, making note of which one's were burnt out, and sent the list to Joe Casazza, the grizzled leader of Boston Public Works Department, saying "Turn on my district's lights." I was frustrated and then realized, in the spirit of image and theater, that what was best was to put in new bulbs myself.

Gary and I got a ladder and bulbs and Mobile One (Gary's old car) and went up and down Commonwealth Avenue where the biggest problem was.

I was a spectacle, Gary's car pulling up next to a burnt out streetlight (imitation gas lamps that dotted the Back Bay), out with the ladder, me in my suit, take out the old put in the new, somebody in the media finds out and I bet Ray got embarrassed. The mayor is responsible no matter who was responsible if you know what I mean.

Gary and I went from dark lamp to dark lamp and started putting the new lights in, and Casazza said he considered my report (and my actions) "friendly fire." The city moved fast and all the burnt out lights were replaced in a flurry of activity.

93 /   Marriage

David Steinberg and me. God, he's cute.

Cultural institutions are difficult to change. And they don't just all of a sudden collapse or morph. Gay Marriage began in a thousand fights. Here is one of them in 1987. It made Dapper nervous because he had suspected that I had targeted marriage all along. This was the smoking gun.

Lesbians were denied couples membership at the community boathouse in Boston because they could not produce a marriage certificate. My Human Rights Commission Director, Fred Mandel, a lawyer who had spent a lot of energy in my election campaigns, informed them, "A Boston organization cannot create a special marriage rate and then deny that rate to two people who are together without a marriage license." I was proud of Fred. He was on target enforcing our civil rights law.

Debbie Bresnahan, the assistant manager of the boathouse said : "I can't tell what we are going to do. We certainly don't want to discriminate against anyone." Many non-profits in Boston had handled couple memberships creatively and inclusively, like the Institute of Contemporary Art and the Museum of Fine Arts which defined eligible couples as "two people living at the same address." This was a small event happening in Boston, but it would grow until it reached the days of the great marriage debate, which impacted even the election of President Barrack Obama, and led to the Massachusetts's Supreme Judicial Court decision to make gay marriage a reality in our state.

The boathouse changed its policy.

They wanted to anyway. The fact someone 'powerful' was telling them to do it gave them a cover to change things and make life inclusive of those who had been excluded because they were 'different.' It was a way to do the right thing and excuse it to those who objected by claiming they were forced into it.

It was not the only thing that Power can led to.

Occasionally it can lead to comedy. On April 28th, at Nick's Comedy Stop's 7th Anniversary Celebration, a place that had spotlighted people like Jay Leno, local politicians were lampooned. Dapper made fun of Barney Frank and me (we were both in the audience at the time) and Marjorie Clapprood, the rather beautiful, charming state representative from Sharon who would spend some time at my house talking to my friends. She was a good legislator, a wonderful person and a comedienne when she put her mind to it. (Once, at the Boston Gay pride event, and wearing a yellow and black outfit with black high heels, Clapprood said, "It takes a lot of effort to outdress a drag queen!") She was to be feared when she had a mind to make a point in a debate and spent time at the mike with an iconoclastic style for which this woman became famous. She eventually ran for Lieutenant Governor and hosted a very well regarded radio show for a long time.

Robert and I liked her a lot.

94 /   Rosaria runs with a rose

Election Efforts: On May 4th we kicked off our 1987 re-election campaign at the Harvard Club of Boston. Senator John Kerry was the big name on the invitation, along with US Representative Barney Frank, State Reps John Businger from Brookline, Kevin Fitzgerald from Mission Hill, Gloria Fox from Roxbury, Saundra Graham from Cambridge, Mark Roosevelt (now a state rep from Beacon Hill/Back Bay), Attorney General Jim Shannon, and many other elected officials, movers and shakers. Each of the over 50 people who donated a total of more than $11,000 for the kickoff were friends with whom I had had a relationship and for each there was a story. It was clear that I would do well in the 1987 election.

Rosaria Salerno was 52 years old. This was actually rather young for politics but she felt she had to do it now before she was too old — at least this is one thing she told me in the alley behind my house where we first discussed her running for city council. I endorsed her, of course, as did virtually all of those who supported me. We were working toward creating a "progressive majority" on the Boston City Council, built on the coalition of minorities, and would eventually get much of the way there during my ten years on the Council.

We had decided that if you can't make a tune work because the piano doesn't have enough keys that work, get some more keys.

The *Boston Globe* described my support of Salerno and another candidate, my first campaign manager, Mike Kane, this way: "David Scondras, who is spearheading the effort, said yesterday that progressives are seeking to elect councilors who will address housing and school issues. Scondras yesterday hired Janice Fine, former staff director for Boston Fair Share, to head his re-election campaign and, in an unusual move, said she would also give technical assistance to Kane and Salerno. He said other groups such as the Massachusetts Tenant Association, Fair Share and the Black Political Task Force would also help the two candidates."

It was an extraordinarily unusual move in a system geared toward personality politics, one for one and all for one, instead of creating teams. On the city level there were no political parties, so coalitions of like minded candidates made sense.

95 /   A Parking Lot

There was an empty parcel of land in the Fenway, which I got agreements to use as a community parking lot to raise money for local non-profits. Robert's sister Sandy helped park the cars, Galen Gilbert helped run the place. It was a good idea and it worked. I mention this because being a politician meant dealing with issues creatively that were multifaceted, taking advantage of opportunities as they arose, thinking out of the box and encouraging volunteers to undertake new ideas rather than repeating what had not worked in the past.

96 /   The Wedding

I never saw Maura so pissed off. She was to be married June 12th and she wanted the council to delay voting on things like the housing bill until after the honeymoon. Maura got pissed off because we decided to hold council meetings and make decisions about things she cared about in spite of the fact she would be on honeymoon at those times. As punishment, she would uninvite us to her wedding.

Rox. TRANSCRIPT 06-17-87

Meanwhile, the fact I sent out seven times as much mail as my colleagues made it into the *Herald*, with Dapper saying, "It's a disgrace, that's what it is. Why should the taxpayers foot the bill for this?" I quickly pointed out that I got the lion's share of the mail, and I responded to all of them and intended to keep doing so. Dapper said, "You should see them at the copying machine on weekends. They go crazy."

Of course no small part of this was because some of my colleagues spent their time in their law practices instead of doing their job as city councilors, and in Dapper's case, he couldn't really write coherently in the first place.

97 / Culture War

Jerry Falwell started using the AIDS crisis to raise money. He used his right wing version of Christianity to get rich off of the pain and suffering of others. He proposed mandatory testing and quarantine of those who "refuse to stop spreading the deadly disease." Basically he said that gays were contaminating the blood supply and were spreading AIDS to everyone and that he had to stop "innocent victims of this perverted and deadly lifestyle. Send me money to stop the homosexuals."

In the meantime across the country gays were under attack — a minister in Maine fired for being a lesbian. Men attacked, arrests in parks and toilets.

During any cultural shift you get positive events (the mayor of San Jose declares Gay Rights Day) and negative events, until eventually the culture adjusts to a new reality. Living through any cultural transition is really difficult, and that uncomfortable period before the new is old continues through today. Gays coming out energized both their friends and their enemies.

The *Boston Herald* continued to misinform in an editorial about Nicaragua, elevating the thugs called the "Contras" to the status of freedom fighters. They were American-paid mercenaries who were trying to get rid of the first elected government of Nicaragua since the overthrow of the dictator Somoza by the Sandinistas. The *Herald* tried to pretend the Sandinistas were a Commie group that hijacked a popular uprising against the dictator. In fact they were the popular uprising against the dictator. They held the first free elections with international monitors from around the world agreeing the elections were open and fair. The *Herald* called for an "election" in Nicaragua to throw out the ruling clique of Sandinistas, ignored the fact there was already an election, and wanted the government to turn over all the state-owned enterprises like electricity etc. to private ownership. In other words, the right wing once again was pushing for private gain trumping public access to the necessities of life.

The media, it is clear, needs some mechanism to force it to tell the truth about what happens in the world. A democracy depends upon accurate information and much of the paid media is indoctrination and propaganda instead of news. Robert's idea is to legally distinguish individuals and companies from each other so that the First Amendment applies to individuals but corporations would be held to a standard of truth with monetary damages for sloppiness or misrepresentation.

Meanwhile my colleagues (namely Dapper) complained I was wired, implying that I was involved in some legal matter. In fact I was wearing a microphone because a local TV crew was filming me for a segment on television series called "Chronicle," a very popular show on WCVB, the ABC affiliate. In articles about the matter, the *Herald* took pains to swipe at Brian McLaughlin (my City Council colleague from Allston-Brighton) who had given back a bribe that he had wrongly accepted from a landlord. It was a stupid mistake on his part but the media enjoyed tormenting him.

99 /   Your Gloves Don't Match Your Shoes

"Fashion is an imposition, a reign on freedom."
– Golda Meir

I went to Washington again. It all started with President Ronald Reagan calling for mandatory AIDS testing. This idea continued the moronic religion-inspired strategy for solving problems followed by right-wingers (Robert calls them the neo-puritans) for pretty much everything: identify whom to blame and punish them. The right wing substitutes revenge for reason.

Vice President Bush supported the Reagan ideas. Then again so did Dapper, which pretty much tells you all you need to know about Reagan.

Governor Michael Dukakis made it clear that Reagan who, for years, had ignored the issue, now wanted to test everything that moves and that Massachusetts would not follow his advice. It turns out that AIDS tests don't tell you fast enough that you have HIV (it takes a while for antibodies to form which is what the assay tested for in those days) and most folks pass on the virus before knowing that they have it. Reagan wanted prisoners, immigrants, hospital patients, and marriage license applicants to be tested. But that list didn't target the high-risk groups that make up most of the source of the virus. Prisoners don't usually have sex with lots of folks not also in prison. Hospital patients, if they have HIV, are past the stage AIDS is very infectious. Very few people who are about to get married are infected with HIV — they were, after all, most likely in 1987 to have been heterosexual. It is not clear how the testing would do very much except create a list that would be turned over to the feds for God knows what reason but it couldn't be a good one.

Demonstrations began across the country to stop this nonsense.

So Robert and I went off to Washington again. And I was among 325 elected officials who got arrested demonstrating at the White House against Reagan's craziness about AIDS.

The police put plastic ties on my wrists behind my back (they hurt) and hundreds of us started to chant "Your gloves don't match your shoes" because the police were given yellow rubber gloves which would protect them from nothing, but from a gay point of view were a fashion *faux pas* given the colors of the uniforms of the police. I was taken to a jail in which my old friend Peter Medoff led a group singing songs, got lots of signatures from friends on my papers about the protest.

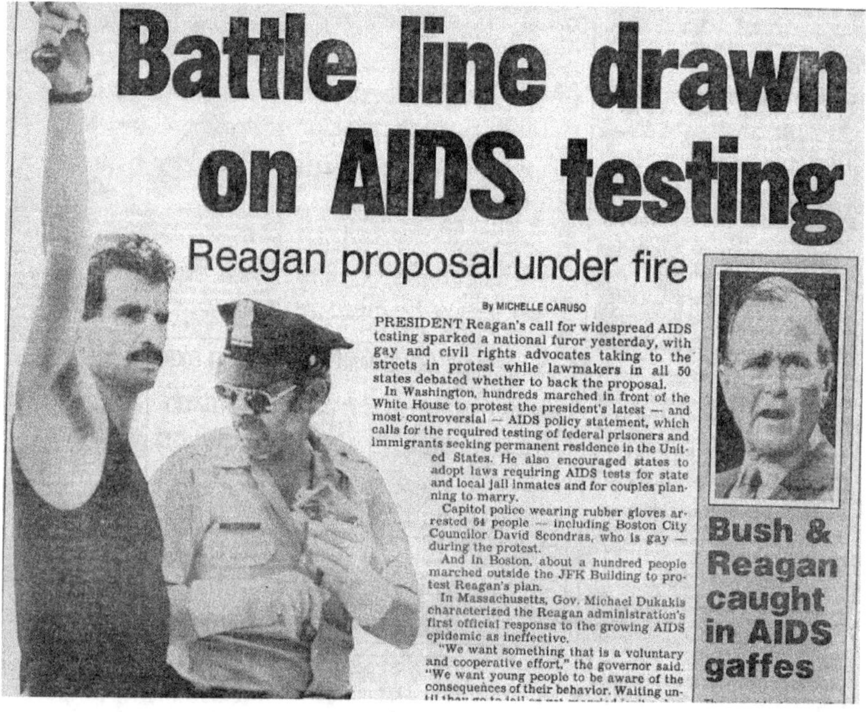

Battle line drawn on AIDS testing

Reagan proposal under fire

By MICHELLE CARUSO

PRESIDENT Reagan's call for widespread AIDS testing sparked a national furor yesterday, with gay and civil rights advocates taking to the streets in protest while lawmakers in all 50 states debated whether to back the proposal.

In Washington, hundreds marched in front of the White House to protest the president's latest — and most controversial — AIDS policy statement, which calls for the required testing of federal prisoners and immigrants seeking permanent residence in the United States. He also encouraged states to adopt laws requiring AIDS tests for state and local jail inmates and for couples planning to marry.

Capitol police wearing rubber gloves arrested 64 people — including Boston City Councilor David Scondras, who is gay — during the protest.

And in Boston, about a hundred people marched outside the JFK Building to protest Reagan's plan.

In Massachusetts, Gov. Michael Dukakis characterized the Reagan administration's first official response to the growing AIDS epidemic as ineffective.

"We want something that is a voluntary and cooperative effort," the governor said. "We want young people to be aware of the consequences of their behavior. Waiting un-

Bush & Reagan caught in AIDS gaffes

Before getting arrested we had called for a "Medical Manhattan Project" on AIDS along with policies barring discriminations against those with HIV, and intensified research, treatment and education. We marched to the White House from a church carrying a black bannered wreath with "20,000" written on it, the number of those who had already died of AIDS, and it was the first time I remember the key phrase of AIDS activists was uttered that "Silence equals Death."

The police dragged me up took me off and into the crowd in the jail who were waiting to be bailed out. Needless to say the *Herald* lost no time publishing pictures of me being arrested saying I had been jailed.

When I got back from Washington, there were cameras and reporters waiting. I said, "We felt we had to send a message to the president that the AIDS crisis affects all of us and his lack of leadership was condemning our children to death. We felt getting arrested in front of the White House was a way to send a message across the country," which it certainly did.

AIDS would become an increasingly important political issue for the next twenty years. I was exasperated with politicians — who did not know anyone who was sick and who knew nothing about medicine — opening their mouths and trashing my friends, proposing ideas that would make things worse and ignoring things that would help.

Needless to say, every article made sure to remind everyone I was gay. The media was doing its part making sure people learned AIDS was a gay disease. In fact in most of the world outside of the United States and Europe, where most people with HIV live, over 95% of those infected were heterosexual. Even in the USA the fastest growing group with HIV in 1987 were black heterosexual women. Statistically, however, in the USA the disease was pretty much restricted to drug addicts, their partners, and gay men. But bashing queers has been long a sport of the right wing. Both Reagan and Bush made HIV a "gay disease" — which would hamper efforts to test for it, treat it, and misled people into assuming that if they were straight they were safe.

When we were in the jail cell we carried around the green sheet on which were our instructions. I attached to it the Metro Police Department's invoice for the $50 it cost me to get out of jail. They of course had my address wrong. In addition, on the sheet were signatures because we used our time between singing protest songs to get each other's names. David Mixner signed mine. He would later be a fundraiser and major figure advising President Clinton about the gay community. Sean Strub signed it, and had started the magazine called 'POZ.' Larry Kramer signed my green sheet. Tim Wofford, whose brother would become a U.S Senator signed it. It is a wonderful souvenir.

100 / The Day After

"Without a plan, there's no attack. Without attack, no victory."
– Curtis Armstrong

The day after getting home from the Washington demonstrations, I spoke out and voted "yea" on a weak housing bill written by Maura Hennigan; it was better than nothing and certainly the best I could get through the Council at that point. I had even driven around with Dapper to show him all the suffering the conversions were inflicting — the tenants who could not both eat and pay rent, older renters becoming homeless. But there simply were not enough people of compassion on the City Council. Even Dapper, who was moved by what he saw, refused to vote yes to my version of a bill that would protect tenants from condo conversion evictions. But Dapper would voted for Maura's version.

Maura's version of the housing bill was so bad that the mayor threatened to veto it. Her version would let tenants stay in their apartments for 60 days instead of 45 days after being told their apartment would become a condo.

I wanted a condo ban. So did Ray Flynn. But I could not get the votes. So I decided to help get more people elected. The only way to win the housing law I felt we needed was to change the City Council.

So I worked to get my good friend and one of my first campaign managers, Mike Kane, elected to the council since a citywide seat had become open. As a graceful way to exit the council Joe Tierney had decided to run for mayor. We needed a liberal majority on the body to get things passed that would help the working people of the city and Michael was bright, energetic and very progressive.

The effort led to a citywide alliance to do a makeover on the City Council.

101 /   Letter from LaFontaine

Letters are among the most significant memorial a person can leave behind them.
– Johann Wolfgang von Goethe

I got a letter from David LaFontaine who was very involved in the Boston Gay and Lesbian Political Alliance who would later play a big role in getting Republican William Weld elected governor, and he was right about doing that.

It was about how important Robert and I were to the Alliance, the group of local politicized gay people who were fighting for gay rights, in the ongoing internal struggle with internalized homophobia and assimilation within the gay community. One sentence was intriguing:

"David's mother has been extremely helpful in collecting letters for the gay rights bill and it turns out she never called Sheehy and never made any kind of a threat, so he (David) must be having some kind of delusion."

Uh, oh. I know my mom.

Representative Sheehy was from our hometown, and I know her well enough to say that if she was asking him to vote for the bill it could easily have sounded like a threat. My mother does not take kindly to fools, wimps or weasels. I recall during the efforts to get the assault weapons ban through the statehouse sending Gary to Lowell to get her directly from her hairdresser and madly driving her into Boston to try to convince her senator to change his vote. My father said he could hear her up and down the corridor while she was inside the inner chamber of a senator's office yelling something about knowing where he lived and who he spent time with in Lowell. I also know that at the time the senator was quoted as saying on the floor of the senate that he was voting in favor of this bill to accommodate Mrs. Scondras.

You really do not want to get on my mom's shit list.

Anyway it was both an interesting and much appreciated letter.

In May Barney Frank publicly acknowledged he was gay. He had been in Congress for four terms. Barney was forced out because Robert E. Bauman, a former congressman, wrote a book in which Frank was specifically identified as a gay member of congress. (Bob Bauman had been outed by the Carter Administration for being so rabidly anti-gay.) Barney got away with it by coming out on a Saturday, and being very upbeat. And he had become quite handsome. He had lost weight, dieted and worked out, got a tummy tuck, contacts. His being out was a high point for me, because I was the point-person for a great many gay people's hopes and concerns and more openly gay elected officials meant more people to share that responsibility. Once again, as happened over and over, the issues raised were about Barney being with a young companion. It was true, but young meant 27 years old, and he was a friend, not a lover. Barney felt he couldn't avoid the gay issue any longer.

In the gay community, Barney coming out was a cause for dancing. The day after the news broke, he got a standing ovation at an AIDS walkathon in Boston.

He also quickly learned how being gay in those days created media obsession. "Playboy called me and asked for an interview," he told the *Herald*. "I said no. But they assured me, 'We'll discuss other things, the issues you are interested in.' So I said to them, 'Then why didn't you call me a month ago?' "

All of us have to learn to use what we have to our best advantage and to the best advantage of those we love. Being gay gave Barney and me more media attention, which we could frame in ways that moved our agendas forward even though most of those agendas were not gay related. I saw the new Barney at the gym under Club Café. He was definitely hot.

103 /   1987: The Quilt and More

Cleve Jones was not full of himself. He was kind and sweet and I liked him. He decided to make a gigantic quilt made up of the names of some 10,000 men and women who had died of AIDS and put it on the Capitol Mall in Washington DC as part of the October 1987 national March on Washington for Lesbian and Gay Rights.

People asked if our office could be March headquarters for the New England region and Gary Dotterman became the coordinator.

People were being asked to contribute a small piece of quilt: a rectangular piece of cloth with a memory woven into it, a memento of someone you loved and who died of AIDS.

The last sentence of Gary's call to action about this part of the March agenda was a note:

"Gary Dotterman's panel in memory of John Cyrus may be photographed to accompany stories on the Names Project (the project to create this giant quilt). Please contact Gary at 725-4225 during regular business hours."

I did not know that Gary's lover had died of AIDS. Gary was not bitter. He was quiet about it.

I felt bad, because Gary was a very big guy with a big heart, loyal, and a good brain and I thought that he should have someone to love him. He didn't.

I guess I thought that he was too out of shape to find some cutie who would love him, and I would find out that this idea of "good looking" was a lot more subjective than I had realized. Gary would find happiness in the arms of an incredible, hot, Brazilian chubby chaser who has stayed with him to this day, but I wouldn't have guessed it at the time.

The Parade

This year 30,000 gays showed up in Boston for the Gay Pride march. I got the crowd chanting, "What do we want?" "Gay rights!" "When do we want them?" "*NOW!*" Not original but effective.

I urged support for the March on Washington. In the *Globe* I said, "We're going to Washington to tell Reagan to tear down his Berlin Wall of Bigotry." I told the *Globe* that Dukakis would make a good president but that I didn't understand why he refused to budge on the foster care issue. He was telling gays who were critical to the Democratic Party that they were defective and that this would undermine efforts to rally them to the ticket.

I said, "We were going to Washington because we are offended and insulted as a community that this country spends more on advertising soap than it does teaching safer sex."

Meanwhile Dapper and I kept up a war of words about AIDS. We got so heated that by June, that pinnacle of media interest was reached — the cartoons.

As chair of the city's Budget Committee, on June 10th I issued an Interim Report on revenue to the city. It had to be one of the most important and careful reports I ever did. I was determined to blend social activism, caring for the poor and a balanced budget. But sex was a lot more interesting and got a lot more press.

Meanwhile the Council chickened out on my effort to create a condo ban. I could only manage to get a weak protection bill through because Mike McCormack, our 7th vote, sided with the big landlord Jerry Rappaport. The new law wouldn't really stop the rapid rate at which rental housing was being sold as condos to speculators across the city. The *Globe* editorialized against condos but Mike McCormack looked to the future and cast his lot with the gentry. But he also got a cartoon out of it.

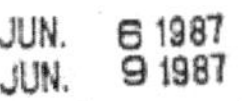

Tearing Up Streets

Carmen Figueroa was a Latino man on Mission Hill who owned a small store called "Casa Chris" on Huntington Avenue, which is also known as Route 9.

The city paid for this major artery to get upgraded, and while it was going on, the store lost electricity; the gas main that went to the store was broken; you couldn't get into or out of the store for weeks; Carmen couldn't get supplies; and customers couldn't get in.

After 13 years of doing business as a neighborhood store, a family business, Figueroa had to close the store. He was $10,000 in debt, unemployed and his family was in a crisis. He said to the *Boston Herald*: "I don't want to go on welfare or be called lazy. I worked seven days a week for my four kids including two who are in college. There is pain in my heart because I feel embarrassed explaining to everybody why I can't pay my bills."

The city as usual told folks what they wanted to hear, but did nothing. Carmen was told to sue the city. Well, Carmen couldn't afford a lawyer and that's the way it is in the land of the free. Expensive.

I put a law in front of the City Council which would require all contractors who rip up streets to pay for damages to stores and businesses, by putting aside cash or a bond to pay for estimated damages to stores before they could get any city license to do work.

Councilor Menino (later mayor) tabled the ordinance indefinitely. Tommy, not a bad person, had an aversion to anything that was out of the ordinary, that pissed off people with big money like contractors.

104 /   Smear Campaign of 1987

"The problem with smear campaigns is that too often they work."
– Mark Shields

On September 19th, 1987, a fuss began that was to frame an issue that kept annoying me my whole life: sex between older and younger people. It seemed everyone was concerned about it except me, intergenerational couples, James Bond, and all of India.

I got wind of it from an article in the *Boston Herald*. Dapper was quoted saying, "I want those two birds removed from the city payroll. I don't want them (sic) people around here. They support civil liberties and sexual freedom for homosexuals who want to have sex with teenagers."

Dapper put in an order to fire two of my staff, Gary Dotterman and French Wall. Dapper was asked by the *Herald* reporter about me and said, "I don't speak with him. I don't see eye to eye with him on anything. As a result I try to steer clear of him. But I'm not going to tolerate this."

The *Herald* said that Gary and French were members of a group that supported the rights of homosexuals to have sex with teens. Actually, this committee, which was **not** about gays having sex with teens, also had people from the Mayor's office on it, as well as many other well known folks all of which the *Herald* ignored. The *Herald*, to build up the perception that even I thought something was wrong with the committee, said that I had ordered Gary and French to resign from the group. (I most definitely had not.)

I hadn't had time to check out what the hell was going on when the *Herald* started calling me demanding to know what I was going to do about it. I had no idea what they were talking about and I got pretty angry with French and Gary for blindsiding me in the middle of an election. Turns out they had joined the group months earlier and everyone ignored it for months — so they were caught by surprise too. The preliminary election was in a few days.

Bob Parks, a mover and shaker on Mission Hill, laughed when I saw him at Mission Park, shook his head smiling, saying, "Grasshoppers?"

He was reacting to me mouthing off to the press when they asked about Gary and French — I had said that I didn't care if they joined a group advocating fornication with grasshoppers; it was their business. I had recently looked out of my office through the window across the hall and noticed the grasshopper weather vane on the top of Faneuil Hall – it must have still been in my mind when they phoned me – anyway, the grasshopper line was the thing most people remembered about the whole affair when all is said and done. It was quoted rather widely in the press and Robert occasionally uses the quote to this day.

Anyway, from documents I got from the gay news magazine called *The Guide*, I learned in retrospect how crazy, fast and furious the events unfolded and how off guard I was.

First, Gary and French were members of a group called the Committee for Civil Liberties and Sexual Freedom (CCLSF). There were 22 members of the committee listed on their letterhead, and the Committee had a statement of purpose, to wit:

> *"To aid both defendants and alleged 'victims' in legal cases*
> *which allege nonviolent, non-exploitative sexual activity*
> *between gay men or lesbians and teenagers…. The committee is*
> *necessary because of the current hysteria about adolescent*
> *sexuality and rampant homophobia, especially among police*
> *and prosecutors."*

The CCLSF group noted that the conviction rate for men who violently rape women is less that 50% at that time in 1987, the rate for men accused of sex with boys is more than 80%. They infer that this stems from both homophobia and the refusal on the part of legislators to equate violent rape of young children with non-violent, consenting sexual activity with teenagers. The penalty for these very different activities is the same under Massachusetts law, life in prison. The group stated that the gay community needed to protect itself especially given the biases involved.

My first response was to stand by my staff: I said that my staff has a right to participate in any committees they choose. I had a serious problem with the idea that freedom of speech and association could be curtailed by anyone for any reason, and I reacted on principle.

The Boston Herald

The Boston Herald, Saturday, September 19, 1987

'Dapper': Fire 'gay-flap' aides

BOSTON City Councilor Albert L. "Dapper" O'Neil wants to fire two aides to a rival councilor who have been members of a group supporting the rights of homosexuals to have sex with teens.

The conservative O'Neil yesterday said he will file a proposal to "terminate" two aides to Councilor David Scondras, a liberal who is the council's first openly gay member.

"I want those two birds removed from the city payroll," O'Neil said. "I don't want them people around here. They support civil liberties and sexual freedom for homosexuals who want to have sex with teenagers."

O'Neil said he will file his proposed order on Monday. The order calls for a public hearing on the termination of the two aides.

O'Neil said his proposal has nothing to do with his long-running feud with Scondras.

"I don't speak with him," O'Neil said. "I don't see eye-to-eye with him on anything. As a result, I try to steer clear of him. But I'm not going to tolerate this."

Scondras two days ago ordered aides J. French Wall and Gary Dotterman to resign from the group, known as the Committee for Civil Liberties and Sexual Freedom.

Scondras said he has taken "appropriate discipline" against the two aides and will keep them on his staff.

Scondras called O'Neil's proposal "a last-ditch smear campaign."

"It's no secret that Councilor O'Neil has been against everything I do with regards to both housing and human rights," Scondras said. "He'll use whatever he can to get back at me."

Bruce Bolling, the President of the council, came to me and said I needed to fire my staff, for my political health. I told him I really couldn't do that, that it really wasn't right.

Over the next few days I learned a lot more about the issues surrounding the chaos. A friend of Gary's named Donald Dobson, a bank president and long time civil rights and human rights activist, was arrested in February of 1987 and charged with oral sex and fondling of two Puerto Rican boys aged 14 and 15. With permission of their families, the boys had lived with Dobson since December and Dobson had placed them in school immediately and got them English tutors. Dobson pleaded innocent.

The two Puerto Rican "victims" were held in locked facilities against their will for six months. At one juvenile detention hearing the court-appointed lawyer said, "Going to the can might be good for the boy." When one boy cried out that his own lawyer was sending him to jail and that he wanted another lawyer, he was placed in leg irons and manacled.

The CCLSF felt the boys' rights were being violated and tried to get a lawyer for the boys and get an investigation of their treatment. The mother of one of the boys said that she wanted him to be free and to get a new lawyer. She wanted the boy to return to Puerto Rico. Talking directly with the boy who was in a large locked juvenile facility in Boston, the boy stated his desire for freedom, and his belief that he was being punished though had done nothing wrong.

When the CCLSF contacted US Assistant Attorney Via to tell her of the boys' requests for independent attorneys, she refused to help and claimed that the boys might have been wrongly treated but faulted the Massachusetts Department of Social Services (who actually wanted the boys freed and, if they desired, returned to Puerto Rico).

All of this originated with a tip the *Herald* got that I was involved in a "gay sex defense group" advocating sex with children. This led to the articles in the *Herald* about me advocating sex with children (I don't advocate sex with children; I do advocate defense of gay sex).

I told Gary and French that I was pissed off at them not telling me about all this, that I would appreciate their leaving the committee until the dust settled and I could figure out what to do, that I would never fire them, and that they did not have to resign from the CCLSF as a condition of employment with me. The issue for me had become more being left out of the loop and not able to define my own causes more than anything else, and being as a result unprepared for the onslaught of lies, innuendos, accusations etc.

To deal with the effort being made to fire Gary and French, I started studying relevant constitutional law and found an important precedent: "a public employee's statements of public concern which are found to be false are constitutionally protected" (Pickering v. Board of Education, 391 US 563, 568 [1968]) and many other decisions to the effect, as I suspected, you can't fire someone because of what they say or groups that they belong to.

It was interesting how wrong the media got most of the things happening. For example, Peggy Hernandez of the *Globe* had an article on September 19th saying that Gary had resigned from my office but French didn't show up to work implying that he had resigned. She got it right when she said I was angry that the men did not notify me of their membership.

The Alliance, the political arm of the gay community, got involved. On Saturday, Sept 19th they issued the following press release:

The Alliance denounces the recent articles in the Boston Herald.
The Alliance views the Herald's *coverage of the issue as a
transparent smear campaign against Scondras, CCLSF and the
lesbian and gay community. Avoiding the critical issue of the
CCLSF's constitutional right to exist, the* Herald *has viciously
injected the issue of sex between adults and minors into the
public debate. Sex with minors has been historically used to
justify the persecution of our community.*

The CCLSF has been in existence for months and yet the Herald
*has chosen to publicize it days before Scondras faces an election
in which a homophobic bigot opposes him. The timing suggests
that the* Herald *articles are a thinly disguised attempt to
discredit Scondras by inducing public hysteria.*

*We urge councilor Scondras to reject the unsound and
unconstitutional advice offered in the* Herald *editorial*

The *Herald* actually got it more on the mark on the 18th saying I had asked my staff to quit the CCLSF but even then they missed the point that it was not an order, as they suggested, but a request, which I made sure was understood by my staff not to be an order.

That Friday night September 18th, I had a meeting at my house, which was emotional and full of pain. Robert had put it together, mostly of campaign staff, but he felt it didn't turn out too well. People were confused, upset, and did not give us a clear direction to move towards.

Galen Gilbert (my treasurer) came over from two doors down on Edgerly Road, and said, "You don't support sex with children, right?" I said that I did not, but I did think that two issues had not been dealt with yet, the age of consent and the right way to manage issues around sexuality. I thought that criminal law was not the right context in which to resolve conflicts about sex. But I had not yet developed a clear philosophy on it.

I did find out that the two boys involved were pressured by prosecutors into saying they had sex with Dobson and that they had attempted to retract their earlier statements, which they claimed were made to avoid being forced to go back to Puerto Rico (as one of the boys did not want to return to Puerto Rico).

It became apparent that the boys were being punished with jail for non-cooperation, and the key to their freedom would be given only if they gave testimony sought by the prosecution. This troubled me deeply — it is the kind of behavior that police states engage in.

It was quite ironic that virtually no one in the media was concerned about the way the boys were being treated except the CCLSF!

On September 30th, Dapper put in a Council Order to fire Gary and French. Only Yancey and me stood up and cast a no vote against firing French and Gary. I gave an emotional 10-minute speech, according to the *Boston Globe* saying that French and Gary were entitled under our constitution to belong to the Committee for Civil Liberties and Sexual Freedom. "I find it offensive, frankly, that the press and certain individuals have chosen to frame a very complex issue as though it is over support for a 'child molester.' "

Immediately after the vote, French hugged me quickly and then left the Council Chambers. He never came back and I missed him over the years. He is a brave, clear, committed, caring, smart man.

This event was traumatic, revealing, and helped show the way personal lives interacted with the media, politics, sociology and ethics to create that soap opera we call 'public lives.'

The Boston Herald. Friday. September 18, 1987

Scondras orders aides to quit gay-sex defense group

SCONDRAS

By JOE BATTENFELD

CITY COUNCILOR David Scondras, in a reversal of a previous position, has ordered two aides to resign from a group supporting the rights of homosexuals who have sex with teens.

Scondras announced the move just two days after expressing support for aides J. French Wall and Gary Dotterman, who belong to the Committee for Civil Liberties and Sexual Freedom.

"I have since instructed them to resign their positions on this committee." Scondras said in a statement yesterday. "I have reprimanded them for joining it without my knowledge."

The committee was formed two months ago to support gays and lesbians accused of having illegal sex with minors.

The group claims accused child molester Donald Dobson has been railroaded by authorities for allegedly luring two Puerto Rican teen-agers to his home and having sex with them.

Sources in the gay community say gay leaders have been reluctant to support the committee's goals. Under state law, sex with children under 18 is statutory rape.

Just two days ago, Scondras, who is running for re-election, said: "I agree with what they (his aides) are working on."

But in his statement yesterday, Scondras said, "I am opposed to exploitative relationships of any kind, including those between adults and minors."

Lessons from the Dobson Affair

This traumatic event in my life actually contained a few useful lessons to begin with, about the media. Note that the media, having lost out on sex being inherently evil (not as much market share in sex-bashing) was losing its punch. So was being gay. But farsighted Howie Carr, to this day the moral equivalent of a character out of the horror movie 'Halloween' or some similar clichéd but effective piece of garbage, saw to it that I would be constantly framed as a child molester. That had punch!

It was astonishing this could be accomplished given my lack of interest in sex with kids, my lack of familiarity with same, and the absence of even a single person in my entire seven decades of life that has ever said I tried to get sex from them when they were under-aged.

In any event, the media said I flip-flopped, that I fired my staff, that I didn't fire my staff, that I ordered my staff to resign from the committee (I didn't), that I had a dilemma (true, caused entirely by the media), that I was supportive of the 'most heinous kind of conduct a society is faced with,' etc.

There were indeed issues being raised of some importance but none of them got any public discussion. Among them were:

- Why were the young people involved put in jail and why didn't they get to choose their own lawyer?

- Why did the prosecutors try to exchange damaging false testimony for freedom, which the young folks had a constitutional right to, and no one at all on the state level investigate these claims coming from, among others, the parents of the young people?

- Why is there no distinction made between rape and having consensual sex with young people older than the average age at which people historically got married?

- What data exists that supports the notion that consensual sex initiated by teenagers and others of any age causes any harm whatsoever to the teenager?

But there was no context in which to raise these issues or look into the questions, because the country, the society was then and is now, gripped by hysteria about sex with children. And I doubt in practical terms older folks having sex with teenagers will be a very common event in the culture with or without rules — teenagers prefer younger people in general and oldsters get tired of teens rather quickly (they have too much energy and too little experiences to be of long lasting interest) so the culture's panic attacks about sex and teens are as insane as the detention camps for the Japanese, the McCarthy hysteria, and the many other witch hunts the USA has been prone to.

What is particularly disturbing however about this continuation of gay bashing, is the new dress it walks in. While the fictional James Bond or the real Harrison Ford have much younger heterosexual mates with or without marriage involved, gay guys get arrested for child molestation with or without any actual children involved and by defining age of consent over puberty, long after the same young people could get married to the so called 'molester.' That is, if gays could get married at all.

More hypocritical crap from the same source that brought us Jerry Falwell and Anita Bryant.

Well, I learned when you are labeled into a cultural myth it is next to impossible to get free from it. Howie Carr has spent the past 25 years regular as clockwork figuring out new ways to abuse truth and print lies about me. (Since much scientific evidence shows homophobic behavior correlates with homoerotic attraction, should I be flattered/worried that Howie Carr has a crush on me?)

My only comfort lies in knowing that, like Dapper and Kelly, he will eventually die. I need to live long enough to dance on their graves.

36 The Boston Herald, Thursday, September 17, 1987

Scondras' dilemma

WHAT consenting adults do behind their bedroom doors is one thing. What happens when an adult attempts to exploit a child is quite another. Under the best of circumstances we're talking here about statutory rape, a crime as defined by state law. Under the worst of circumstances we're talking about the most heinous kind of conduct a society is faced with.

There are two men currently working in the office of City Councilor David Scondras who are involved actively in the support of the efforts of the Committee for Civil Liberties and Sexual Freedom. That two-month-old group is dedicated to supporting gay men and women prosecuted for having sex with minors.

The group's current efforts are devoted to helping former bank president Donald Dobson, who is charged with luring two boys to his home and sexually assaulting them. The charge, if proven, would put Dobson among the lowest form of human life. And yet the CCLSF maintains Dobson is being railroaded. That gives you some idea of where this group is coming from.

The CCLSF and other fringe groups that advocate or support the sexual exploitation of children are an embarrassment to responsible gay men and women. Such groups and the people who belong to them ought to be an embarrassment and a cause for indignation on the part of Councilor Scondras as well.

An elected city official ought to have the moral sensitivity to know that there is no place on a public payroll for anyone who would support or protect those accused of abusing children in this manner. If Scondras can't see that, perhaps the voters ought to take another look at his candidacy.

Boston Herald

PATRICK J. PURCELL, Publisher

KENNETH A. CHANDLER, Editor

ALAN S. EISNER,
Managing Editor

PHILIP BUNTON,
Sunday Editor

RACHELLE COHEN,
Editorial Page Editor

Official blasts new gay-sex defense group

By JOE BATTENFELD

A STATE social service official yesterday blasted a newly formed group dedicated to helping gays accused of having sex with teen-agers, calling their goals "crazy."

Department of Social Services spokesman Joseph Landolfi said the group, which includes two members of City Councilor David Scondras' staff, is promoting illegal activity.

"Sex with a child is a crime," said Landolfi. "We're obviously opposed to that — it's crazy." Group members say the Committee for Civil Liberties and Sexual Freedom was formed to prevent unfair prosecution of gay men and lesbians who have sex with adolescents.

Under Massachusetts law, sex with a person under 18 years old is considered statutory rape.

According to the committee, gay men and lesbians who have sex with teen-agers "face an increasing risk" from federal authorities.

A number of gay leaders have been reluctant to support the committee's goals, according to sources in the gay community.

Scondras is not part of the committee, but said he supports the right of the group to exist.

The group has focused on the case of former bank president Donald Dobson, accused of luring two Puerto Rican boys to his home and engaging in sex with them.

Group members say Dobson was railroaded and the victims have been held against their will by the U.S. Attorney's office.

Landolfi, however, said the boys are in custody of the DSS at foster homes.

"They're in our legal custody and receiving the treatment they obviously need," he said.

The staff members in Scondras' office, J. French Wall and Gary Dotterman, said their work with the committee is separate from their City Hall jobs. Wall defended the group, saying consentual sex between adults and teen-agers "is not that harmful."

The Herald's view: Page 36

105 /   Carpe Diem: AIDS

For gay people, life was already painful before AIDS — those who would not let us eat at the table of life were demanding they get to tell us the proper ways to eat the scraps they allowed us to have. The table was off limits and the alley was painted as beneath the dignity of man to eat in. A United States Senator from Idaho, Larry Craig, was arrested for foot tapping in an airport bathroom. The young Barney Frank was too fat to be appealing to the crowd that defined good looks, was accepted as a bachelor with no love life but crucified for an affair with a male prostitute. Congressman Gerry Studds was censured for an affair with a 17-year-old *aide-de-camp*. Men across the country were arrested for gay sex in the quiet of the woods, at rest stops, in bathrooms, even in their own bedrooms. Banished from home and bedroom, dates and talking to peers about our lives, gays were told their youth should be spent in the closet and their aging years in silent contemplation of their unrealized sins.

We already lost our youth to the need to hide, to be invisible. We lost the times we could have discovered love, the quiet connections with romantic music, never learned the nuances of dating, never had conversations with young friends about our awakenings.

We lost love.

We lost fun.

And instead we got fear and fists.

And then AIDS.

AIDS killed the majority of Robert's and my friends. In Robert's weekly call to his grandparents, they would spend most of the conversation talking about the friends and funerals they had attended – a 30-year-old comparing notes about dead friends with 80-year-olds.

It was a nightmare. It was a killing spree that turned the some of the most intelligent wonderful, amazing, compassionate people we knew and cared about into thin, skeletal tired versions of themselves full of a variety of excruciating pains and then drained them of life like a vampire sucking out their blood. We lost Fred Mandel, the man I picked to run the Human Rights commission to it.

Peter Medoff, our loudest activist friend, died of it.

Stephen Gendin, our rabble-rouser who I met at Brown University, had it. His sleeping face would be the front cover of POZ magazine after his death on July 19, 2000.

Our doctor friends tried everything to save our friends and failed. Our friend, Dr. Ken Mayer said, shaking his head in an emotional moment, "We should have been able to save Fred Mandel." I know that the docs did everything they could.

It seemed so unfair to have society rob us of our youth and then nature of our future.

Jerry Falwell's team called it divine punishment, and we had to be especially strong not to be seduced by our need for approval to succumb to this rhetoric, to become like Heracles and let the voices of the sirens lead us to a shipwreck of our self-worth, already fragile.

I remember being with Barney Frank at a small apartment in the South End of Boston. He was uncharacteristically quiet, saying to me, "He doesn't look good," as one of our hosts paced the room, his hand rubbing back and forth on his hair, a repetitive motion I had only previously seen at Mass Mental Health Center. It was clear that there was pain around.

The purplish spots of Kaposi's sarcoma were on many faces and bodies or camouflaged as best as possible.

I understood how my father suffered when his two brothers were killed, stationed in Hawaii, unable to help them as they died, buried in graves in Lowell, one of them with the name one of them shared with me. My mother never knew that sometimes I would go to visit my high school math teacher Victor Luz who lived where the Luz monument company is (his family made the monuments for the cemetery) and I would go and look at the white simple stone with my name carved in it, David Scondras.

I wondered if I would be next.

Steve Colarusso, who lived on the ground floor of our four-unit row house, got HIV. He was a quiet, handsome, smart, sweet man. I watched him get thinner and sicker and die over the next five years.

Our sweet angelic friend Charles died. I do not think he reached thirty years old. He was perhaps the sweetest, most innocent man Robert and I had ever met, and one of Robert's closest friends. His lover gave Charles AIDS. Charles got sicker and sicker with the virus. We loved Charles. Robert spent years listening to his pain, holding his hands, laughing with him and caring for him, and when the time came, told him when he was dying, tubes in his arms, that it was alright to let go, to die. He needed the permission. Charles sighed and let go.

It was not the only time we helped our friends die.

So although we were in our thirties and forties, we were old, going to funerals every week. Carrying our grief. Crying in silence and drinking a lot. There was really no point talking much about it, because once begun the words would never stop.

I felt like my world was slowly being exterminated.

Of gays.

Later I would learn that Africans were harder hit, and the future for me would be on continents I had never known in causes I had not imagined.

AIDS began to redefine the gay movement in fundamental ways.

Just as this disease was the beginning to redefine gay power and life, we learned love is a lot about taking care of each other and not much about the chemical bonding of intensities that for a moment flower in youth between strangers and is endlessly sung about. We learned to live with each other taking care of each other as families do, supporting each of our right to do what we must to be happy, and not define our relationships in terms of sexual fidelities or the moments of heady fun that happen from time to time. We learned that tops and bottoms have different needs, that life and love are far more complex than they are portrayed in the media, that the cultural norms are not actually obeyed by the vast majority of people and that true love is really about supporting each other's search for happiness.

AIDS redefined the gay movement, the National Institutes of Health (NIH), immunology, in fact even the way research was conducted. It introduced new concepts like safer sex, evolved into a fight about giving sex education to children supported even by Ronald Reagan's Surgeon General, C. Everett Koop.

It became part of our lives. And it brought together the gay community in ways not foreseen. Lesbians, who did not get HIV for all practical purposes, took on the roles of leadership and began to fight for all of us as the quiet killer silenced the voices of male gay activists one by one. And gay men started taking breast cancer, that so afflicted women, more seriously.

Larry Kramer began ACT UP and the gay community itself got noisier and angrier as its leaders died, increasingly leaving only those who identified with assimilation as the tactic for survival into the next century. Sexual liberation would die off as well.

To this day I carry grief in my body like a bag of rocks that sometimes makes me cry. And, although it was incredibly difficult for both of us, I realize that Robert and I grew beyond the confines of the straitjackets, which defined what we were supposed to feel and think into a world more real, but also more unexplored than the one most of us attempt to live within.

Robert and I have been family to each other for 38 years. The epidemic shaped our lives for the remainder of the century. Its power only began to wane on an extraordinary day in Vancouver in 1996 when David Ho announced to a crowd of thousands of doctors and people with AIDS that a way to stop the virus from killing had been discovered.

Robert and I were there. But by then, most of our friends weren't.

"Do you ever get the feeling that the only reason we have elections
is to find out if the polls were right?"
– Robert Orben

Larry DiCara, a short thin man with dark hair and a compelling stare who had been a Boston City Councilor when he was in his twenties, offered me time to debate my opponents on his political cable television talk show. I liked Larry. I was always impressed that when he ran for mayor he spoke in the language appropriate to each neighborhood — he spoke that many languages fluently. It amazed me. He was a lawyer, a person who helped negotiate conflicts, a smart and caring man.

I often went on his show, got myself powdered by the fix-your-face person, and took a seat talking for what seemed like ten seconds even though it was a half hour. Larry used his show to continue to be a force in the political life of the city. I usually took him up on coming on his show because in general I never turned down an opportunity to talk. But this election it would not happen.

I always felt ambivalent about being on air with my opponents because it felt like a fight, like a contest, like the guy games I avoided all my life. On the other hand, it was a useful way to communicate with voters.

Glen Fiscus and Jack Molesworth were my opponents in the Preliminary race.

Boston does not have partisan elections, with political parties like the Democrats and Republicans holding primaries which decided a party's candidate. Instead anyone could run as there were no party affiliations. However many seats there were for the job (like mayor was one seat for example) the top two vote-getters in an election called the 'preliminary' would get to have a run off and the winner would get the seat.

Since there were four at-large city council seats, there would be eight winners of the preliminary and the top four vote getters in the final election would get those seats. Since the district seats (there were 9) had only one seat per district, the top two vote-getters in the preliminary would run against each other in the final.

For this reason the finals were particularly brutal, expensive, and energetic.

I did not want to debate Molesworth or Fiscus. The latter was apparently a member of *Opus Dei*, a Catholic, conservative private club of true believers. Some call it a 'conspiracy' to make the Catholic message more powerful or more pure or something like that. I had no idea what the club was about. Irrespective of details, it was clear that its members were secretive and leaned to the right politically.

What I did know from meeting and speaking with Glen Fiscus many times, was that Glen was angry and stupid and Jack Molesworth was superficial and homophobic. Both of them were more interested in distorting information to suit their right-wing world view than solving problems: in other words, they were true believers.

So I refused to 'debate' them. I said that a 'debate' with Molesworth would degenerate into name-calling and given his media attacks on my support for gay rights, I said, "You can tell there would be nothing to debate."

As a practical matter their name recognition was zilch and I wanted to keep it that way.

In the preliminary election, held a few days after the Gary and French firing crisis began, I won 70% of the vote and Glen and Jack divided the remaining 30% between them. I could never seem to get above 70% of the vote in the district as a whole but, hell, that was pretty good. My Uncle Joe pointed out that you only have to win by one vote.

I was so pleased I smiled. I had won pretty much every part of the district. Of course most of that was probably due to the weakness of my opponents. I always got the feeling that making sure we looked invincible and keeping anyone with money and sanity from running was the best way to win an election, short of keeping everyone else from running at all.

On the citywide front, our friend Rosaria Salerno came in third place in the preliminary election. You needed to finish in the top four in the final to be elected, as four at large candidates are elected, so this looked great. I was surprised, but not surprised. It was a city of many Catholics that would, if they could, vote for a member of the clergy. Rosaria was the nun whom you confided in. Judgment-free and caring, she emanated concern and understanding. And it was a heavily Catholic city. Added to this, there were many progressives with energy, money, time and political skills who supported her. The combination made her a terrific candidate.

Joe Casper, the school committee guy who hated me, finished sixth in the at large preliminary election, behind Freddy Langone, a previous city councilor from years earlier.

He said that Rosaria comes from the "fruit-loop district of the city," [where I lived as well] according to a direct quote in the *Herald*. He continued, "That's where the political crazies are. If Salerno is elected there will be a swing in the council in favor of people like gay Councilor David Scondras."

I hoped so. I was working hard to get the Boston City Council to lean left so I could get my housing legislation passed, among other things. But in spite of the fact I understood what Casper was doing, appealing to the right, it still made me mad. I had spent my life teaching math and economics, writing papers, starting a health center and a day-care center, fighting arson, developing the arson early warning system, getting laws changed, people into housing, delivered hot lunches to the elderly for five years... and these guys as far as I could figure never did anything except gripe that lefties were ruining the universe. They were worthless parasites who spent their time projecting their miserable, mean little lives and their miserable mean little problems onto everyone else, and blaming people like me for their self-generated frustrations.

Better I should shut up and not talk about them — I needed to at least sound gracious even if it was a challenge given the personalities of these swamp creatures that ran for office every two years.

I noticed that Althea Garrison, who was actually a black transvestite, got 6,000 votes in her run for council. Althea would eventually win a seat as a state representative, which would last a short time. She was an impressive example of how far you can get if you are sufficiently persistent and if the electorate is sufficiently out of touch. She was a good friend of Dapper's. Figure that out. I never did, although it did get to be a big media thing later.

Anyway, after I won the preliminary election which gave me a sense of huge relief given the nightmare of the past few days with all the lies about Gary and French tied to me. the *Herald* said in a huge headline, probably reflecting their disappointment "SCONDRAS TAKES PRELIM IN CAKEWALK."

The *TAB* said, "Back Bay City Councilor David Scondras' landslide win in last week's preliminary race indicates that controversial media reports just days before the voting about two of his aides had little effect on the election, say political observers."

But they did have an effect on me. My stress levels were rather high. I was really wondering how long I wanted to go through this crazy election cycle.

Tip O'Neill was wrong. All politics is not local. All politics is ***personal***.

Running for office feels like walking over a canyon on a wire in a hurricane. But I found time to pass an ordinance requiring residents to put their trash in rodent-proof containers which Ray Flynn vetoed. Rats outnumbered Boston residents by 2-1 according to stats from public works in 1987. I met with residents at the Boston Public Library to draft a new rodent container law that would affect Back Bay and Fenway only.

Barney Frank warned me not to show up to every event. He said people would come to expect it and then I would get criticized if I missed one. Be selective, he counseled, but I didn't listen and later came to regret not taking more of his advice.

Taking Over the City

After winning the primary, I looked at a *Boston Herald* with a big editorial in it by a right-wing fanatic named Don Feder, columnist for the tabloid. On October 14th he wrote an article entitled, *"'Radicals' attempt takeover of Boston's City Council."* It was mostly about me, really.

I wondered, "What does the word 'Radical' mean, in quotes? Mostly it means, 'people who aren't like us.'" I felt that if they couldn't kill me because I was gay, maybe they would get me because I was a Commie. Of course that was a little harder, since I was a landlord and not a Commie, but I figured out long before Karl Rove that lies that worked were the right wing's stock in trade. They used them all the time. Said Feder:

> *A battle is brewing for the soul of Boston's City Council. David Scondras, radical councilor and gay activist, is intent on gaining control of the Hub's governing body.*
>
> *Scondras' vehicle for the power grab is a seemingly innocuous ex-nun named Rosaria Salerno. Salerno surprised observers by coming in third in the preliminary election for four at large council seats.*
>
> *Should she win in November, it will shift the council's ideological center of gravity far to the left.*
>
> *In the past, moderates have stemmed the tide of lunacy. By subtracting Tierney (who is vacating his seat for a mayoral quest) from the conservative column and adding Salerno to the radicals, the Scondras forces will have an invulnerable majority.*
>
> *The roster of those endorsing Salerno's candidacy reads like Jane Fonda's Christmas card list; Americans for Democratic Action, NOW, the Boston Gay and Lesbian Caucus, U.S. Rep. Barney Frank, Mel King and David ("I don't care if they advocate fornicating with grasshoppers") Scondras.*
>
> *The latter isn't just a Salerno backer; he's her political mentor. Scondras has put together a radical coalition to push Salerno's candidacy, provided staff support and even held joint fundraisers with her.*

Suing The City

French and Gary filed suit against the city for firing them. Of course, the *Herald* covered it extensively, giving them the chance to repeat over and over that I was connected with sex with children.

This court case was to have a profound effect on the Council in the long run. Meanwhile I was being trashed by those who grew increasingly worried that 'my' power was getting too big. In reality of course, I was just reacting to situations and getting power was to me getting a tool to rectify injustice, not reaching for an addictive drug. Also power was a bit of an illusion. People kept thinking that because I believed in what the groups that supported me thought, that therefore they were my willing tools as opposed to the other way around.

The *Herald* and the newspaper called the *South Boston Marshall* trashed me for supporting Gary and French, but the *Globe* printed a letter pointing out that John Adams defended British soldiers accused of murdering patriots in the Boston Massacre and Boston attorney Joseph Welch defended men accused by Joe McCarthy of being communist traitors. The letter basically called the Council cowardly for not supporting the 6th amendment, the right to a lawyer when you are accused. The committee Gary and French belonged to were trying to get legal help for the accused, the two boys still in jail for no reason.

Using Gay As An Attack

A flyer appeared in five Boston neighborhoods that said Salerno was gay. That would be a big surprise to anyone living in the Fenway who watched the love affair between Rosaria and Bob Case over the decades, and knew that Rosaria was a loving, caring woman who happened to be heterosexual. When asked is she was a lesbian, Rosaria said she wasn't and was not planning to be. I laughed. It was a little disheartening that lies about me and my staff was now indirectly being used to try to tarnish Rosaria. You could see how those who were about protecting existing interests used sex as a tool to defeat those who were trying to change these interests, to make the ladder a little easier to climb or at least less likely to fall from.

107 /   The March On Washington

"There is nothing more American than peaceful protest."
– Russ Feingold

It was Sunday, August 23rd, and Whoopi Goldberg was the inviter for the National March on Washington for Lesbian and Gay Rights luncheon. I was the special guest, the luncheon speaker, and there was a $100 minimum donation to show up. Organizing the March needed a lot of money. *Impulse* magazine wrote a summary of the speech that went:

You and I live in two Americas.

One America has enshrined theocracy, constantly devalues women, enslaved people of color, placed profits above people and equated sex with sin.

But the other America, our America, has fought back — and won. As Puritan theocrats sought to enforce an old world order on a new continent, our Thomas Paine was there with his fiery prose, arguing that men and women should participate in decision making, whether or not they owned property.

As privileged elitists sought to curtail liberty in the new constitution, our freedom fighters drafted the Bill of Rights, seeking to expand freedom of thought.

As their America forbid women from owning property, from entering college, and from voting, our America responded with figures like Elizabeth Cady Stanton who convened the first women's rights convention at Seneca Falls in 1848, and Susan B. Anthony who launched a half century struggle to win, finally, the vote for women in 1920.

As propertied racist interests consorted to maintain slavery, our abolitionists fought a civil war to end it.

As their America replaced slavery with Jim Crow, our Rosa Parks sparked a national revolution with her simple act of self-definition. By not marching obediently to the back of the bus, back to her closet, Rosa Parks ignited a successful 381 day strike against the Montgomery bus system and became a symbol for an entire generation seeking freedom and social justice.

And as their America terrorized lesbian and gay people with bar raids and mass round-ups, our America, embodied in drag queens and street dykes fought back at Stonewall.

We are the true freedom fighters of our times — we are facing the disease of the century, confronting the Dred Scott decision of our time, living with the accumulated indignities and oppression of generations.

So join us to make our America a reality, to work until all of us are truly free at last, able to say to that other America with a smile on our face, this is what our country stands for. Love it, or leave it.

In 1987 America reeked of homophobia.

Robert had received a letter from the Young Americans for Freedom, one of the front organizations of the old America, offering a full color autographed copy of a picture of Nancy Reagan if we would contribute ten dollars to their fund to "keep the homosexual Communist conspiracy from undermining the Reagan Administration."

Reagan was a horrible president. His administration worked to dismantle civil rights laws, tried to get religion taught in science classes in public schools, illegally armed Contra thugs to overthrow the Sandinistas, and had the unmitigated gall to appoint Illinois Representative Penny Pullen to the National AIDS panel. Pullen had written that she saw AIDS as "God's visitation on gay men and 'due penalty of their perversion.'"

I felt we needed desperately to get gays to become political, following the lead of other minorities to take action to break the oppression.

The March on Washington was the event that would crystallize gay power in the minds of politicians and I hoped it would move us closer to freedom in America.

October 11th, 1987, Washington, D.C.

7:13 a.m. My friend Cleve Jones walked to the podium which faced the U.S. Capitol dome. He read a list of names starting with the name of his closest friend who died of AIDS a year earlier. I spoke with Cleve often, as he planned and executed the creation of a patchwork quilt, each square of which was a memorial to someone who died of AIDS created by those who loved them. There were over 2,000 panels stretched in front of the Capitol, two football fields filled with memories of the dead. Cleve had arranged for each of many of us to read off the names one at a time — congressmen, friends, parents, myself. It was difficult to walk among the panels and read the goodbyes. It was quiet except for the sounds of people weeping.

Quilt containing names of 1,920 persons who have died of AIDS stretches for two blocks along the Mall. It was unfurled in a sunrise service yesterday.

You could see men walking quietly, wearing the lavender triangles that reminded us of the badges Nazi's forced homosexuals to wear in concentration camps where they were murdered. Some of the panels were anonymous because even in death some parents did not want their child's name used publicly.

Some of the people I saw were in wheelchairs, or used canes and had faces with the bluish spots of Kaposi's sarcoma, a cancer which people with AIDS sometimes got.

There was no treatment and no cure. In 1987 AIDS was a death sentence.

The March on Washington began with the memory of those who had died. The quilt, 3-and-½ tons of it, was put together the previous night by 500 volunteers. The patches of the quilt had flowers and boas, baseball jerseys and stars, children's animals and messages. We love you. We miss you.

Even the members of the press were quiet.

It was a somber beginning to the huge march which the *New York Times* estimated to be 200,000 people prior to the march, and the police estimate was 750,000.

I remember how difficult it was for me to read the names assigned to me. I felt incredible sadness and surprising guilt. Had I done enough?

The mood would change during the day from sadness to anger, but it began with mourning. It was the right way to begin a march to end the pain that hate brings to people.

And many, many people who are not gay joined us that day. And for many people, it was their last chance to speak out, for they were dying.

The March

I remember the poster that was made of the beginning of our march which said, "For Love and for Life we are not going back." Robert had it framed and it has hung in our house for years. You can see on the poster I was helping hold the parade banner, with Whoopi Goldberg,

Harvey Fierstein with his amazing voice, César Chávez and many other famous folks. I love that poster. We walked for miles and the entire mall filled up.

Whoopi Goldberg spoke and I was on the platform with all the gay elected officials being presented to the crowd as the first elected officials our community had.

It was strange and awesome to hear hundreds of thousands of people cheer and clap, like waves of an invisible ocean passing through us. I felt quiet inside, listening and feeling for once a part of the group, a member of the tribe, at peace.

I felt the movement, the sense of history. Every major news outlet in the United States was there, filming the moments, filling the pages of what people would be reading for a week.

After marching from the White House, about 200,000 people rally on the Mall. One demand was for more funding for AIDS.

On Monday the Supreme Court would shut its doors as the largest number of protesters ever arrested demonstrated against its anti-gay decision in the Hardwick case.

On Sunday night, DuPont Circle and all of Washington became gay. It was the first time I ever felt really at home. The first time I was walking in a crowd of people as part of the majority.

Robert took my hand. We had never in our years together held hands in public. We were too afraid, knew too well that we enticed violence if we did that. For several magic moments we felt safe, like the world was the way it was meant to be. We have never felt truly safe before or since, for we have truly not been safe before or since.

I have never forgotten the feeling of being free. And I hope some day it comes back again.

Many gay activists felt the need to form a national organization of progressive gay Democrats in order to have a focused effort on issues affecting all of us.

On November 14th, 1987, at the Wellington Avenue church in Chicago, I began the keynote speech to 150 key leaders from across the United States. It would lead to a constitution for gay Democrats, which married the issues of gay oppression to ending all oppressions of all kinds. I felt then and feel now that injustice anywhere to anyone breeds injustice everywhere to everyone — that injustice is a cancer and must be cut out to save all of our political body precisely because it spreads.

The crowd was buoyant, full of energetic and smart people of all ages. I felt happy that my family was so strong and principled.

My speech was a distillation of what I had come to understand over the years of working and growing. I said that we needed a vision of a new kind of world, which would include real social and economic justice. I pointed out the unique role that gays had as a result ironically of their being closeted putting them across many cultures in positions of responsibility, of by their nature being men and women, black and white, red and yellow, belonging to all religions and groups thus more able than perhaps anyone as a group to cut across the labels that divided because gays belong to every group and thus can speak with every group.

I said, "Power, it's wonderful stuff," as I challenged people to get political to break the chain of centuries old oppression. I focused on our own internal obstacles. "All power begins with an act of self-definition," I said, which I had learned from Mel King. "You don't get what you don't demand, and you don't demand what you think you don't deserve." I said that the "real miracle of Rosa Park's refusal to give up her seat on a bus was the insight that she deserved to remain where she was." Her act of self-definition was the necessary precursor to her decision to stay seated, a statement that sent "echoes throughout history."

Boston City Councillor David Scondras was the keynote speaker at the Progressive Dems convention last weekend. See article p. 12.

Datelines

Gay and lesbian election news

BOSTON--On Nov. 3 openly gay City Councilor David Scondras was returned to office with 64 percent of the vote, and progressive Rosaria Salerno was elected to the at-large seat formerly occupied by conservative Joseph Tierney, *Gay Community News* reports. Salerno, a newcomer to the council, was attacked after a strong showing in the Sept. 22 primary by her opponent Joseph Casper, who claimed she was an "ultra-liberal" from "the fruit-loop district of the city." Shortly before the Oct. 11 March on Washington flyers appeared in the city designed as if from Salerno's campaign office that stated "Show Your Gay Pride"; the leaflets encouraged people to participate in the march and quoted the candidate as asking in a speech at a walk-a-thon for lesbian and gay rights, "Why aren't there thousands of US here?" Salerno stated in response to the flyers that she is heterosexual, but that if she were lesbian she hopes she would be proud of her sexuality. Scondras has recently been under fire from the media and the city council for the membership of two of his aides in the Committee for Civil Liberties and Sexual Freedom, a group advocating the fair treatment of all parties in cases where sex is alleged between gay adults and minors. The aides were recently fired from their positions by the Council; the Civil Liberties Union of Mass. is considering filing a suit in opposition to the Council's actions.

Nadine McGann wrote up a summary of my talk for the November 19th *Chicago Outlines*:

> *"From the beginning," Scondras said, "lesbian and gay children live a double life because they know they will not get approval at home. A heightened need to develop ways of seeking approval begins early as a survival tactic. In addition 'acting' becomes part of the 'fabric of life.' These strategies for survival, which in many ways have allowed the community to live and grow over the years, are, however, at the same time obstacles to self-definitions and empowerment.*
>
> *"For example," he said, "many lesbians and gays consider that the ability to go to a bar on gay night represents a freedom. We think this is normal," said Scondras, "but in fact it is 'apartheid.'" The denial system that is in part a product of living a double life allows gay men and lesbians to continue "tracing the edge of the wall of the prison they are living in, and calling it freedom".*
>
> *Approval seeking divides us against ourselves. "We internalize the heterosexist value system," he said, and in seeking approval our actions often replicate the moral codes of that value system. Embarrassment about out "image" often induces the community to polarize along the lines of "good guys vs bad guys." The question of sin and sexuality is yet another example. "Viruses don't give a shit about sexuality" he declared, referring to the society's homophobic response to the AIDS epidemic.*
>
> *"As long as we adopt the moral code of the straight population instead of looking at reality, we'll be in trouble." In a challenge to those who recommend caution in the fight for lesbian and gay rights, Scondras asserted that that adage "don't rock the boat" is "only relevant to people who have been allowed on the boat. When they let us on we will stop rocking it."*
>
> *"I focused on the issue of the source of the anger and uncomfortable reaction to gays as a reflection of a weakness in the mainstream culture's definition of meaning. That when the reason to exist is summarized as reproduction and family as male, female and children, we endanger the underlying rationale for existence itself," [he said]. Insofar as the "purpose of life" is to have children, he said, the heterosexuals believe that they have a monopoly on it. Observing that it "only takes*

I ended my address with a reiteration of gay pride coupled with an appeal for action, "We are the new constituency. If the battles for justice are ever won, it will be because we decided to participate. Neither the community itself nor the rest of the population yet appreciates how important the gay and lesbian community is to the survival of the planet."

I guess I was still in my "Let's save the world" phase. I do not think I have left it actually. But my rhetoric has become more catholic, more inclusive and better informed from the many battles that were yet to come after 1987.

I was not the Messiah. Oh well.

Letters

Being gay I experienced injustice and this led me to spend my life helping people get what they needed, go where they wanted to go, do what they wanted to do, not work on gay issues exclusively. Some of the letters I got during 1987 shows the range of our team's efforts. I felt that fighting for justice included all kinds of unfairness.

- From the South End Historical Society thanking me for helping keep a Church landmarked;

- From Bob Gallagher, a broker at Century 21 for my law stopping run away condo conversions;

- From the Pine Street Inn for getting more shelter space for the homeless, for stopping a car alarm that kept a group of people from getting any sleep (I got a tow truck to take the van away);

- From Ken Hudson for helping him get a room part of which read, "Finally I found a rented room near the Prudential Center in an owner-occupied building. After having been treated like a leper by white male absentee landlords, it felt good to be treated like a human being by a black lady (I am of a pinkish complexion)." Kenneth had been homeless for six months before finding a job;

- From the Boston Food Coop for resolving the conflict between it and the Health Department;

- From the Back Bay Association for our new rules to end the rat infestation;

- From the Audubon Society for money I put in the budget to match private donations for a cleanup of Boston Harbor;

- For helping get affordable housing built on behalf of Sociedad Latina on Mission Hill;

- For helping fund a state-of-the-art fire station, and the first downtown ambulance facility, by cutting through the red tape at City Hall from the various companies collaborating on the project;

- A note from the French Library for making its Bastille Day celebration an event all of the Back Bay could support;

- From Roxbury Community College for getting the parking ban lifted so students could come to school;

- From a dozen condo associations thanking us for helping them in a variety of ways;

...and on and on. People reached me from wherever they were, thanking us for helping many people in many ways. I mention these things because most of our time was spent dealing with the hundreds of issues that mean so much to people and which never get much attention. I felt it was my job to pay attention and deal with everything that falls through the cracks as the media and the important folks deal with big issues that are of course important but which do not deal with the myriad of problems that our society visits upon folks day after day.

And also to make it clear that while my work trying to create a new reality for gay people was central to much of my work, that it was nevertheless a small part of what being a city councilor was, of what I had to do to make life better for the people I represented.

109 /   The end of 1987

The Conference of Gay Officials

I was getting used to death threats and being placed on pedestals. The year was getting old, and so were the hatemongers, but I paid some attention to the hate, just in case some wing nut tried to actually kill me.

Funny, but I had lived so much of my life in danger that the death threats were just an expected part of life for me by the end of 1987.

The world was changing. I knew that being gay was becoming a voting bloc when I went to the November 20th third annual conference of Gay/Lesbian Elected and Appointed Officials, Candidates, Prospective Candidates and Campaign Workers.

Nobody wanted anyone who was part of getting elected left out of this one.

I remember that both Alan Spear (smart, short, balding, cool, shy), a state senator in Minnesota, and Elaine Noble from Massachusetts, our first ever-gay official, were there. Alan told about the first time he spoke to at a Students for Democratic Society conference. They were not convinced about electoral politics being the road to social change. The second he was up on the stage they started to boo and heckle him. He eventually gave up and stepped off the podium. Elaine, not to be deterred, charged up onto the podium, grabbed the mike and yelled "If I hear one more peep out of any of you I will come down there and shove this microphone up your ass!" He told us they immediately shut up and listened to her speech.

We Won

Truly issues just won't die. They keep popping up again. But unlike the usual horror movie, in this case Coors rose from the dead smelling like a rose [see chapter 89 above]. After declining offers to be wined, dined and who knows what in Golden, Colorado, we did not know what form the future would take. New England refused to go along with the AFL-CIO settlement of the Coors boycott until one day we won. I still don't know exactly how this all happened.

Here is the letter from Ray Tye, owner of United Liquors speaking for the Adolph Coors Company.

UNITED LIQUORS LTD.

Wholesalers and Importers

DATE: November 20, 1987

TO: City Councilor David Scondras

FROM: A. Raymond Tye

The Adolph Coors Company announces the following corporate policies due to extensive negotiations between the executives of the Adolph Coors Company and members of the Gay and Lesbian Community. Among the input from community members has been that of Boston City Councilor David Scondras resulting in the following:

A basic policy, in writing, that Adolph Coors Company prohibits any discrimination because of sexual orientation.

The policy states: "It is the policy of Adolph Coors Company to provide equal opportunity for all employees and to hire and promote qualified applicants without regard to race, creed, color, sex, sexual orientation, religion, national origin, handicap or age."

This policy extends to non-support of organizations that advocate discrimination because of race, creed, color, sex, sexual orientation, religion, national origin, handicap or age.

Lie detector tests are not part of any current or future employment requirements for any position at the Adolph Coors Company.

Through the Adolph Coors Company local distributor, United Liquors Ltd., resources are and have been committed to the Gay and Lesbian Community as an expression of sincere interest in furthering a relationship with the Boston Gay Community.

It is the sincere hope of the Adolph Coors Company that the noted items will be put to rest in the past and a working relationship will continue to develop toward a more productive future.

The Adolph Coors Company and United Liquors Ltd. would like to recognize the tireless efforts on the part of one particular gay advocate, Councilor David Scondras. It is due largely to the negotiations generated by his office that such accommodations have been fashioned.

From *Bay Windows*: December 17, 1987:

Scondras Announces Ceasefire with Coors

At a City Hall press conference last Wednesday, City Councilor David Scondras announced an end to the New England Coors Boycott. Ray Tye, president of United Liquors, Coors' New England distributor said that Wednesday's announcement followed negotiations in which "Scondras talked to Peter Coors directly….At one point last week we were actually faxing back and forth"….most gay businesses are already stocking the product again. "They were just waiting for an official announcement," he comments.

Coors contracts now include a statement prohibiting "race, creed, color, sex, sexual orientation, religion, national origin, handicap or age" discrimination…

Coors says it has also permanently discontinued funding for what Scondras describes as "right wing hate groups." According to the company it has also implemented affirmative action and job training for minorities and will allow the AFL-CIO to attempt unionization of its brewery workers.

Clearly the most unexpected and significant development announced by Scondras is "a commitment by Coors of resources to the constituencies who have been involved in the boycott."

"I think there's a time to fight and a time to declare peace." Scondras told the press.

Brian Delaney, a public relations representative for Coors concluded, "Without Councilor Scondras' ability to communicate, what happened today just couldn't have happened. Corporations have a responsibility to do things to enhance society. The result of all this? I think we'll be a better company today."

I remember how difficult the talks had been, and how illuminating on all sides. I learned a lot about the history of the Coors family and came to understand the way the aftermath of the murder of one of the earlier members of the Coors family had created a sense of understandable paranoia and anger that worked its way into policies that needed to be re-examined in light of the changes that time brings.

The *Herald* ran a story that the Fenway beer boycott was over.

I thought about the voices against me the days I was characterized as bludgeoning the company unfairly and had to laugh. While I was flattered by the characterization of having good communication skills, it was the coalition of unions, minorities, the gay community and the distributors at the Red Sox that got the attention and created the conditions that led to a settlement.

You can't arrive at a treaty without two sides, and my diplomatic skills could not have had any effect without the united front represented by the coalition — to trade you have to have something to trade with.

The New Year's Party at our House

"In One Year and Out The Other" — From The Invitational Flier

We had Carmine, our tenant on the second floor apartment of our home at 34 Edgerly road dressed up with a turban to do tarot card readings. There was food over a huge table, a barrel with champagne bottles in it, live music on the top floor, tables with candles throughout the basement floor and over 400 people came to our third annual First Night Open House. It was the last day of 1987 and the first night of 1988. Each floor (apartment) had a different function, readings and talking, food, dancing. Maybe lectures on topics of interest.

I loved the party – 400 of my best friends all at our house doing tons of interesting things. What could be better?

It was a wonderful way to end the most amazing year Robert and I had lived as a family together.

110 / 1988 Part One: City Hall for Sale

"Politicians all too often think about the next election.
Statesmen think about the next generation."
– Linda Lingle (Democratic Governor of Hawaii)

It all started with a reporter from the *New York Times* who asked to see City Hall. I don't know exactly what got into me. Perhaps it was the memory of Mayor Flynn giving me his electric heater to help us keep warm that first winter. Perhaps it was the umpteenth person trying to find the fourth floor that didn't exist on the Council side of the building. The elevators went from 3 to 5. No 4. "You can't get there from here," was a phrase characteristic of jokes about Maine and Boston City Hall. Perhaps it was the arrogance of a monstrous building that made you feel it was at any moment going to crush you. Or getting lost constantly. Or being cold in one part and hot in another. Or the famous missing room somewhere in the building that became part of Boston's urban legends.

Robert asserted that the architects were simply trying to build an apt metaphor for Boston City Government – scary to approach, impossible to navigate, with departments unknown to each other.

I ventilated about the building with this *New York Times* reporter. The building's skylights were blocked by concrete passageways so that the artistic effort to create the feeling of a cathedral jutting toward the heavens was ruined but the huge space had to be heated anyway. The grand staircase that led nowhere but to a dead end wall looking over Faneuil Hall Marketplace. The concrete cubicles difficult to work inside. the City Hall chambers with gigantic rectangular solid columns made it impossible to see the theatrics on the floor of the council from most angles. The depressing gray of the concrete walls characterized the architectural style of the building aptly called the "new brutalism."

For a few moments the building was visually interesting but for most of the people who worked in the place, it was a depressing mess. Hard, cold, cubical, an elevated dungeon.

I told the reporter that we should sell the thing and build a new place closer to the section of the city that needed the most investment and where most lower income people lived instead of downtown where no one lived.

THE MUSE OF THE WEEK IN REVIEW

Halltercation

Councilor Scondras has cast a pall
On Boston's gargantuan City Hall.
"Too ugly," he calls it, "too big and too small."
Councilor Scondras is having a ball.

Councilor Scondras demands that we sell
Our city's municipal citadel.
"We can't fight it," says this zealot,
"What we've got to do is sell it."

Come now, sir, though we've outgrown it.
Sell it? No! We can't condone it!
City Hall deserves obeisance
As the start of our renaissance.

Though it is the place in Boston
That so many have been lost in.
Looks less friendly than monastic,
, Your proposal's too Scondrastic!

Sir, if sold, it might become
A mammoth condominium!
That's a frightful fate from which
We could save it by a switch:

Let's not let our thinking harden.
Let's exchange the Boston Garden
With its Brobdingnagian sprawl
For the Boston City Hall!

Councilor, upon my oath
'Twill be better for them both
When beer and sweat aromas lurk
To beguile the city clerk.

While the Bruins pass the puck
Where so many passed the buck.
And where useless space delights
In the Bird's inspired flights.

— Felicia Lamport

Globe staff photo/Bill Greene

I thought we could get a good price from a corporation that wanted to build a hotel on the spot and use that money to build a real office building with public spaces and hotel like conference halls, places to sit and restaurants — a City Hall that welcomed the people of the city.

I didn't really think my tantrum was a big deal, but it created a landslide of public reaction.

The *Herald* put a cartoon out of City Hall with me in front and a for sale sign on the building.

The *New York Times* wrote a big article entitled "Bostonian Fights City Hall." They wrote:

What's bigger than a breadbox, leaks, has stairways to nowhere
and has been described admiringly as a representative of the
school of 'New Brutalism'?

Boston's City Hall.

This strange concrete edifice, which looms above a forbidding
brick plaza, has won architectural prizes but not the hearts of
Bostonians who often liken it to a parking garage.

Now a City Council member has proposed that, in the name of efficiency and economy, the building be sold and the government moved elsewhere.

What a fuss. Another article in the *New York Times* was headlined, *"If You Can't Fight City Hall, Here's a Different Idea: Sell It."* The *Boston Globe* on January 12th put together an article that underlined the issues around the building. I said, "If function is beauty then this place is ugly." Dozens more articles followed. I introduced an order into the City Council calling for hearings on the subject.

I learned from all the fuss that if you wanted a *LOT* of press, find something everyone has an opinion about but no one is actually affected much by and you can count on an outpouring of opinion, loud but not very deep. I started the longest running, loud and public controversy in years over a whimsical set of honest reflections to a *New York Times* reporter. It kept growing bigger and bigger.

The *Ledger* published a humor column entitled "Take City Hall, Please!" It was by Daniel M. Kimmel. It went like this:

"Well, he's done it again," crowed Mishkin, a great fan of City Councilor David Scondras.

"How is that?" I asked.

"He's put his finger on one of the major eyesores in the city of Boston and placed himself in a position of leadership on the issue."

"Slow down, Mishkin, What are you talking about?"

He pulled out an article where Scondras announced that he wanted to look into the possibility of selling off City Hall on the grounds that it was ugly and inefficient.

"You see, Dan, he hit the nail right on the head."

"...What do you propose doing with it?

"Well, we could use it to replace the Charles Street Jail and save ourselves the cost of building a new one...

"Consider, Dan, the building is like a fortress sitting on its demilitarized no man's land. It's a great design if you're a cement manufacturer. The addition of machine gun turrets and barbed wire could only improve the way it looks"

It went on endlessly, suggesting finally that we move burlesque shows into the building, and massage parlors. This was a tip of the hat to the old Scollay Square that used to be where the City Hall Plaza presently is located, a square noted for girly shows, bars, sex and outlets for the libertine in us.

I wrote an op-ed in the *Globe*. I decided to use the opportunity the press gave me to talk about the sociological changes in the urban fabric of the city caused by bad urban design:

Many have pointed out that the building is the symbol of the age of renewal. They have pointed to City Hall as the pearl of I.M. Pei's Government Center Plan, the embodiment of hope for economic renaissance at a time of center city depression. However, this building also symbolized the discontent of the ethnic neighborhood that were displaced by the forces that urban renewal unleashed. It was an age destructive of the fabric of neighborhoods to the extent that in the early 70's neighborhood activists, dressed up as native Americans, invaded a planning convention and pleaded their case. That convention voted to condemn Boston's age of renewal as unethical. Activists then went to the federal courts which ordered that renewal be halted until community input could be organized and formally become part of the process.

As a sculpture City Hall entertains and is applauded by the artist in each of us. But like the age it memorializes, it is indifferent and harsh toward those it purports to serve. Some have suggested these are the thinking of a contemporary Philistine whose concern for technocratic function has cause him to ignore the importance of architectural statement and form. Not so! I have never met a person who was bored with City Hall, but I have met people lost, confused, hot, cold, hurt, discouraged and alienated by the building.

Soon Bob Campbell, the *Boston Globe* architectural critic got in the act, writing an op-ed spanking me. The article, *"It's time we started treating Boston City Hall with pride,"* made many good points.

It is true that Boston City Hall, as a work of art, is extraordinary. But architects can miss the point. It is a dysfunctional building, and to work there is very trying. I felt that there were ways to create beauty without sacrificing function, but the subtleties of my arguments were condensed into construing my position as reflecting the personality of a Luddite.

Then Campbell came over to our home and had dinner with Robert and me — Robert is an architect from Harvard's Graduate School of Design, hardly a neophyte to architecture or saboteur of good design. Campbell, and sometimes Robert, tried to convince me that the importance architecturally of this piece of concrete was vast. I thought he had a little of it right: the piece of concrete was vast.

I generally agreed, but in fact the building badly needed to incorporate elements that welcomed the public and were functional for those who had to work in it. And the interminable gray interiors and exteriors and darkness needed to be opened to light and color.

I suggested having the building house art from every neighborhood of the city as a starting point, a gallery like in Lincoln Center of New York. Up-lighting the variegated surfaces to emphasize the cubistic forms that created visual texture and hanging banners from the heights that would enliven the building and cast it as a place of activity rather than a tombstone.

Robert was pissed off at me because my proposal was published in "Progressive Architecture" magazine which he had read his whole career and aspired to someday to get published in himself.

The architects who worked on the building and who had designed it were all still alive and still practicing in Boston. I got Kallmann and McKinnell, two of the original architects, to come to City Hall to explain what went wrong with the building. Their firm won a design competition over 265 other entrants. Kallmann was short, German-sounding, and grumped a lot; McKinnell had his nose in the air, was English-sounding, and clearly annoyed at me.

I learned a lot and decided that we needed to finish the vision they originally had for the building.

They claimed that former Mayor Kevin White never finished the building they had planned which was to have colorful banners and a beer garden, imitating many German City Halls, which I applauded. It sounded like City Hall was originally intended to be a building a lot more user friendly than it turned out.

All in all, we got more press coverage about my idea to sell the City Hall building than almost any other issue we ever pushed.

Jesse Jackson

In 1984 I was responsible for the Alliance, the gay political group in Boston, endorsing Jesse Jackson for President. So it probably should not have come as a surprise to get this phone call in 1988. But I was surprised.

May Louie, who was the director of Mel King's "Rainbow Coalition," asked me to come by the Sheraton Hotel (which was a few blocks from our house) on January 24th. She said that the Reverend Jesse Jackson wanted to speak with me if I had time to share with him. It was clear he would ask me to work on his campaign for president.

May had gotten deeply involved in the Jackson presidential campaign, as did another friend of mine, Janice Fine. May was short, sweet, Asian and a person with great clarity. Janice was brilliant and full of fun and had a satirical sense of humor.

Jackson was a huge guy. I stand 6'3" and he was taller than me. He had a great smile, and the voice of a black preacher. I heard the famous voice speaking to staff people, asking for orange juice, saying how he felt, asking for a call to be made to the host of an event he would be attending later in the morning. May Louie said, "He has 15 minutes or so until he has to leave, is that enough time?" I nodded. Then the door behind Louie opened up and Jackson slid through, holding a glass of orange juice, then stopped for a second, nodded at me, took a sip.

He was dressed informally, having just finished a shower, clearly getting ready for the next event. I felt more at ease than if he had appeared in formal garb. It made me feel like I was part of the family, not part of the folks that needed to be impressed.

He sat across from me, bent his body forward and looked at me straight in the eyes. "I want you to help me," he said.

news notes

PHOTO: DON WEST

David Scondras with Jesse Jackson

Scondras Officially Endorses Jackson

Following a meeting on Sunday, January 24, Boston City Councilor David Scondras has officially endorsed Jesse Jackson's candidacy for president. Scondras, who flew to Iowa last week to assist in Jackson's campaign efforts before the primary, says of Jackson's commitment to the gay rights movement, "I think he's learning, growing, and open.

"We must gain the power to end homophobia, racism and sexism, to bring about social and economic justice for all," Scondras states in his press announcement. "I am supporting Jesse Jackson for President—because we need him and he needs us. Every candidate was welcome to come to the March on Washington. Only one came. Only one touched the thousands of people with AIDS. Only one committed himself to supporting us and has spoken forcefully for us since."

Randy Miller, the staffer Jackson hired to direct the lesbian and gay issues desk in his Washington, D.C. campaign office, reports that the candidate was "impressed by Councilor Scondras and grateful for his endorsement."

filed by John Perry

Gay Scientists, Scondras to Speak

The National Organization of Gay and Lesbian Scientists and Technical Professionals (NOGLSTP) will present a paper on "Sexual Orientation and Computer Privacy: The Social Impact" at the annual meeting of the American Association for the Advancement of Science (AAAS) being held this week at Boston's Hynes Convention Center. NOGLSTP Co-Chair Joseph Schreiner will read the paper at a the 11 a.m. to 1 p.m. session on Saturday, February 13.

On the following day, February 14, City Councilor David Scondras will speak on "The Social Impact of the AIDS Epidemic on the Gay and Lesbian Community" at a joint social and business hosted by NOGLSTP from 6 to 8 p.m.

For more information on NOGLSTP or the AAAS conference, contact David Wypij, group coordinator, at (617) 732-1056.

I asked him two things: would he support gay rights and give me time to give him feedback on gay issues before taking a public position? I also asked him for an agreement that when I needed him he would come to one event which I would hold at some point in the future, perhaps a fundraiser, perhaps a speech. He said yes. He was serious and it became clear as I listened to him that he was extraordinarily attuned to the feelings of the people with whom he spoke. He had the ability to see through tangential issues to the core of a problem.

I endorsed his candidacy for president, notwithstanding the fact that Michael Dukakis, then the governor of Massachusetts and a Greek like me, was running for president. I felt that the future for many of those alienated from our society depended upon the development of a coalition of minorities whose banner Jackson held, and there was no clear interest in this from the behavior or speeches of Michael Dukakis.

In my press release I said that Jackson was "learning, growing and open" and I meant it. I began to speak out across the United States pushing for the election of the first black Presidential candidate who had a real chance to alter the dynamics of the Democratic Party in fundamental ways. My analysis was repeated across the country in hundreds of gay papers and mainstream media. My remarks, which were published in many papers under the banner "Two Americas, One Choice for President," were:

Anita Bryant, Jerry Falwell, and John Briggs will be thrown upon the trash heap of history along with the Ku Klux Klan and the Nazis.

But only when we act.

Today, their America benefits from policies, which bring us rivers without fish and beaches with raw sewage.

Their America benefits from hazardous waste, racism, run away shops, and from the suffering of the sick who cannot afford medical care. Their America sells arms to all sides of wars. Their America profits from the balance of nuclear terror and from arming thugs in Central America.

Their America teaches its children to devalue women, seniors, Jews, people of color, gay and lesbian people, and anyone who does not fit into their narrow vision of our country. Their America would rather see our children die of AIDS than teach them safer sex.

It is up to us to fight for ourselves and the children of our future.

We must move beyond hollow victories in which we win the rhetoric — but not the laws, the programs, the money, not the power to address our human rights agenda. We must gain the power to end homophobia, racism and sexism, to bring about social and economic justice for all, to clean up and care for our environment and to end policies of foreign intervention and nuclear terror.

Their powerful club is run by those who are married to the bankrupt policies of the past.

We must join those who have not benefited from these policies, a "majority of minorities" who are ready to come together and who know that each group needs the other.

I am supporting Jesse Jackson for President — because we need him and he needs us.

We can count on a friend we empower — a friend whose supporters need us. We can count less on charity from friends whose supporters fear us.

Every candidate was welcome to come to the March on Washington. Only one came. Only one touched the thousands of people with AIDS. Only one committed him to supporting us and has spoken forcefully for us since.

Can you believe that candidates who didn't even have the guts to show up at our march will have the guts to fight for us? What will happen when they have to stand alone?

We need a President who will lead a war against AIDS of the scale and determination with which President Kennedy made America the first country to reach the moon.

We need a leader who will win the fight for civil rights, one who will stand with the gay and lesbian people of our country and end the social apartheid that poisons America.

We need a leader who knows that teaching children to devalue and hate themselves because they are "different" is an act of child abuse.

Led by Jackson, those who historically have been devalued and left out of the mainstream of American life can address our community's needs and America's needs. A coalition is growing that respects each of the member groups because each group is necessary to its strength, and it is getting stronger every day.

An AIDS program based on this coalition would never be marginalized. The civil rights of gay and lesbian people would be ensured. Rather than being discussed as acts of charity from well meaning liberal leaders, our agenda would be addressed as acts of necessity, the bottom line demands of a core constituency central to Jackson's coalition.

Support Jackson and our issues will be made part of the debate among the candidates and part of the Democratic Party's agenda. Jackson will make sure of it — because he needs us.

Before the year was over the Jackson campaign would have me in many states, on buses, at the Democratic National Convention and learning about the lives of people from coast to coast.

Meanwhile, Our Office Tackles Noise

It was January the 3rd. I was determined to stop the noise. I think that noise is the biggest problem in cities after you deal with food and housing. Car alarms that went off all night were a nightmare for people who needed to sleep.

Mark Roosevelt was now the state rep from Beacon Hill, and we co-sponsored a state law to deal with the problem. I got a flood of calls especially after baseball games when out-of-towners with fancy cars used up every space they could find in my neighborhood and weren't around to shut off their alarms if they went off [see chapter 62, "Car Alarms"].

So I got Mark to help out. The new state law, which we got passed, gave permission to the police to tow away cars whose security alarms weren't shut off by their owners.

It was one of my best "quality of life" laws and eventually, car alarms automatically terminated after a few minutes. I think the companies that made them realized that they would make less money if their buyers had their cars towed.

111 / 1988 Part Two: Clean Needles

For the most part, there were two ways virtually all people with AIDS got the virus that causes it — needles and sex. Keep in mind that in 1988 we were all still very unsure how this disease works — although cases of AIDS were noticed by 1978, the virus that caused it was not identified until 1983. There were a lot of theories on how AIDS worked. It was originally called GRID (Gay Related Immune Deficiency). Most people did not understand that the 'slim' disease, the wasting disease that affected millions of heterosexuals in Africa, was the same illness.

Because in the U.S. the folks who first were identified with the disease were gay men (as opposed to heterosexuals, who are 95% of the total number of cases worldwide) the disease was thought of as a "gay disease" which gave a field day for bigots and right wing Christians to blame the disease on homosexuality and as a punishment for the sin of being gay.

Some Haitian men got AIDS and the finger was pointed at Haiti, whose government claimed that "we don't have any gays here."' Americans looked for someone to blame, in this case Haitians, and the Haitians were outraged that a gay disease was assumed to come from the island of 'normal' people. Having spent time in Haiti I can tell you they were either lying or detached from reality. In Port-Au-Prince boys offered gay sex for money with alarming regularity.

Anyway, eventually reality unraveled the mythologies that had spread, for example that gays used sex drugs like poppers (nitrates) which, according to the gossip among the 'phobes. caused AIDS by depressing the immune system. It was also the beginning of the "anti-sex, drugs, and rock and roll" reaction to the '60s and '70s. It is an irony to watch the same anti-gay groups being preached to by Republican presidential candidate Robert Dole to buy and swallow Viagra to get erections. As usual the "good guys" get to do whatever makes them feel good and the "bad guys," whoever they are defined to be by whoever has power at the moment, are degenerates for doing exactly the same things.

Throughout American history, from the days Puritans coming to America to stop the folks who had fun, sex and dancing around the maypoles, which were all cut down, to the white slavery panic of the 1920's, to the sex with kids craziness of the 2000's, there have been periodic binges of demonizing dance and sex, drink and play, accompanied by attitudes of moral superiority about the sex and play habits of one group or another.

It was always rather odd to hear a guy in a bar swigging a Budweiser and smoking a Marlboro, sneering at the fags getting AIDS because they did stuff that was unhealthy and wrong, just wrong.

Anyway this prelude might seem gratuitous, but it is not. The biggest obstacles to dealing with AIDS has not been finding medicines or figuring out how to stop transmission, but rather the prejudices and panic that characterized a lot of public reaction to the disease. And the war on drugs, the most worthless, self-destructive, expensive, and failed public policy ever undertaken in the United States, which demonized drugs and addicts, fueled gang wars, destroyed countries, and enriched the coffers of pushers and producers and the Taliban, was four-square opposed to the biggest single thing we could do to fight AIDS among addicts: give them clean needles.

This led to one of the most tumultuous efforts I ever made to get legislation passed. An effort which would finally get the support of the White House 21 years later.

We Decide To Intervene

There was a guy from South Boston named Jon Stuen- Parker, who was president of the "AIDS Brigade," an organization focused on helping fight the epidemic that was brewing. He was brave and he wasn't waiting on government or religion or any other institution to take action, so he started distributing clean needles to drug addicts along with bleach and training them on how to clean a needle. He would get periodically arrested, but nobody really wanted to prosecute him. He was trying to help save lives. He was a brave person, and I admired him and tried over and over to get the police to ignore him, let him do what he needed to do. He was determined to protect addicts from getting AIDS.

He set up a place addicts could go to get needles and training. I have no idea where he got the clean needles.

Parker wrote a book called *From Jail to Yale*, the converse of Dellinger's book *From Yale to Jail*. It was a letter to Norman Mailer, whose book *Belly of the Beast* had inspired him. Parker's book is an amazing account of a complicated person.

Anyway it motivated me to learn about shooting galleries, the social context of drugs and needle sharing, and how to effectively help out. I had floated the idea of clean needles during a hearing in 1987, but got so burnt by even mentioning the idea that we back-burnered it until I had had a chance to study where anyone was trying it and any data on it I could get my hands on. The February 24th *Globe* article on the issue mentioned that two addicts, T-Baby and Dennis, a 30-year-old recovering addict with AIDS, said "sounds like genocide to me" when I first brought the idea up at the hearing the summer of 1987.

I decided that I would talk to Ray Flynn about this.

Depending on which statistics you looked at, somewhere between 20% and 60% of AIDS was being transmitted by drug addicts sharing hypodermic needles with each other, a particularly effective way of transmitting HIV, the virus that causes AIDS. There was a secondary effect: people who had sex with HIV-infected addicts, and ex-addicts, like wives and girlfriends for example, often ended up getting HIV as well.

Data from Europe, and some American cities in which buying a clean needle was legal, showed it was an astonishingly effective way to protect drug addicts and those who loved them from getting HIV.

Ray Flynn was a courageous man. And guided by Neil Sullivan, Ray Flynn's public policy czar, Flynn decided to frame legislation that would allow a pilot city program to distribute clean needles to drug addicts.

It Hits the Fan

The "needle exchange" program was how the press characterized the new proposal. It got a big boost when New York City health officials announced that they were trying to institute the nation's first clean needle program. Mayor Edward Koch and the Health Department Commissioner for the city fought those opposed to the plan, including New York Governor Mario Cuomo.

The commissioner said, "There are an estimated 200,000 intravenous drug users in New York City, 50% of whom we believe to be carrying HIV antibodies, up from 4% in 1980. Without the program there will be a guaranteed eight percent increase in AIDS transmission among addicts per year."

Studies showed that the new programs would not lead to an increase in heroin addiction.

In addition, in an act that surprised me given the fact he was a Reagan appointee, the U.S. Surgeon General C. Everett Koop gave his support to the needle exchange program and suggested that the program should be instituted nationwide. It was believed at the time that as many as 25% of those with AIDS got it from not having access to clean needles.

In central Massachusetts, Worcester health officials announced that the AIDS infection rate among that city's addicts had apparently doubled within the past year. Dr. John Sullivan, who would be a part of my life later dealing with AIDS vaccine development, said that 15% of the city's drug users were infected.

In spite of all this, the program faced a lot of opposition. Governor Michael Dukakis, who was running for president, was dead set against it. This did not endear him to me, and showed me my decision to back Jesse Jackson for president was the right one.

Dukakis slightly increased funding for ending waiting lists at drug treatment centers — not enough. He saw this as a substitute for clean needles, arguing that treatment on demand was a better way to proceed to fight both AIDS and drug addiction simultaneously. I think it was mostly a chicken-hearted way to avoid the needles issue — the years of propaganda about drug use created a loud voting bloc opposed to anything that looked like sanctioning of drug use.

The usual cast of American moralists characterized drug addiction as a character defect instead of an illness. Just pray your way out of heroin. Just say no. I wondered if Nancy Reagan got that advice from her astrologer?

What was especially concerning to those of us who were trying to save lives was the refusal of legislators opposed to clean needles to provide enough state money to make sure anyone who wanted to kick the habit could get into a drug treatment center. The very fact there were waiting lines was morally reprehensible.

Ray Flynn sent Dr. George A. Lamb, a city health expert, on a fact-finding trip to Europe to analyze needle exchange programs.

The mayor pointed out that the governor's drug programs have had no impact on drug addiction or AIDS among addicts, "The state treatment programs just haven't produced. There is still only one treatment facility for addicts in Boston with only 25 beds and a limited number of methadone clinics."

It was necessary for the city council to pass any such new program, and you can be sure Dapper opened his mouth as soon as he got wind of it. "It won't get my vote," he said, "I will not condone drugs or drug addicts. And if it does win in the council, I'll make sure there is an amendment attached. Drug addicts will have to give officials their names and addresses. This where we'll know who they are and where they live." This was the same sick thinking that launched the creation of CORI reports and later created our "sex offender registry" which haunts us to this day, making keeping track of actual pedophiles impossible, and caused Human Rights Watch to label it as a violation of human rights.

I replied to Dapper, "AIDS is a serious, out-of-control medical epidemic, and politicians have no business standing in the way of medical programs that experts say are necessary to protect us. Opponents of the program are passing moral judgment on this issue, as if drug addiction was not a disease, but an evil choice of lifestyle. What are we, barbarians? One out of every 60 babies are born with the AIDS virus. I suggest that those who want to interfere with expert medical advice on the issue consider whether they themselves should be held responsible for the further spread of this epidemic."

I could tell this was going to get nasty. The *Herald* attacked me again, and *Bay Windows* responded:

By Mark A. Perigard, February 25:

What is this paper's problem anyway? It's now obvious to even the more kind hearted among us that the paper has a vendetta against Boston City Councilor David Scondras. Is it because David is so unabashedly leftist? Or is it just that he makes no apologies for being gay? The Herald *doesn't devote a tenth as much coverage to the antics of the other 12 city councilors.*

The latest felony in print, headlined 'Scondras' attack' appeared February 18th. The excuse for all this wasted space was to rebut a talk Scondras gave to a group of gay scientists in which he compared the fight against AIDS to the fight against the Vietnam War.

The Pundits blustered "ending the war in Vietnam, like ending any war, was a tremendously complicated task; AIDS is a different matter entirely. Gays know precisely why AIDS has spread in the homosexual community. And they know how to stop it in its tracks."

Duh-h gee, Wilbur, what do they mean by that ? Are they aware that the gay community has led the country in reducing the spread of AIDS. Do they know about the assorted studies which show that gays have dramatically altered their sexual behaviors?

Herald *writers don't keep up with current events.*

The editorial also warned that Scondras' words "have done his own cause no good." Oh, now the Herald *is giving us advice on how to fight for our rights, isn't that convenient? About as trustworthy as a Nazi telling a Jew the way to spiritual redemption.*

By February 25th Mayor Flynn sent the needle exchange legislation to the council. If it passed the council it would have to go to the statehouse and pass that body as well. I chaired the committee that the bill was sent to.

We began with only four supporters: Rosaria Salerno, Travaglini, Tom Menino, and myself. We needed seven votes to win. Three more to go.

The Backrooms And The Hearings

On February 24th Peggy Hernandez and Bruce Mohl wrote a huge article on the fight headlined *"Dukakis, 7 Councilors oppose Flynn needle exchange plan."* In the article it quotes Dukakis as saying: "I don't believe it's the right way to go. I don't believe we ought to be encouraging people to shoot up with heroin." He said emphatically that he would veto any home rule petition (a city bill that required the state's approval which is what needle exchange would require). Dukakis said he doubted he would have to veto anything because the state would not pass Flynn's bill.

It made it clear to me that we would have to put on the most amazing education campaign and find ways to get political pressure on the council as a starting point.

We decided that the more we pushed the debate toward what makes medical sense the better off we would be — there was a tendency on the part of the public to support public health officials, or at least to think twice about contradicting them. Public health officials could help us mainstream the idea.

Some folks would pay attention to data showing that the proposal worked to cut down HIV transmission, and that would help some support it.

Some folks would pay attention to how much more it cost taxpayers to deal with someone infected than prevent the infection in the first place.

We felt that we could peel off each of the groups that objected to the program one at a time. I said I would need several weeks to assemble the specialists and data needed for the public hearings.

My staff and I decided that we had to campaign on this issue — that the usual method of organizing existing public support wouldn't work when the public was pretty clearly against the idea. We had to educate.

Education

I set up a meeting on March 2nd that was covered by the *Globe* — in fact, for several months the clean needle issue dominated much of the press in Boston.

Allan Parry was a health coordinator from Great Britain who came to one of the meetings I set up with most of the City Council and another 25 key people. He told us that the availability of clean needles is one reason Liverpool did not have as big an AIDS problem as Boston. Miraculously, I got nine of my colleagues to attend at least part of the multi-hour session. Several councilors said that they were concerned that distributing clean needles appeared to condone drug use. "Syringes don't make people take drugs," said Parry. "Drugs make people take drugs."

I told everyone that this was the first of many sessions I would be holding — and in private told several of my colleagues that they should deal with this now and asked them what I could do that would persuade them to give me a vote.

I was pretty upset with Charles Yancey, who was not going to go along with our so-called liberal coalition. It was clear to me that Christianity was a two edged sword, making people both more inclined to helping folks and more inclined to judging them. There was no reason Charles would be against the bill except for preachers being against it, and they were against it for mythological reasons like needles causing drug addiction or for thinking that supporting clean needles made you look like you supported drug pushers, which upon a moment's reflection becomes absurd.

The Parkman House

Ray Flynn invited a group of Boston's leaders to the Parkman House on March 3rd. He decided to invite the Cardinal Bernard Law and the governor to the meeting. Dukakis couldn't make it because he was campaigning for president in Texas. Law sent representatives. Many people did come however.

I went and listened carefully to the non-verbal language of the folks who came. Philip Johnston, who would later run the Democratic Party in Massachusetts, came as the state's Human Services Secretary to promise that the 1,200 waiting lists for treatment would be eliminated by summer. The commitment to end the waiting list, to focus on making sure treatment on demand would happen was a way of undercutting those who said we were not concerned about the health of drug addicts and to try to move the issue off the table so that the issue of AIDS could have center stage.

John Silber, President of Boston University, said that the ultimate solution to the problem of drug abuse lies in changing the hedonistic attitude of a society in which people believe the only goal in life is to have pleasure. (He clearly fell in with the "judge and punish" wing of Christianity!) He would again and again cross swords with me and many others whenever an opportunity existed for him to exercise the judgmental and punitive thinking supported by him and so many others. I wondered what, exactly, Silber thought the goal of life actually is? To have pain? To build up brownie points so God gives you a good seat in the football stadium of the afterlife? To accumulate power and money but not use it? It was certainly not the Christianity I was taught.

Anyway as subtle a part of human thinking as one's philosophy about the point of life had entered into the debate on clean needles.

I heard from Phillip Johnston that the state was 'exploring' ways to alter Medicare policies to allow third party payments for those enrolled in methadone maintenance programs. This would be a big deal. I learned over the years how talk was cheap, how expensive programs were, and how hard it was to find the cash to make talk reality.

Change

The key to the clean needles bill was always to move it away from the frame of "cops and crime" into "health and help" — a difficult transition in a puritanical society, but religion like everything else in human sociology was inconsistent about this — and we used the religious commandment to help your neighbor and to take care of the sick to counteract the subterranean but all too real idea that "the sinners deserve to die, the wages of sin is death."

We were starting to win.

Bruce Bolling, a black member of the council who had been its president for two years, said on March 6th that he was inclined to be supportive of a needles exchange program. He was an example of how agreeing with those who said expanded drug treatment should be the main weapon in the two front war against AIDS and drug abuse could win over some to the sunny side. The treatment issue had always been a way to not discuss the needle exchange program and we ended it as a vehicle people could use as diversion.

During the first hearing, Ray Flynn made a surprise appearance and testified. It was virtually unheard of for a mayor to make such a move.

He pointed out the program would cost what one person with AIDS costs the state to treat. That he would support the distribution of condoms in connection with the program. I know this seems small, but keep in mind that in 2004 the biggest obstacle to AIDS prevention in Africa has been the Catholic Church and George Bush refusing to allow condoms to be distributed through federal programs. The compassionate Catholic Ray Flynn in 1988 was ahead of where the Pope was in 2008, twenty-one years later.

The American Jewish Council and the Massachusetts Council of Churches voted to endorse the treatment and clean needle combined program.

We Win

U.S. Senator Edward Kennedy used a parliamentary move to make sure U.S. medical money could be used for clean needle programs, getting around an amendment sponsored by the right wing crazies that presently dominate the Republican Party. This became relevant to us because one factor in getting Boston to adopt the clean needle program was getting the Feds to allow federal money to finance the programs, which would include treating drug addiction.

On the federal level, Edward Kennedy not only stopped conservative lawmakers from inserting language in the one billion dollar appropriations bill for AIDS treatment, research and education which would stop any money being used for distributing clean needles, he also included language that would allow Koop to determine the effectiveness of needle exchange programs.

But ironically, it was Michael Dukakis who would become the biggest problem for us about clean needles.

We Vote

An April 28th article by M. E. Malone summarized the extra-ordinary day. It said:

> *Boston yesterday became the first city in the nation to endorse*
> *a pilot program for offering clean needles to drug addicts to try*
> *to slow the spread of AIDS. The City Council voted 8 to 5 to*
> *approve it.*
>
> *At a state house press conference yesterday, Dukakis reiterated*
> *his opposition to the plan which he has said would send the*
> *wrong message to drug addicts.*

Our strategy was to have the Boston delegation argue to their colleagues that since the bill only affects Boston and all Boston legislators want it, that they should defer to the Boston delegation about a Boston specific bill. Then approach Dukakis from the point that the legislature is united that Boston should have the right to its own opinion in matters affecting only Boston. Such an approach might work, but our own delegation in Boston was in fact *NOT* united.

I said that I hoped dialogue on the subject would lead to some kind of program to address the spread of AIDS. I told the *Globe*: "They either have to pass it or they'd better come up with something better."

I felt politically they would have to deal with the fact that a growing number of people wanted the pols to deal with stopping the spread of the virus and just saying no to ideas would not sit well with many constituents.

Neil Sullivan said the Senate's action would help us at the Statehouse. But Dukakis and the police were major hurdles.

In 1988, demonstrations about the Boston program were held against Dukakis at his national presidential headquarters and at Michael's home in Brookline. We had done a great thing. We had overcome a great deal of ignorance and fear. And were on the way to helping a lot of people that not too many people were very keen to help.

The battle continued

President George W. Bush was opposed to such a program but then again so was Bill Clinton. I will never forget the anger at him from public health officials when I was at a meeting between Clinton and them at the White House. Clinton apologized years later, saying that he had made a big mistake.

The first President to support clean needles and the removal of federal bans was Barack Obama in 2009.

"Divide and rule, the politician cries;
unite and lead, is watchword of the wise."
– Johann Wolfgang von Goethe

On February 17th-18th Robert and I went to Airlie, Virginia near Washington, DC where lesbian and gay leaders from around the country held the "War Conference." Over 121 action items were dealt with at a meeting including Barney Frank, who suggested how to pinpoint districts in which gay and lesbian candidates might best serve our interests. Keep in mind that as a community, gays and lesbians had perhaps 5-10% of the population. If we were represented in accordance with our numbers, we would have 90 Mayors of the 900 largest cities (we had one), 40 congress people (we had two) 500 state representatives (we had perhaps 10) etc.

The conference was one of many national meetings of gay and lesbian people, unthinkable ten years earlier and would become regular events in another decade.

The community struggled with how to move forward on the issues of great concern to our community. Two national organizations had formed, the National Gay and Lesbian Task Force (the 'activist' organization) and the Human Rights Campaign Fund (the 'insider' organization). They would continue to lead on national issues for over 20 years.

Together

Inspired by the "War Conference," on March 9th my office called together Massachusetts gay and lesbian community leaders for two meetings. They were fighting too many times with each other, and I decided the time had come to get people to work with each other. *Next* magazine summarized my efforts: "The intent is to coordinate the efforts of all segments of the community into a cohesive force," I said, and to a large extent, we would succeed. Already, in Massachusetts, we had at least a dozen different organizations dealing with separate issues and we needed to find a way to communicate and work together.

Hospice

All of the city's best interior designers were given a separate room to design in the city's first AIDS hospice, which was built on Mission Hill. Many of them worked to get parts of their designs donated. I held an open community meeting on April 7th to which over 100 people came. The neighborhood asked good questions about trash, noise and parking but what was wonderful was that they supported having a hospice for people dying of AIDS. It was a beautiful home.

I remember saying that while I was excited and happy that we would open a home to those dying of this disease, that my happiest day would be when we would shut that home because we had found a cure.

And Robert and I would live to see that day, unlike so many, many of our good friends.

The Trashman

We also dealt with other issues simultaneously, as usual. Like trash. I had put together a city ordinance as a result of studying the Buhler-Miag plants in Europe, which automatically sorted out trash and packages recyclables without source separation, but the city wanted to move along with source separation. I couldn't get colleagues unstuck from the "do it or else" model of getting your way. They could not accept a law unless it punished people for breaking it instead of incentivizing people to obey it.

Rosaria and I had studied a town in Illinois in which the mayor had decided on a totally different reward-oriented approach. Joe Sciacca outlined it in an April 20th article called, "Hub may cash in on trash deal." We wanted Boston to follow that lead. It read in part:

The program was advertised with music videos with the
Trashman, a guy dressed up in an orange sports coat wearing one red and
one blue shoe. $36,000 were given out from the fund and $250,000 was
spent advertising the program and not one cent came from taxpayers: the
companies that hauled trash put up the cash.

Rosaria and I were pushing to reopen a Boston paper mill
formerly used by the James River Company for use as a paper recycling
plant. We located a company, the Conservatree Paper Company, that was
interested in the lottery project, and which would employ over 200
people. The recycling plant would consume 160 tons of waste paper daily,
up to 20% of Boston's solid waste according to company estimates.

I was shown in detail the different automatic plants which did
separation in Europe, and was stunned to find out that Massachusetts,
which had a bottle bill, took the 5 and 10 cent deposits to create a
company called Krink that started a state of the art separation facility in
Rhode Island. Rosaria and I sat on benches made from the recycled
plastics and we knew from what we had seen that transforming trash
from something to get rid of to something that was a resource was where
the future lay.

The news of our efforts made it into the *Lowell Sun* and slowly
filtered out to many news outlets across the country.

Drugs

My staff was not too happy, but I decided to fight for legalization of drugs. On May 19th I said that "the collective acceptance of an underclass is an acceptance of drug abuse. The most effective war on drugs is a war on poverty. Legalization is just one small piece." I found myself in the company of William F. Buckley and Milton Friedman, perhaps for the first time, but all the data pointed in the same direction. Making drugs illegal fed gang wars, built a huge drug busting industry, left a big business untaxed (think liquor sales taxes), made unnecessary foreign policy problems issues from dealing with Afghanistan to Columbia, and an endless series of kids arrested for smoking dope, arguably the least harmful recreational drug available in the society while allowing the most dangerous, cigarettes and alcohol, to be freely legally sold and used.

Addiction has natural limits: studies showed that 5-10 percent of cocaine users become addicted but 6-8 percent of people who drink alcohol become addicted.

To my surprise, I got a lot of support for legalization from the police. But the anti-drug industry included jailers, police, federal bureaucrats and many others who would never support taking away their money and power by legalizing drugs. Making drugs illegal is just a protection racket that never helped anyone using drugs. We demonize marijuana no matter what studies say about the actual danger of the drugs. The Aztecs kept throwing virgins into volcanoes no matter what the data says about it's effectiveness at ending drought. Likewise, the obscene anti-drug rules feed the drug enforcers, the only people that benefit from the war on drugs.

It is always fascinating to watch Americans consuming McDonald's to the point of obesity, diabetes and heart disease, cigarettes to the point of hundreds of thousands a year dying from smoke caused death, and alcohol — the single biggest killer of kids — refusing to legalize drugs that would probably reduce the real killer drugs, undercut the organized crime that kept the drugs flowing, and move addiction from jail cells to hospital wards.

Welcome to the land of the brainwashed.

"On Beacon Hill we have our own jokes," said State Rep. Marjorie Clapprood during the political stand up comedy show that raised money for the Jimmy Fund. "We call them colleagues!" WRKO talk show host Jerry Williams put the show together. "What a great gathering this is," said Clapprood. "Imagine on the same stage — a Neanderthal chauvinist for whom walking upright is an effort, and your basic liberal pinko." (Dapper was the Neanderthal; I was pinko). Robert and I had a lot of fun.

My Colleagues Get Fed Up

Chris Iannella quashed my resolution on a troop buildup in Honduras. I was getting sick of Washington squandering our money but Chris felt it was "not city business." Rosaria understood the connection: "Boston will be affected when we have to send our boys over to Honduras," she said. I saw the connections on many levels, including the fact that people from South America migrated to the USA and became part of our fabric and would not be happy with the adventures conducted by an out of control military money-eater, with the way their home countries were being treated. "Why doesn't the federal government take the money it's squandering over there and give Boston a $10 million grant?" I asked.

I was annoyed that a council that met only one day a week pretended that it was too busy to comment on world affairs. One of Rosaria's staff people summarized it this way: "What you read in the paper on the front page ends up in the metro section." I felt that patting yourself on the back because you got an elderly woman a space in affordable housing instead of an equally deserving elderly woman was not what a local pol should be doing: he or she should be yelling at the Feds that there wasn't enough cash going toward housing for all of us and too much toward stuff like troops in Honduras.

I said to the press: "As long as Washington keeps taking money from my pockets and from the pockets of my constituents and keeps spending it on things I don't agree with, addressing those issues on the council is my job."

Trust me, Washington would love it if cities and towns and governors would shut up and go away, but fortunately they don't. Incidentally, the whole fuss was a farce because when issues affecting Northern Ireland or Italians surfaced, like Columbus Day for example, Chris and Kelly, who hated my stances on countries like Honduras, rushed to get the council to make statements on behalf of the home countries of the ethnic groups to which they belonged. Apparently, hypocrisy was a central ingredient of local politics.

ACT UP

"Silence=Death" was the signature of ACT UP. (AIDS Coalition To Unleash Power). ACT UP is still around, still needed, but in the beginning it was alone as the force that pushed for medicines and fair treatment.

I got a letter from Harvey Fierstein. I had marched next to him in the 1987 parade in Washington D.C. He was a New York producer and playwright. Some of his letter was painful:

> *The dedication to my play "Safe Sex" read as follows: 'To my little Christopher. You will live to celebrate life again. Trust me on this one.' It was a promise I could not keep. Within ten months of my writing that, Christopher was dead. At the time of his death he was almost totally paralyzed, incontinent, demented and in great pain. He was twenty-six years old and had AIDS. He was one of four members of the "Torch Song Trilogy" company to have died of AIDS. We lost another five people from the companies of "La Cage Aux Folles."*

Harvey demanded that we all get together and force the government to release drugs for Americans, like AZT which was available in Europe, and spend money on testing treatment methods using other new drugs, and stop the discrimination against people with AIDS that was growing ugly.

32 Arrested at an AIDS Rally in Manhattan

Demonstrators holding hands during a moment of silence yesterday in Foley Square. A march and rally sponsored by the AIDS Coalition to Unleash Power (Act Up) ended in a sit-in outside the United States Court House. Police arrested 32 protesters for disorderly conduct. They were demanding increased Government involvement in the fight against AIDS.

ACT UP has changed America. At their first demonstration on Wall Street they hung the commissioner of the FDA in effigy, 17 members getting arrested. Within one week the FDA announced rules for swifter drug release and the NIH released two of the drugs that ACT UP had been fighting for. Dan Rather gave ACT UP credit for this.

ACT UP organized political protests everywhere and contributed more than any single organization to the changes that are now part of the way the government does medical research, including giving patients new drugs before they are released in 'compassionate use' programs. I saw my former staff aide French Wall in a photo at a sit-in in Manhattan. We were everywhere.

Harvey Fierstein was one of many, many well-known figures who fought for making AIDS a national priority, and in the end, they won.

Grandma Krebs

We stayed in the finished basement because I didn't want to rub Robert's grandmother's face in our gay relationship, but I found out later that she had thought we would be staying together in a large bed upstairs. Grandma was sweet and open-minded and kind. She sent us a clipping from the local paper, the *Colfax Tribune* —

> *Monday, April 18th the Congregate Meal Program celebrated their tenth year in Colfax. Piano music was played by David Scondras. He is a friend of the Krebs' grandson Robert who is an architect in Boston. Mr. Scondras played piano duets with Eleanor Howell. A sing-along followed.*

I found a goat loose in the town of Colfax and chased it everywhere. Perhaps my Greek heritage included goat herding. Anyway, everyone in town knew about the guy chasing the goat (the goat won) and I learned how quickly a small town learns everything about newcomers. Especially such an odd one.

Grandma sent a note with the clipping: "We enjoyed your stay so much. I just wish you lived closer. Come back soon. Love you both. Everyone enjoyed you two, especially David's piano playing. Grandma K."

My big surprise: Grandma, a life long Republican, supported Jesse Jackson but wasn't too vocal about it to avoid a discussion with Grandpa about it.

Campaigning Schedule

- April 29th Delta 271 to Cincinnati; party at a local black judge's house; reception of University Faculty Club; speak about Jesse Jackson during the shows from 10 to 1 on a bar disco tour; go to the Omni Netherlands Hotel for a speech.

- April 30: Delta 425 to San Francisco interviews all day about Jesse Jackson, including with *Bay Area Reporter;*

- April/May 1: drive to Sacramento. Brunch with the "River City" Democratic Club 75-100 people will be there. Take a plane to Los Angeles and contact Robin Podolsky of the Jackson Campaign;

- May 2: Interviews with local news at Astro's Coffee Shop, Glendale Boulevard; AIDS hearing in Plumber's Park; Stonewall Democratic Club speech in North Orange Grove in West Hollywood (where my old friend and former porn star Steven Shulte was now Mayor);

- May 3: Greater Los Angeles Press Club speech; catch a flight to New York City on Pan Am.

We campaigned in Ohio and Michigan, California and Iowa, and I came to understand the amount of energy you needed to campaign across our country. I stood on stages behind Jesse Jackson and was carried away by the river of words that took us out to sea, our chance to sail across the oceans of misunderstandings and fear. I stood behind the singer Holly Near as she sang to audiences, and I felt outclassed and somehow not strong enough to carry off the transformation we were trying to get to, that we are still trying to reach. To calm my nerves, I drank — too much. So I left California without having spoken in the way I wanted to the crowds — I was there, I said some things, but I had not yet reached a place clear enough inside me to get out the words I needed the world to hear. That would come in time.

Police Spying at the State House

On May 26th the chief of the police that patrolled the Statehouse said they had infiltrated 'secret' meetings to spy on gays to "thwart protests." We were annoyed and a bit confused, as the chief of police himself said "they advertise these meetings on hotlines and in newspapers." In other words, far from being "secret meetings" they were open to whoever we could get to show up.

There was never a secret about the meetings, or for that matter about what was decided, and it was unconstitutional to "thwart protests." Just as a reminder, the relevant Constitutional amendment reads: "Congress shall make no law… prohibiting the free exercise thereof; or abridging the freedom of speech…; or the right of the people peaceably to assemble, and to petition the Government for a *redress* of grievances."

In essence, Police Chief Dan Skelly specifically wanted to abridge freedom of speech, freedom of assembly, and the petitioning of the government for a redress of grievances, but hell, what's a piece of paper when compared with the lust for control that police around the world have always tended toward?

I was not pleased. I was quoted in a May 28th *Herald* article: "The surreptitious monitoring drives a stake through the heart of the democratic process. The issue is that it is un-American to have secret police invade organizations that are discussing political actions. That is totally intolerable."

The police chief admitted that his officers had sat in on planning sessions, wore civilian clothes, did not announce that they were police. He claimed that there was nothing 'sinister' about it, thus proving he really did not understand *in any sense* what the phrase "free society" means.

The National Gay and Lesbian Task Force in Washington said they were distressed that Governor Dukakis had not condemned the action (because it took place at the State House).

It amazed me that people did not get it, that people could not freely discuss what they wanted to do politically among themselves if they thought that police would be spying on them. It put a cloud of silence in any room with strangers in it, and could easily end the fragile freedom at the heart of America. Our founding fathers would rather have no government than no freedom, and here it appeared that to some extent we were being told that freedom was going to be sacrificed for some vague notion that safety came first.

Ray Flynn supported the filing of a civil rights complaint with the Human Rights Commission that had an impact because I did not hear about any other kinds of meetings that the police infiltrated. Representative Byron Rushing said he would launch an investigation.

We decided to sue to find out what other groups the police were infiltrating, if any. It was just wrong. It was hard enough to get folks to meetings: they were already nervous about being 'out,' and the police had no business interfering with freedoms.

After the Civil Liberties Union sued for information from the Capitol police, it turns out that the information they got about the gay demonstrations were provided to the police voluntarily by one of the groups under surveillance. John Reinstein, the legal director for the Civil Liberties Union of Massachusetts, said that it wasn't clear that there was any need for them to go to the meetings.

We gave anyone who wanted any info they wanted about anything we planned to do because we wanted everyone to know about it. The whole episode was weird, reflecting the fear response that seemed to characterize 'protection' rackets that we call police and prosecutors.

The Homeless Move to City Hall

In front of Boston's City Hall is a red brick desert. It extends to beneath the gargantuan overhang of concrete that demarcates the edge of the superstructure of the building, creating an area protected from the rain and snow. The red brick desert has an urban legend associated with it. Apparently the designer wanted the bricks placed randomly (there are more than one color of brick). But the workers, probably bored out of their minds, started to make designs with the bricks which you could see if you looked from a balcony overlooking the desert.

The designer one day noticed the brick diamond patterns and had a fit. He told the workers to stop, and the bricks were torn out and replaced randomly. However, I noticed when walking around the desert that from time to time a design escaped the purview of the Brick Gestapo. I smiled, thinking that no matter what you do, humans will insert their mark on everything.

Homeless people congregated on the brick steps at the edge of the brick desert, beneath the concrete protective canopy of City Hall. The homeless felt it was a political statement, a use of political free speech, complete with a demand: that the city give the homeless the deeds to 10 abandoned buildings and the money to fix them up.

Between 30 and 60 "Homefront" members camped out on cots and in sleeping bags on the steps.

Rosaria and I stopped the police from evicting the homeless at first by joining them and making it clear that we would be hauled off to jail along with them if the police made arrests. Salerno said, "City Hall is a public building. There is no reason for them not to be there. And every day they are there, it reminds us all of a problem that won't go away until we solve it."

Of course Kelly and Dapper had a different take: "They are a blight to City Hall Plaza," he said. I smiled. I considered the plaza a blight to the city. Dapper said, "Enough is enough…. I'm going to do everything I can to get them out."

After a week of this, the police decided to move the homeless out. They sat down on the steps and waited for the arrests to begin. They sang another tune adapted from the sixties' civil rights movement:

No More homeless, no more homeless
No more homeless over me
And before I'll be your slave
I'll be buried in my grave
And I'll fight for my right
To be free

Salerno made it clear the police would have to arrest her, so they instead picked up the cots, blankets and other supplies, and drove off in two police wagon without a word. No one was arrested but eventually everyone decided to leave.

Meetings continued and Ann Maguire — now the mayor's person on homeless shelters — did everything she could to figure out a way to get housing for everyone.

It did not work completely, but it helped.

The city pointed to the state which pointed to the Feds, but for those who had no place to stay at night in the winter, that was poor consolation.

It is a fact of life that in a nation able to spend trillions of dollars on projects ranging from protecting the habitats of wild condors to giving guns to both sides of wars, we don't have a way to deal with the homeless the vast majority of whom have no way to survive.

One day in the alley behind my house, I saw a small truck stopped. In it were a guy, his wife and a baby. They were scouring the alley for bottles to return to pick up enough change to pay for gas and food. They could not get enough time and money to find a place or get a job which there were few of to start with.

I thought about it, and wondered why the country we called America, which needed to be judged by how it treated its most vulnerable, was considered 'great.' In Holland the constitution provided a guarantee of safe, decent housing for every person. In the United States, in Boston alone, over 100 people died of exposure every winter. The homeless and the sick that no one wanted, or wanted to know existed.

I thought the camp was a reminder to those who wanted to live in the wonderland created by the media that the real world was beyond tough for a lot of people we called 'ours' or pretended were somehow at fault for being sick or overwhelmed by an economy that had no protection for those who fell through the cracks.

Well, get on welfare, you might say. But it does not exist for most people. Here is an irony: to get most government help, you have to have an address!

The homeless put up a memorial to all who died on the streets. I went by it every day, and I decided to push for year-round shelters, food, and medicine for everyone who needed it. Before I left City Hall, this was what we accomplished.

Christian Science vs. Reality

I was a city councilor in Boston but I also lived a couple of blocks from the Christian Science Church. I also counted as a friendly acquaintance John Selover who was to become the chairman of the five-member board of the Christian Science Church.

The principal of 'freedom' of religion has never sat well with me. It amounts to the idea that people have a 'right' to believe whatever they want, which I have less concern about than the corollary, the right to 'do whatever I want.' Lately it has also come to mean that people can be hateful, cruel, and discriminatory in the name of their 'God!'

The connection between belief and action is the crux of this debate. Take the following event, which was reported in the *Boston Globe* on May 3rd:

This is more than a small event — underlying the event is a fundamental issue. Can you really accept social policy, law, institutions, interventions, education, investigations and the actions of governments, which are based on mythologies, things that are simply not true, or which interfere with actions that are known to work?

I thought about it, and have concluded that by the same reasoning that brought the Christian Science Church into conflict with law, there was a serious question as to whether churches and other institutions which teach young people that being gay is sinful, bad, sick or evil leading them to psychological problems, suicides and to suffer other kinds of damage in spite of medical knowledge that it is a sexual orientation established by nature in every higher species could be subjected to damages suits and restraining orders. Shouldn't the parents of kids who kill themselves because they are gay, who were taught by churches that they would go to hell, have the right to seek redress in court, to restrain institutions from those types of teachings that doctors, psychiatrists and child development specialists all agree are the source of the damage done to the child?

In general, should we allow institutions, which disseminate information known to be false to be free from the consequences of that dissemination? To yell fire in a crowded theater where there is no fire? To teach that you will die miserably and alone, and suffer the fires of hell in the afterlife if you are gay?

Anyway, the underlying issue is even broader: Can a world whose only hope for its future is the reach for reason embodied in the enlightenment afford to have freedom of lying without consequence? To paint, as if in dispute, matters not in dispute? To base decisions on things that are just not true, when the facts are available?

This is the central issue of this and previous generations, for everything from global warming to the way women are treated in some countries, all are connected to social/public policies based upon a fabric of mythology and lies rather than fact and experience. I fear for our species.

Freedom to believe in nonsense and preach insanity was to be preserved for individuals, not for institutions paid to provide us guidance and make decisions affecting millions, not for companies or people paid to know the facts. It is interesting that we would never allow a group of people at an airport to decide who could fly the plane. We know better. And to allow a group of priests in drag swinging pocketbooks on fire to decide what is and what is not acceptable sexual or other behavior is equally irresponsible.

No More Condos

On Wednesday, June 29th, the Boston City Council with its new representative, Rosaria Salerno giving us the seven votes we needed, passed a sweeping new housing law. We protected some 70,000 tenants from being evicted for condo conversion, the process by which landlords and developers were evicting tenants and selling off apartments, usually with little or no cosmetic improvements and virtually no real improvements, to speculators driving up the price of housing, displacing long term residents, uprooting relationships that were at the heart of what made neighborhoods communities.

The final vote was 9 to 4, because when it was clear that there were seven votes, two more councilors decided it was better to be on the winning side of this one, given the tenant vote.

We made the law retroactive to May 4th to help some 450 apartments where eviction proceedings had already begun.

The *Globe* article of June 30th said "Yesterday's City Hall drama was enlivened by impassioned speechmaking and punctuated by numerous recesses while councilors were heavily lobbied by Mayor Flynn's top aides and real estate representatives."

Over a hundred people were at the meeting, which went on for hours. There were 15 amendments attempted to undermine the new law, and we used Nancy Reagan's "Just Say No" as our mantra to kill every one of them. One of our colleagues, Jim Byrne, said "I just wish some of our colleagues would stand up and think for themselves. They were better trained than circus poodles." Of course in reality Jim was a guy who ran and ask Jerry Rappaport, one of Boston's biggest landlords, what to do whenever the issue was about housing.

Mayor Flynn had been working on trying to protect tenants for many years. When he was a city councilor, he pushed over and over again to protect tenants. Once, he said about those who cared so little for the poor that "they must go straight to hell when they die." And he meant it literally. Ray believed in the afterlife and in divine justice.

The *Herald* said "Salerno and Scondras led the floor fight for Flynn's proposal, heading a coalition that included Bolling, Yancey, Travaglini, McLaughlin and Iannella.

Flynn called the law "a breakthrough" and landlords referred to it as "devastating." The new law allowed a rental building to go condo if the majority of tenants who had lived in the building for over a year voted in favor of it.

There was no way to continue to pretend that housing used as investments as if they were stocks and bonds, bought and sold on the speculative market, was acceptable to a society that wanted stability, neighborhoods, and to avoid a price balloon.

Like all victories, this one would prove to be temporary, but for years it would keep Boston's neighborhoods more stable than they had been during the years of rapid conversion, and would fuel the construction of new housing because we purposefully said that if you build new housing, it would not be under any controls pushing the developers and speculators toward increasing the supply of housing rather than recycling old buildings.

Real estate interests, before now just annoyed with me, now focused a good deal of energy trying to get me out of office. On the other hand, the tenant organizations gave Rosaria and me plaques and applause.

Since most of my friends were tenants, I was happy. I did not want to see another friend losing their home.

"He has a right to criticize, who has a heart to help."
– Abraham Lincoln

For half a century the reeds at the edges of the park in the Fenway we call the Fens, part of Olmstead's "Emerald Necklace," has been a cruising area for gay men. The adjacent parkland contains the last remaining large number of "victory gardens" — small plots of land where local residents grow flowers and vegetables.

Over the years the city tried idea after idea to get rid of gay cruising. The city invented ridiculous ecological arguments to justify killing the reeds which live on the waters edge of the Muddy River, such as they were 'invasive' (they haven't changed where they are for 150 years) or they "slowed down the flow of water" (which might suggest dredging the river not cutting down the reeds along the edge where they actually hold back the land from filling the river in).

The city used poisonous plant killer to kill them which freaked out the gardeners; tried burning them down (which led to better blooms the following year); cutting them down with machetes (too much work with people up to their knees in mud), digging up the roots (the remaining roots just spread filling in the holes); to using police to arrest gay men (which is what they really wanted to do in the first place).

So when a stabbing occurred in the Fens in 1988, the Boston Deputy Superintendent of Police James Claiborne said he would patrol the fens and arrest any men having public sex, as opposed to finding the stabber. [See chapter 77, section "A Maniac in the Reeds," when a killer hunted gay men in 1986 in those same reeds].

I said publicly, "If gays are arrested for public sex (out of view of anyone else, mind you, as private as kissing on a remote beach at two in the morning) then the police should also arrest straight people down at Castle Island (a heterosexual cruising area where people had sex in cars) and that if there was not a uniform policy about public sex then it was discriminatory and a violation of civil rights."

Interestingly, the state Supreme Judicial Court (SJC) agreed, ruling that the police had no business arresting anyone for sex if they were not trying to make it public, that is to say, if they were out of view conducting private business. The SJC underestimated the number of ways the police could interrupt gay behavior, like parking police cars in the park and shining lights on people who were cruising.

Some would say "how disgusting" that gays had sex in the Fens, and after the well-known sportscaster Bob Gamere was stabbed while he was cruising, the police got aggressive about ending the cruising.

I intervened and eventually the stabbings ended, the young people involved were caught, and life went on.

This became another chapter in the book of sexual freedom issues that have never been resolved. The problem was that in the absence of social acceptance of gay life and sex, and the continuation of closeted behavior as a result, things like cruising in parks at night out of sight would continue as the only option save for abstinence which, apparently, was required only of gays.

It was not acceptable, as an example, for a boy to bring home his male date to meet the family, or neck in the family car, or dance on the heterosexual bar floors for that matter. There was a social apartheid going on, and the pretense that this was an abstract issue, some liberal silliness that was not substantive, protected the illusion that laws and rules were fair for everyone.

I remember saying that they won't let you eat at the dinner table but were disgusted when you ate in the alley. So don't eat?

A city in which in 1988, 10% of girls between 15 and 19 had a pregnancy was hardly in a position to pretend that out-of-marriage sexual behavior among heterosexuals was not happening. But the city was determined to make sure that gay sex was restricted by rules not obeyed by anyone else in practice.

In the end the attack on the reeds was an attack on gay men and gay sex. In fact, if the neo-Puritans had it their way, there would be no sex at all.

The SJC ruled that the right to sex in private included public settings in which people were not trying to impose their behavior on others — in other words if you go to the woods to neck on a blanket at midnight you couldn't be arrested for 'public' anything because 'public' means that the behavior was being imposed on an unwilling public which simply did not exist at two a.m. in the middle of nowhere.

Part of the difficulty stemmed from hypocrisies around sex itself — a behavior demanded by nature and suppressed by bigots resulting in confused public policies that attempted to do battle with nature itself.

It would be like demanding that people not eat or pee and then being upset that secret peeing and eating were happening all over the place.

No surprises here. I had the courage to speak publicly about sex arguing that it was natural, fun, and that the society had no business putting rules around it beyond those needed to make sure it did not interfere with what we all needed to do to keep the necessities of life produced and distributed. If it didn't stop the food from getting to the table, leave it alone.

On July 20th, they came again, this time the poison "Rodeo" in hand that kills plants. They tried. They lost. The reeds have so far successfully overcome 80 years of efforts to get rid of them driven by a desire to get rid of gay men cruising in them. Neither the reeds nor the gays have left. A group of volunteers from my office went into the reeds at night and gave out whistles, and leaflets on using whistles to protect each other, figuring that they were practical, and the other stuff wanted by the bigots were never going to succeed anyway. No point even arguing about it.

Atlanta: Democratic Convention

The Democratic Convention was July 16-22. I reviewed the dozens of speeches I gave on behalf of Jesse Jackson, and listening carefully to the negotiations, which led to changes in the party led by Jackson.

I got a lot of pressure from friends and heavyweights in the party to support Michael Dukakis, now the nominee. It was ironic but my very pointed visibility and anger at Michael could be of great use to him in shoring up the left.

I felt that George Bush was really not someone I could in good conscience support and that keeping out of the race was self-destructive. Barney Frank in one speech said, "Think of it as a one-night stand. It's two minutes to two and there are only two dates left, George and Mike." Or something to that effect.

I finally decided that I had to support Michael Dukakis and put out a press release that got coverage across the country.

This really was difficult for me. But I remembered Barney pointing out that supporting someone for office was not getting married to them, it was a decision on which person would be best for you. By that standard, George H. W. Bush would be not as good for us as Michael Dukakis by any measure.

So I bit my tongue and swallowed, suppressed my ego, placed pride aside and published my decision on who was best for us. It went like this:

Why I am voting for Michael Dukakis
by Boston City Councilor David Scondras

We have spoken out across the country hoping to get the Democratic Party leaders to reject the policy of courting Archie Bunker Democrats at the expense of progressives. The party had chosen not to listen.

We argued that many of those who have been historically devalued would stay home if the party did not reach out to them and their concerns.

People of color, gay and lesbian people, and progressives made their concerns very clear by supporting Jesse Jackson. This message was heard by many, and is reflected in the Democratic Party platform and rules reform. Our message will continue to be heard as we grow stronger.

Jackson lost the nomination. Dukakis won the nomination.

Integrity made us work for Jackson. Now, integrity calls upon us to work for Dukakis.

There are some who feel progressives ought to intentionally stay home to "teach the Democrats a lesson". They feel this is a way to get more power.

I disagree. But even if this were true, who would pay for the lesson?

I'm sure the hungry and homeless, the sick and the old, those living with AIDS and those who are frightened at the pollution that is killing the seas — those who have suffered in so many ways from the Reagan-Bush policies of the past eight years — would wonder why we decided to desert them. I'm sure those who fought for eight years to stem the erosion of progress for people of color under the Reagan-Bush administration would wonder why we decided to leave.

I'm voting for Michael Dukakis because I'm voting for the children whose school lunch was under attack by a presidency that declared ketchup an adequate vegetable.

I'm voting for Dukakis because the Reagan-Bush years offered us sun screen as the antidote to the disintegration of the ozone.

I'm voting for Dukakis because the children in the towns of northern Nicaragua want an end to a war that has them jumping in and out of trenches to protect themselves from Bush-Reagan sponsored terrorists.

I'm voting for Dukakis because children who are dying at the hands of drug dealers need a leader who will dump Noriega, not support him.

I'm voting for Dukakis because people with AIDS need a president who will fight to get new drugs out to people with AIDS, to cut FDA red tape without using the AIDS crisis as an excuse to deregulate the drug industry, and who will protect people with AIDS from discrimination — instead of dragging his feet in spending money already allocated by Congress. That man is not George Bush, who sent a letter to gay elected officials focusing on testing as a key response to the AIDS crisis.

We're voting for Dukakis because the oceans that are dying cannot wait four years for Jackson to save them from Bush's commitment to offshore drilling.

We're voting for Dukakis because the homeless who sleep on City Hall steps all summer need the federal government to build 200,000 units a year — as they did before Reagan — rather than the 20,000 a year that have been built under Reagan-Bush.

Vote for Dukakis because you do not want to be a part of a presidency that offers women the coat hanger as their only choice to an unwanted pregnancy, a presidency that would bring back the nightmare we remember.

Vote for Dukakis because he has openly gay men and women in his campaign, because when a gay rights bill passes he will sign it.

Vote for Michael Dukakis because Ronald Reagan in eight years has appointed more than half of all the judges in the federal courts and you don't want George Bush to appoint the rest.

Vote for Dukakis because the three most liberal members of the Supreme Court are in their 80's; because you do not want to be part of a decision that will shackle the next two generations with a Reagan-Bush court that has already given us Hardwick and is itching to overturn Roe v Wade.

I know Dukakis is not the Savior. But it is a mistake to look for salvation in a president. It comes from within each of us.

I will vote for Michael Dukakis because he is a good man. And we can help him become a better man.

I hope you will join me.

I joined the Dukakis campaign. This was significant because it was long before it was popular to get gay support. Soon I would be traveling again across the United States, this time for the governor of my state.

I could tell that our cat, Nixon, wanted to jump through the window to attack the newcomer, but the white wavy line down the back of the big black furry animal told me it was a skunk and I didn't care how much Nixon growled, he wasn't gonna go out, piss off the skunk and stink up our house.

But my self-destructive tendencies tended to piss off a variety of skunks, such as *Herald* reporter Howie Carr, and I sometimes ended up smelling like their piss. When you have been the victim of so many injustices, managing the anger can be difficult.

So can staying sober.

Because two things about being gay are never fully mentioned or widely understood — you learn to feel you are a fake and have no self-esteem because you have banished your self.

When I was on stage my senior year at Harvard, playing the part of Malvolio in Shakespeare's *Twelfth Night,* there was a paper called *Boston After Dark* which eventually became part of the *Boston Phoenix.* The first edition of it had me on the front page in costume — A star! But I didn't feel it.

When you spend your life pretending to be who you are not, and people praise you for things, you feel like a fake. The price of the closet, the huge number of ways that gays protected themselves, paid attention to not being noticed (not holding hands in the dark in a movie; having no dates; having 'girlfriends' laughing at jokes implying you were one of the men; playing games you really did not particularly like to play; joining the military; in some instances, becoming a Republican), all these things protected you, but they made it harder and harder to be clear that people actually liked the real you, because they never got to know the real you. In fact, I started to lose the sense of who the real me was as I grew up and went to college, never actually dealing with the fact of being gay. And even if I had, the society would have punished me even more than it did.

So one price of the closet was to not feel, to be behind the mask that was in place for others to see, and to treat the statements back and forth between you and others as lines in a play.

Great for politics. Bad for mental health.

Another price was every now and then deciding that others were better than you, real people, real guys. When you were with the 'real' men, you felt the need to live up to their expectations. Approval seeking. And this created so much anxiety that getting drunk seemed to help even though it didn't. My friend Mitzel worked at the gay book store Glad Day and later started the gay bookstore Calumus. I don't remember him ever really being sober (and not very dysfunctional either, notwithstanding his liquid diet).

Same for Chris Iannella's aide Bob Kaven — I don't remember him ever being sober either. The fact the gay bars were our churches, the centers of our lives, the only places we could be ourselves and live out our gay lives, says something — I mean we didn't pick gay churches or gay movie theaters.

Maybe by the 21st century it has become more complex — gayish gyms and gay games, gay marriage and gay bowling leagues — but in 1988 it was bars, bathrooms, parks, and the nightmare of AIDS.

So I tried to make sure I didn't binge in order to run away from what I never really wanted to do. The stress of my public life was particularly difficult for me as I was ambivalent about my self-worth. There are those who think that I ran to every TV camera in sight. Actually, I spent a lot of my life alone, and wanted for most of my life to be left alone to do my thing. I was a hippie living in a place surrounded by preachers and people quick to punish and laugh at you.

But although it is painful to say, I did drink too much when I felt scared — of not living up to my own and everyone else's expectations.

Some people would like to say, 'He's an alcoholic.' Not so. Been to enough meetings to understand the thinking. The issue is sometimes we abuse what ordinarily we use appropriately, and to understand why this happens is the road to success, not magical thinking that creates another religion out of abstinence, another facet of the same Puritanism that believes blame and punishment, rules and obedience leads to salvation.

I never thought anyone had to be saved. Stopped sometimes, but never 'saved'.

I did not feel compelled to get drunk, but sometimes I decided to. There is a big difference. But they can both get you into trouble.

Water, Water Everywhere

Ground water levels were starting to hurt more housing (if you recall lower ground water meant buildings foundations sinking and walls cracking; see chapter 86). Jimmy Kelly and I were worried, proving that in politics there are no friends or enemies, just common interests. In this case, I wanted to maintain leadership over ground water problems and Kelly wanted to protect his constituents — he represented Chinatown. A big headline from the October 6th *Boston Herald* said "Chinatown Under Water Attack — Hundreds of Homes in Danger."

Four brick row houses in the center of the commercial part of Chinatown where the restaurants were had been condemned and dozens more were structurally damaged. The water table was sinking and this meant the wooden piles that held up the buildings were rotting which happened when water that previously covered them fell exposing them to air. In other words, it was very important for the stability of buildings that the water table stayed at the same level.

William Rizzo, the Chairman of the groundwater trust which I put in place a year earlier warned that this was the "tip of the iceberg" because as many as 200 to 400 units of low income housing were threatened, wrote Rizzo to Mayor Flynn.

I said that we needed money to study and monitor the whole city because without an early warning system, we would have to wait for buildings to fall down before we realized that there was a problem, a hell of a lot more expensive to repair than putting more water in the ground which is all you had to do if you caught the problem early enough.

I was worried that Chinatown would lose jobs, housing and restaurants and the city would lose tourists, taxes and the fun of visiting Chinatown. I got the city to cough up $25,000, which freed up $35,000 in matching funds from the Four Seasons Hotel. This would fund at least some of the engineering study that was needed.

Pets

I had worked for many years at the Boston Center for Older Americans [see book I, chapter 21], and I came to learn that pets for old folks and the disabled did two things: help with the loneliness and give people a little exercise. Pets were a good thing. Pets were a way people met each other as well. But for some people other people having pets were a nuisance: smells, barking, poop. In any event, we decided that all things considered, for some people asking them to choose between their pets and their home was really not fair.

I remember how long it took for me to convince one landlord to allow a person who was disabled in the Fenway to keep his pet. The tenant spent years after that thanking me. He taught me from his reaction, that it was not about pets. It was about a member of his family.

I thought about the nuisance issues, and concluded that the objections to having them was mostly coming from two groups: First, young folks who got drunk on Friday and Saturday night, which let's face it, led to more nuisances than pets ever dreamed of, including peeing on my back door and keeping me up during party season. And second, from a few older families who for God-knows-what reason didn't think their kids were a nuisance. We might love them, but they are not clean and quiet!

So on October 5th the Council passed a law that Rosaria and I put together which prohibit owners of housing with more than three units from restricting or discriminating against any elderly or handicapped tenant in connection with admission to, or continued occupancy of, rental housing because they own pets.

We got Dapper to co-sponsor this legislation, and when our names were together sponsoring a law, it passed because we covered the spectrum — the message to everyone was that the law was 'safe' for anyone to join. The *Globe* article on the law reminded me that the ordinance was drafted in reaction to the October 9th story of Peggy Hernandez which read:

> *Following publicity this year 91-year-old Alice Stacy was evicted*
> *from the former Columbia Point housing project because she*
> *would not give up her Afghan dog 'Good Boy.' The dog died the*
> *day Stacy was moved from Columbia Point. The woman was*
> *later moved back into a new apartment at the complex, now*
> *known as Harbor Point.*

At the same meeting that passed the dog law, there was a fight over who would get to have hearings over an idle paper mill involving 200 union workers — I got the council to send the matter to me, to my "special committee on waste management." I wanted to see if we could help get a recycling business set up requiring that paper generated under I law I wrote be recycled as material from which to make new paper.

Anyway council meetings dealt with issues from whales to recycling, pets to gay rights. It fit well with my tendency to be interested in everything, and my ADHD.

"A lie can travel halfway around the world
while the truth is putting on its shoes."
—Mark Twain

The right wing was at it again, and I finally figured out that they really weren't just stupid; they were driven by a desire to make everyone obey them, believe in the values they espoused. They were all "true believers" and this is what made them so dangerous. I use he term as defined in 1951 Eric Hoffer's social psychology book called *The True Believer: Thoughts on the Nature of Mass Movements.*

True believers think they have a duty to convert everyone to their truth. For them, there is no truth except their truth. The biggest threat to world peace is people who believe that only they have access to the truth.

The Republican Party in the U.S.A. is increasingly a captive of true believers, which our society incorrectly calls 'religious.' This is a misfortune because if we were to be accurate about it, the people of the evangelical Christian and fanatical Muslim movements are not engaged in a search for truth which would be the common ground between science and religion, but rather in a search for converts, control, condemnation, punishment and power. And they are not sane. To label these mobthink gangs 'religious' is to grant them a freedom to spread, which is dangerous to freedom itself.

Anyway, in the fall of 1988 a film called "The Last Temptation of Christ" hit Boston (in the film, Jesus, while on the cross, imagines a future in which he marries Mary Magdalene and lives a long life with her and their children). I will never forget the fuss. We debated it at the city council with Dapper and the other right-wingers denigrating those who went to see the movie.

The Catholic Church organized their fruitcakes into mass protests while the city and state officials accommodated their insanity by blocking off whole roads to accommodate them.

I always thought the entire movie issue was ridiculous.

First, you have to go find where the film is playing, then pay money to the theater, and go in to watch the movie. You are not grabbed while shopping somewhere, dragged into the trunk of a car, and then tied to a chair and have your eyelids propped open and forced to watch the movie against your will. It is a voluntary act that costs money.

Second, if the Church really wanted to stop the film they would shut up about it, which they didn't because it gave them fuel to continue their insanities, a *cause célèbre* that provided a focus for action. It exemplified the necessity of the enemy, of the Devil, without which why have a God? Without evil there is no need for salvation.

Anyway, I decided to go see the movie (I went alone; Robert felt it was sadistic), and realized I had been duped. Not because it was terrible — it was passable I suppose, but I never would have bothered to watch a bunch of guys in dirty rags wandering around a lot of sand and rocks except for all the advertising that the Church got from their picket lines.

What is important to remember about this episode is that the protestors never bothered to get permits, and yet the city and state blocked off roads to accommodate their nutty demonstrations. This support for freedom of expression did not extend to a coalition of AIDS groups who staged a noisy protect October 6th at the Westin Hotel. They were protesting the Anti-Defamation League (ADL) giving Cardinal Bernard Law an award when Cardinal Law would not support help for AIDS. I knew quite a bit about this protest because I had to intervene to get a permit for it. The Catholic protestors of "Last Temptation," you'll note, had no permit at all, which was okay in this Irish Catholic and Italian city. In spite of the permit for the AIDS rally, when five folks got into the cocktail reception area of the hotel, shouting slogans to conference attendees, Boston plain-clothed cops handcuffed the five protestors. The five protesters were kept at the police station all afternoon.

To understand how hypocritical this is, compare the following: if you tried to see the movie "Last Temptation of Christ," you had to run a picket line of protestors who handed you leaflets and yelled at you, you could not park near the theater because the public streets were shut down, and you were yelled at leaving the movie. But if you tried to protest the Cardinal who was opposed to stopping AIDS, who demonized being gay, who fought tooth and nail to stop the gay rights bill for the previous 16 years, and who was responsible for a great many young gay people committing suicide, you got arrested for using your freedom of speech and assembly.

The public assumes that police, prosecutors and judges try to make the world safe and fair, while in practice they try to curry favor with whoever is in power. They allow power to do what it wants and punish everyone else.

Cardinal Law was a man I met, spoke with, and had little patience with for the simple reason he was smart enough to know better. He was not a captive of the irrational, he was a schemer and his rise in the ranks was his objective, just as prosecutors often seek votes, not justice. He was not about love, he was about exploiting hate. And exuding unctuous moral superiority. He told me he was worried about his reputation by meeting with me. I said I was worried about my reputation by meeting with him.

I think a persuasive case can be made that one dead guy would agree with me, a Jew named Jesus.

Timothy Harris did an interview with me and I realized looking at it that I was and am a radical and a subversive — at 46 years old I was an aging lefty hippie agitator. In fact the title of the lengthy interview was, *"To the Barricades, Councilor Scondras!"*

The article was in a publication that stemmed from Home Front, an organization that started at the gazebo on the Boston Common where we held a memorial service to the homeless people who had died of the cold in Boston. The Q and A used 'Street' as the questioner. Some of the interview went like this:

Street: You said then that there was a need to value human rights over property rights...

Scondras: It's a question of what things are for. Clothes are to keep people warm. You don't cut someone's arms and legs off when they don't fit a suit. You change the suit, right? So you tailor the suit to fit the person.

Street: So, institutions need to change rather than neglecting those that are left behind by changes. Is that what you mean?

Scondras: Well, you've got essentially two models of human behavior going on. One is social Darwinism that this country got infected with. I consider it a kind of disease. That model of society says, in effect, that everybody's on their own, and the way progress is made is that you weed out the weak; you create a hostile, competitive environment in which the strong survive. Well, of course this leads to people that are not particularly good at cooperating with each other, who are overly competitive, and it should be no surprise to people that with that kind of an ethic you end up with self-centered so-called Me Generation people. All of the myriads of small things that make up what we call a community are completely destroyed. People increasingly view themselves as enemies of each other, or as competitors in a world of scarce resources.

The other model of society, which I think is much healthier, is one in which the workforce feels it is part of a team. What you find is that those societies that have the most amount of personal security around issues like healthcare, education and so forth are the societies that end up being by far the most productive. West Germany, Holland, Japan, France are examples of societies with some extraordinary benefits that they've given to working people that are consistent and predictable.

The justification people give for social Darwinism is that a rising tide lifts all boats. A rising tide drowns all people who don't have a boat would be a more correct observation. This trickle-down nonsense is very simple: it isn't true. It's a rationalization that people who are doing well in this economic structure give for maintaining an essentially exploitative, cold and inhuman structure.

Homelessness is an example of a problem that has its origins in greed. We had over 20,000 lodging houses in Boston ten years ago. We have two thousand now. We lost ninety percent of our lodging house units. The bulk of these units housed elderly and poor and were turned into luxury condominiums. In other words, the dramatic increase in homelessness is not in the alcoholism and deinstitutionalized group; it's in the growing number of people who work for a living or did work for a living and are no longer able to afford a place to live.

Street: *My understanding is that when Home Front was negotiating with the city that you and Councilor Salerno were essentially the middle people between Home Front...*

Scondras: *...and the Mayor's office. That's true. It was a perfectly reasonable thing for me to do. Boston's not owned by me. The city government is a place where I try to advocate on behalf of the people who live here and try to get the city to change to accommodate their needs.*

Street: *To bring it back to Home Front, It seems like after Mayor Flynn spoke at the opening memorial service, that from that point on the mayor distanced himself from the Home Front demonstration and never commented on it publicly and never spoke with them. Do you have any idea of why that was, because this has some people confused?*

Scondras: I pointed out Mayor Flynn was chair of the National Democratic Party's platform committee and he was in Atlanta or Michigan most of the relevant time. Also he wasn't sure how he could solve this because the city did not have enough money.

I pointed out that a Dukakis presidency would give us a better shot at solving homelessness.

I painted a picture of the USA as a place in which folks had choices in the national parties between bad and not as bad. I framed it as a society that was like an automobile rushing toward a wall, and the two parties saying, "Let's go faster" and the other "Let's go fast, but not quite as fast as the other party wants to" and a lot of folks are saying "Hey, there is this brick wall up here, hasn't anyone heard about the brakes?"

The reporter asked me if I thought that a fascist revolution would happen, or that when the shit hits the fan things would turn our way. I said no, that we get marginal shifts, slow erosion. We have managed capitalism. There's a wonderful poem of T. S. Eliot about the end of the world that says it's "not with a bang but a whimper."

I felt that the polarization between those who felt plugged in and were essentially content with the system and those alienated was deepening and eventually would create a shift toward a more populist politics. I pointed out that Jesse Jackson getting thirty eight percent of white people in Maine in the primaries was an example of how a pragmatic populism could overcome racism. I predicted a shift in power by 2011, the year that a majority of minorities would demographically occur.

I was naïve in many ways, but Obama's election in 2008 is the proof that the end of factionalism on the grass roots level can lead to extraordinary shifts in power on the national level.

Recycling Bill

Rosaria and I got a recycling bill through the City Council that would mandate separation of trash and recycling, showing that the way we were doing it now, dumping into landfills, was actually wasting a lot of money, was more expensive as well as bad for the environment. Ray was annoyed that our bill had high fines in it for not recycling, but we felt that a 'voluntary' program would not work. I tried to get the council to use positive reinforcement in the bill without much success.

The recycling bill which I cosponsored with Rosaria, was called the "most sweeping recycling bill of any city in the nation."

Ray thought it was too radical. I mandated the city buy things made from recycled waste, that a fee be paid to finance recycling, that bond authorization be given to a new waste management commission whose job would be to target 100% recycling and to build whatever facilities could be financed toward that end.

Ray was probably right that the bill was too much but, you know, you can't really solve some problems halfway and the environment was one of them.

Gays and the Police—Again

Finally, I got totally fed up with the police — no big surprise. In this case they put a guy who was drunk and was arrested in a cell in which he promptly hung himself. I called for a full investigation of why the guy wasn't taken for counseling instead of jail for drunk driving. I said, "People who are sick, mentally distressed, on drugs or drunk out of their minds need medical attention or counseling immediately. They don't get that in a police lockup." What I didn't mention is that what they do get is lip, stupidity, prejudices, a predisposition of violence, shame, self accusations and a variety of other things that help no one and harm people who are picked up by police. Harold J. Christensen was 36 years old when he hung himself. It should not have happened and if the police had treated this as a medical emergency it would not have happened.

Christensen was a white gay musician and carpenter. The police kept refusing to answer simple questions about the suicide. The belt that was used was not Christensen's, could never have fit him and his friends seeing the belt had a gold colored designer type buckle understand that it could not have belonged to him. So where did he get it?

The police station had a reputation for abusive treatment of gays, blacks etc., not a particularly unusual condition in 1989 given the composition and lack of training of the police force. A guy named Hawkes, Christensen's love of fourteen years who lived with him during the previous eight, was pre-empted by Christensen's mother, whom the victim had only seen two or three times during the previous five years. Hawkes could not arrange his own lover's funeral. He said, "As a gay person, I feel like everything's been ripped out of me, and I feel complete and utter frustration because there's nothing I can do about my rights or at least no one is telling me what I can do."

The lesson here is more profound than it might appear: like Ezekiel's wheels within wheels the threads of public policies based on lies, on religion rather than fact, led to innumerable abuses. The fact that Christensen had been a hustler meant that he and his friends had many run-ins with the police. The same police who abused prostitutes, traded blow jobs in police cars in exchange for not arresting prostitutes, and shaking down gay bars for cash. I demanded a full investigation but never got one that satisfied me. The police like most of the institutions of our culture spent a lot of energy protecting themselves from the public, who they, like most institutions, considered the enemy.

Once again I was fed up with how our institutions misread events, abuse the tools they had for the jobs we entrust them with. For God's sake, where was the humanity? I noted that the police station was in violation of several state laws that would have protected Christensen, such as a requirement that hard, clear plastic Lexan sheets be put over jail cell bars to prevent suicides. It is, however, the rule rather than the exception that the police and their institutions, including the courts, can lie, break the laws, and get away with what they make everyone else go through hell obeying.

They make me sick.

Index

A

B

Bolling, Royal Sr.: State Senator and father of Bruce Bolling; i:142

Borge, Tomás: Interior Minister of Nicaragua; ii:85

Bozzotto, Domenic "Dom": leader of Hotel Workers Union Local 26; ii:105,iii:132, iii:174

BRA: Boston Redevelopment Authority (now the Boston Planning & Development
    Agency); i:82, i:102-6, i:109-11, i:116, i:122-3, iii:26, iii:38, iii:188, iii:195

Braude, Jim: Cambridge City Councilor; New England Cable Network News reporter; iv:145

Britt , Harry: Succeeded Harvey Milk as San Francisco County Supervisor; i:177-8

Bryant, Anita: anti-gay activist; ii:151, ii:225, ii:261

Bucke, Rev. Gerald: West End community activist; i:105, i:111-2, i:164

Bulger, Billy: president of the Massachusetts Senate, 1978-1996; i:14

Bunker, Archie: bigot from 1970s TV show, "All in the Family"; ii:297

Burbank, Liz: Fenway community activist; i:153

Byrne, Garrett: District Attorney of Boston; i:188

Byrne, Jim: Boston City Council colleague; i:6, ii:29, ii:121, ii:292, iii:91-2, iii:100

C

Caffrey, Andrew: Federal District Court Judge; i:124-5, i:192-3

Campbell, Bob: *Boston Globe* architectural critic; i:257-8

Carr, Howie: *Boston Herald* columnist; i:6, ii:23, ii:223-5, ii:300, iii:30, iii:172, iii:181,
    iii:191, iv:53-5, iv:191

Casazza, Joe: head of Boston's public works department; ii:199

Case, Father Robert: priest; Fenway community activist; i:75, i:99, i:109-12, ii:184, ii:236

Cathcart, Kevin: GLAAD activist; i:151, ii:45

CCLSF, Committee for Civil Liberties and Sexual Freedom; ii:218-22

Chávez, César: labor activist & founder of the United Farm Workers; i:15,
    ii:92-6, ii:241, iii:192
        photos: ii:96

Chomsky, Noam: MIT professor and political writer; i:67, iv:219

Clapprood, Marjorie: State Rep.; radio host; ii:201, ii:280

Coggins, Copper: Scondras BFF from college; i:5, iii:41

Commerford, Betty; Social worker in Mission Hill; iii:195

Condlin, Robert: Boston College Law School faculty; i:111

Contras: U. S.-backed militia opposing the Sandinista government; ii:81-4, ii:109, ii:190,
    ii:206, ii:238, iii:72, iii:193, iv:170

Coors, Peter: beer magnate, target of the Coors boycott; ii:101-4, ii:188-91, ii:249-52, iv:6

Cox, Helen: Fenway community activist; ii:46

CPPAX, Citizens for Participation in Political Action; i:90, iv:220

Crisp, Quentin: British writer and raconteur; i:13

Cristiani, Alfredo: President of El Salvador; iii:62-70

Cronin, Mike: Boston City Council candidate against incumbent Jim Kelly; iii:126, iii:143

Crumb, Fritz, director of the BCOA; i:96

D

Daher, George "Eddie": Chief Judge of the Boston Housing Court; ii:111

Dapper; *see:* O'Neil: Albert

Day, Debbie, Christian Scientist activist: i:97, i:117

D'Elia, Christopher: manager of Deak-Perera currency company; ii:78

Combined index for i:The Beginning; ii:The Kiss; iii:The Coup; and iv:The Long Way Home

---

Frank, Barney: first openly gay member of Congress from Massachusetts; i:157, i:190, ii:37, ii:51, ii:55, ii:201-2, ii:212, ii:227-8, ii:234-5, ii:276, ii:297, iii:2, iii:7, iii:161, iii:176, iii:181-2, iv:103, iv:112
    photo: iii:182
French: *see* Wall, French (Scondras staffer)

G

Gallagher, Tom: State Rep. from Allston-Brighton; ii:122
Gandhi, Mohandas "Mahatma": political leader of India; i:155, ii:213, iii:195, iv:91
Garland, Judy: actress and singer; i:22, i:177, i:179
Garneau, Ernie: Fenway tenant activist; i:134
Gates, Bill; philanthropist and founder of Microsoft; iv:21
Gaydar: ii:57, ii:61, iii:164, iii:183
GCN: *Gay Community News*, a Boston-based weekly newspaper; i:162, i:165-6, i:172-3, i:197, ii:11-2, ii:62, ii:175, iii:185-6
Gilbert, Galen: Fenway community activist; Scondras campaign treasurer; now director of the Water Table Trust; i:171, ii:118, ii:203, ii:222
GLAAD: Gay & Lesbian Alliance Against Defamation, legal organization to defend LGBT people; i:151, ii:45
Goldsmith, Larry: reporter at *Gay Community News*; i:173, ii:12
Gordon, Jesse: political activist and editor of this book; i:2,ii:1, iii:3, iv:2, iv:198-9, iv:220
Gore, Al: Vice President and environmental activist; iv:219
Guide, The, gay news magazine; i:200, ii:218, iii:126

H

Hall, Jackson (Jack): Scondras staffer; ii:10, ii:31-2, ii:53, ii:92
    photo: ii:32
Hattam, Nick: poet and friend of Scondras; ii:16, iv:159-60
Hay, Harry; founder of Mattachine Society; i:181, ii:68
Heilman, John: Mayor of West Hollywood California; i:177
Hennigan, Maura: Boston City Council colleague, ii:29, ii:59, ii:104, ii:121, ii:142, ii:158, ii:204, ii:210,
Heritage Foundation: conservative think tank; ii:191
Hernandez, Peggy: *Boston Globe* reporter; ii:221, ii:270, ii:304
Higgens, Carol: Scondras high school crush; homecoming queen; i:32
Hirschfeld, Magnus: founded the Scientific Humanitarian Committee in Germany and organized the first Congress for Sexual Reform; i:181
Hoffman, Abbie: 1960s radical; i:127
Hoffman, Julius: right-wing Judge; i:125, iii:179, iii:256, iv:322-3
Holland (the Netherlands): ii:289, ii:309, iv:29, iv:152
Holmes, Dan: chef and founder of the Downtown Café; ii:94, ii:145
Hougen, Ed: minister and founder of gay news magazine *The Guide;* i:200
Hughes, Langston: poet and social activist; ii:58, ii:63-5, iii:161
    photo: ii:65
; i:173, i:179, i:214, i:219
Hurley , John J. "Wacko": anti-gay activist; iii:157
Huynh, Marylyn: political activist Robert called Marylyn Spacecheck; i:30-1, iii:29

I

Iannella, Chris: Boston City Council colleague; i:111, ii:29, ii:122, ii:280-1, ii:293, ii:301,
        iii:12, iii:62-3, iii:122, iii:280, iii:293, iii:301
Isaacson, Arlene: Co-Chair of Massachusetts Gay and Lesbian Political Caucus; i:157

J

Jack: *see* Hall, Jackson (Scondras staffer)
Jackson, Bob: Boston firefighter; ii:172-3
Jackson, Rev. Earl: anti-gay activist; iii:105-6
Jackson, Jesse: political activist; candidate for president, 1984 and 1988; i:15, i:73,
        ii:8, ii:259-63, ii:267, ii:283-4, ii:296-9, ii:310, iii:182, iii:194
        photos: ii:260, ii:284
Jackson, Michael: singer; ii:17-8, ii:20, ii:26
John Birch Society: anti-Communist advocacy group; ii:190
Johnson, Helene: Boston community activist and state rep candidate; i:188
Johnson, Lyndon: President from 1963 to 1968; i:72, i:78, i:96, i:111, ii:161
Jordan, Robert: *Boston Globe* reporter; ii:13
Joshi, Shashank: M.D. in India; iv:76-8, iv:85
        photo: iv:76
Jurkowitz, Mark: reporter for *the Boston Ledger*; i:202

K

Kallmann, Gerhard: Boston architect; ii:258
Kameny, Frank: Early gay rights activist; i:181
Kaven, Bob: openly gay Chris Iannella aide; ii:122, ii:301
Keane, Tom: City Council opponent who unseated Scondras; Rep. Moakley's staffer;
        iii:165-7, iii:171, iii:177-81, iii:186, iii:190, iii:195-6, iv:8
        photo: iii:171
Kelly, Frank: Boston vice squad police officer; ii:88
Kelly, Jim: Boston City Council colleague, i:6, i:193, ii:26, ii:29, ii:84, ii:98, ii:110,
        ii:122, ii:133, ii:225, ii:281, ii:288, ii:302, iii:10, iii:53, iii:99-103, iii:120-1,
        iii:128, iii:143, iii:158, iii:173, iv:91
Kennedy, Edward "Ted": Senator from Massachusetts; i:14, i:124, ii:138, ii:140,
        ii:274, iii:92
Kennedy, Joe Jr.: U.S. Rep.; father of U. S. Rep. Joe Kennedy III; ii:139-40, iii:62-4,
        iii:67, iii:83, iii:189, iii:195
Kennedy, John F.: President and Senator from Massachusetts; i:23, i:32, i:52-5, i:67,
        i:168, i:196, iii:160, iv:54
Kennedy, Robert F.: Senator from New York; i:79, ii:36
Kennedy School of Government and Library: Harvard University, i:104, ii:108
Kerry, John: Senator from Massachusetts; i:126, i:183, i:198, ii:202, iii:62-4, iv:103, iv:112
Ketover, Dede: staffer in mayor's office; AIDS activist; ii:148
Keverian, George: speaker of the Massachusetts Statehouse; iii:7-8
Kimmel, Daniel, campaign volunteer and copy-editor of this book; ii:256-7

King, Mel: Director of the New Urban League of Greater Boston; candidate for Mayor;
    i:7, i:137-8, i:155-6, i:161, i:178, i:198-200, ii:8-9, ii:13, ii:21, ii:78-80,
    ii:130, ii:235, ii:243, ii:259, iii:17, iii:57, iii:189, iv:218
    photo: ii:80
Klavens, Dr. George: Scondras psychiatrist; i:60-1
Kozachenko, Kathy: first openly gay person elected to public office; i:177
Kramer, Larry: gay playwright; founder of ACT UP; ii:185-6, ii:209, ii:230
Krebs, Robert: architect; Scondras' life partner (major citations); i:2, i:18, i:153, ii:14,
    ii:31-2, ii:37-45, ii:48-50, ii:72, ii:283, iii:65, iv:184-5
    photos: ii:cover, ii:32, ii:48,

L

LaFontaine, David: activist with Boston Gay and Lesbian Political Alliance; ii:211
Langone, Freddy: Boston City Councilor from the North End; ii:58, ii:233
LaRouche, Lyndon: perennial candidate & founder of LaRouche movement: ii:131, ii:151
Lennon, John: founder of *The Beatles*; i:69, i:71
Levenson, Norman: real estate developer; Fenway landlord; i:134, ii:109-10
Levine, Marsha: co-founder of the Boston Lesbian and Gay Political Alliance; i:178, i:187
Liakos, Dennis: Fenway landlord convicted of arson; i:132-3
Liberationism: idea that gays are inherently different from straights and those differences
    should be respected; ii:168, ii:168-70, iii:23, iii:45, iii:170, iv:230
Log Cabin Republicans: gay conservative political group; iii:99, iii:195
Lucas, Peter: columnist in the *Boston Herald*; i:173
Lyons, Pat & John: Fenway real estate and nightclub owners; ii:102

M

Maguire, Ann: City of Boston gay liaison; i:187-8, ii:67, ii:288
Malewezi, Justin: Vice President of the African Republic of Malawi; iv:100,
    iv:111-2,iv:141-6, iv:150
    photo: iv:111, iv:142
Mandel, Fred: Boston Human Rights Commission Director; ii:92, ii:200, ii:228,
    iii:156, iii:193, iv:5
Mandela, Nelson: leader of the African National Congress; first black President of
    South Africa; ii:80, ii:227, iii:193, iv:100, iv:121, iv:137-8
    photo: iv:121
Mapplethorpe, Robert: photographer and gay activist; iii:95-103
    photo: iii:96
Martin, Gaye: Fenway activist; i:129-31, i:136, i:146, i:153
Martorelli, Tom: Fenway Health Center board member; i:89
Matewan: Scondras familial home in West Virginia; i:40-4, iii:37
Mattachine Society: early pro-gay rights groups, founded in 1950s; i:181, ii:68
Mbeki, Thabo: President of South Africa who denied that HIV caused AIDS; i:6, iv:94,
    iv:100, iv:116-21, iv:124-5, iv:131-3, iv:135, iv:144
    photos: iv:200, iv:121
MBTA: Metropolitan Boston Transit Authority, Boston's train system, known
    as "the T"; i:183, ii:7, ii:98, ii:136-41

N

Combined index for i:The Beginning; ii:The Kiss; iii:The Coup; and iv:The Long Way Home

O

P

Q

R

T

U-V

W-X

www.ingramcontent.com/pod-product-compliance
Lightning Source LLC
Chambersburg PA
CBHW060037260726
48658CB00004B/1085